The Superpowers and Africa

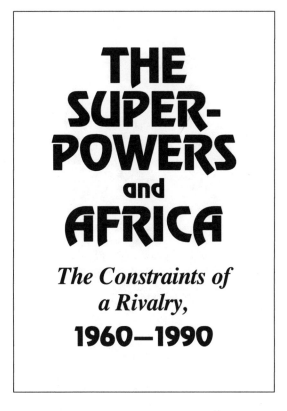

THE SUPER-POWERS and AFRICA

The Constraints of a Rivalry,

1960–1990

ZAKI LAÏDI

Translated by Patricia Baudoin

The University of Chicago Press

Chicago and London

ZAKI LAÏDI is a research associate at the
Centre d'études et de recherches internationales,
and teaches at the University of Paris I.
He is cofounder of the journal *Politique africaine*;
editor of a collective work, *L'URSS vue du tiers monde*; and
author of *Enquête sur le Banque Mondial*.

The University of Chicago Press, Chicago 60637
The University of Chicago Press, Ltd., London

© 1990 by The University of Chicago
All rights reserved. Published 1990
Printed in the United States of America

99 98 97 96 95 94 93 92 91 90   5 4 3 2 1

First published as *Les contraintes
d'une rivalité: Les superpuissances
et l'Afrique (1960–1985)*, © Editions La Découverte,
Paris, 1986.

Library of Congress Cataloging-in-Publication Data

Laïdi, Zaki.
   [Contraintes d'une rivalité. English]
   The superpowers and Africa : the constraints of a rivalry,
1960–1990 / Zaki Laïdi; translated by Patricia Baudoin.

     p.   cm.
   Translation of: Les contraintes d'une rivalité.
   Includes bibliographical references.
   ISBN 0-226-46781-3 (cloth) 0-226-46782-1 (paper)
   1. Africa—Foreign relations. 2. Africa—Foreign relations—
United States. 3. United States—Foreign relations—Africa.
4. Africa—Foreign relations—Soviet Union. 5. Soviet Union—
Foreign relations—Africa. 6. World politics, 1945– I. Title.
DT30.5.L3513   1990
960.3'2—dc20
                                 90-10832
                                      CIP

To my sons

Contents

Maps and Tables

Maps

Tables

Abbreviations and Acronyms

ABAKO   Association des Bakongo
ACP   Afrique-Caraïbes-Pacifique
ADF   African Development Fund
AID   Agency for International Development (US)
ANC   African National Congress
BOSS   Bureau of State Security (South Africa)
CAD   Comité de Aide au Développement (OCDE); = DAC
CDA   Cooperation for Development in Africa
CDSP   Current Digest of the Soviet Press
CEDEAO   Communauté Economique des Etats de l'Afrique de l'Ouest;
                = ECOWAS
CFA   Communauté Financière Africaine
CMEA   Council of Mutual Economic Assistance; = COMECON
COMECON   = CMEA
CONAKAT   Confédération des Associations Tribales du Katanga
CPSA   Communist Party of South Africa
CPSU   Communist Party of the Soviet Union
DAC   Development Assistance Committee (OECD); = CAD
DOS   Department of State (US)
DTA   Democratic Turnhalle Alliance (Namibia)
ECA   Economic Commission for Africa (UN)
ECLAC   Economic Commission for Latin America and
                the Caribbean (UN)
ECOWAS   Economic Community of West African States; = CEDEAO
EEC   European Economic Community
ELP   Portuguese Liberation Army
EPRP   Ethiopian People's Revolutionary Party
ESF   Economic Support Fund
Eximbank   Export-Import Bank
FBIS   Foreign Broadcast Information Service

FNLA	Frente Nacional de Liberação de Angola
Frelimo	Frente de Liberação do Mocambique
Frolinat	Front de libération nationale du Tchad
FSM	Fédération syndicale mondiale; = WFTU
GAO	Government Accounting Office (US)
GNP	Gross national product
GRAE	Angolan Revolutionary Government in Exile
HNP	Herstigte Nasionale Parti (South Africa)
IBRD	International Bank for Reconstruction and Development (World Bank)
IDA	International Development Association
IMF	International Monetary Fund
JMNR	Jeunesse du Mouvement national révolutionnaire (Congo)
JPRS	Joint Publication Research Service
KANU	Kenyan African National Union
MFA	Movimento das Forças Armadas (Portugal)
MNC	Mouvement national congolais (Zaire)
MNR	Movimento Nacional de Resistença (Mozambique); = RENAMO
MPLA	Movimento Popular de Liberação de Angola
NATO	North Atlantic Treaty Organization
NGO	Nongovernment organization
NIEO	New International Economic Order
NSC	National Security Council (US)
NSWFP	National Socialist Workers and Farmers Party (Nigeria)
OAU	Organization of African Unity
OCDE	Organisation de Coopération et de Développement Economiques; = OECD
OECD	Organization for Economic Cooperation and Development; = OCDE
OPEC	Organization of Petroleum Exporting Countries
OPIC	Overseas Private Investment Corporation
OSPAAAL	Organization of Solidarity of the Peoples of Africa, Asia, and Latin America
PCP	Partido Communista Portugues
PCT	Parti congolais du Travail
PRPB	Parti révolutionnaire du peuple béninois
PSP	Partido Socialista Popular (Cuba)
RENAMO	Movimento Nacional de Resistença (Mozambique): = MNR
RTP	Rally of the Togolese People
SCP	Sudanese Communist Party
SDAR	Sarawi Arab Democratic Republic

SWAPO	South West Africa People's Organization (Namibia)
TAD	Trade and Development Board
UNCTAD	United Nations Conference on Trade and Development
UNITA	União Nacional por a Independença Total de Angola
UPA	União dos Populações de Angola
UPC	Union des Populations du Cameroun
UPNA	União dos Populações do Norte de Angola
USET	United States Embassy Telegram
WAMU	West Africa Monetary Union
WPE	Workers' Party of Ethiopia
WFTU	World Federation of Trade Unions; = FSM
ZANU	Zimbabwe African National Union
ZAPU	Zimbabwe African People's Union
ZIPRA	Zimbabwe Independent People's Revolutionary Army

Acknowledgments

This work is the fruit of academic reflections during the late 1970s. They were delineated in the 1979 publication of *Grandes Puissances et l'Afrique* (Paris, Cahiers du CHEAM) and in the defense of my thesis on the same subject for a doctorate in political science. Begun in the graduate school of the Institute for Policy Studies in Paris, this analysis was later pursued within the extremely productive cadre of the Center for International Studies and Research (CERI) of the National Foundations for Political Science.

Throughout those years, I had the benefit of essential support from my research director, Alfred Grosser, as well as the unstinting assistance of Guy Hermet, director of CERI. Without their aid, and without the stimulating comments of J.-C. Gautron, R. Girault, P. Hassner, and J. Leca, offered during defense of my thesis, this work would probably never have seen the light of day.

The product of a personal effort, this work is equally the sum of valuable and often informal reflections exchanged with colleagues and participants in the political life of Paris, Washington, and Brazzaville. It owes much to the effort to renew Africanist research within CERI, to the review *Politique africaine,* and most particularly to the inestimable support of J.-F. Bayart.

To all those mentioned herein, along with C. Perrot, S. Haas, H. Arnaud, and H. Cohen, I express my profound gratitude and friendship.

Alger-Vandoeuvres, August 1985

For this American edition I would like to thank my translator, Patricia Baudoin; Aristide Zolberg, who encouraged the University of Chicago Press to publish the work in English and who made many valuable suggestions; and Priscilla Coit Murphy, who not only edited and fine-tuned the translation but researched names, terms, and bibliographical references for the benefit of the English-speaking reader.

Paris, December 1989

Introduction to the American Edition

On December 22, 1988, the United States and the Soviet Union sponsored an Angolan–Cuban–South African accord anticipating the total though gradual withdrawal of Cuban troops from Angola by July 1991, as well as South Africa's departure from Namibia. Thus ended not only the last chapter of decolonization in Africa but also one of the most acute African crises. In many respects, the Soviet-American benediction in southern Africa confirms the crucial role the superpowers have taken on in the exacerbation and the denouement of African crises since 1975.

The Angolan crisis developed in a context of East-West tensions. It was attenuated in a more serene environment marked by collaboration between the superpowers. Taking this perspective further in the same direction, one might see in this historical agreement the triumph of American policies and the failure of the Soviet Union's. Indeed, after eight years of efforts, the United States achieved recognition by all regional actors of a link between the withdrawal of Cuban forces and Namibia's independence. On the other hand, the Soviet Union had lost all ideological illusions about that part of the world, which some were tempted to see as a possible area for extension of the communist system.

This being said, one might be susceptible to a reductionist view of the dynamics of relations between the superpowers if one insists on a stubborn interpretation of the stakes there as a zero-sum game. One might also be subject to a linear and mechanistic view of international relations if the following essential fact were forgotten: the results of a policy should rarely be measured by original objectives only; results must be interpreted according to the stakes at the time. Let us be more explicit about these two hypotheses. They seem essential, for they will serve as a foundation for the rest of this book.

One fact seems undeniable: the superpowers have clearly managed to synchronize the rhythm of African tensions with the state of their global relations. The tensions have been exacerbated when it was in the superpowers' interest to do so and diminished when it was to their advantage. This mechanical relationship is maintained by the superpowers' ability to control the different economic or military flows to the different actors. But this relationship is not purely material or instrumental. The local actors' perceptions of the international climate and the political risk they can accommodate to advance their own interests is a fundamental element of international reality. It is also one of the most difficult to circumscribe since it rests sometimes so much on subjective elements.

The Dialectic of the Internal and the External

Scientific understanding of this phenomenon is particularly complex because interpenetration of the internal and the external is extremely difficult to measure. Neither the ebb nor the flow of African Marxisms is independent of the political evolution of the Soviet Union; but at the same time, nobody can seriously believe that the international factor was the sole determinant. And what is true for Marxism is also true for South Africa. Its withdrawal from Namibia after so much shuffling back and forth was the result, without any doubt, of the effectiveness of external pressure. But these pressures utterly fail to explain the evolution of South Africa's position. The semidefeat of Pretoria's troops at Cuito-Canavale (Angola) had strong repercussions in South Africa, to the extent that it demonstrated the erosion of its military power before Angola. This erosion was in large part the result of the loss of South African air supremacy, a loss itself largely caused by the effectiveness of the West's military embargo.

The impact of economic sanctions is more difficult to evaluate. Although more than a third of American companies in South Africa left the country, half of them maintained license contracts; and this arrangement is not the only factor to have reduced the impact of sanctions. The precipitous sale of American companies, for example, was transacted below their value, thus creating an indirect subsidy to the economics of apartheid. Added to this must be the renewed shipment of products through intermediaries (Botswana and Swaziland); restrictions on the repatriation of capital; and the possibilities for supplying South African companies through third parties. In reality, as is often the case, sanctions are more important for their induced and unforeseen effects than for their originally intended consequences. Commercial sanctions have had but a very limited effect on South African trade dynamics. They have, however, contributed to accelerating the net outflow of capital at precisely the time when restimulation of private investment is so crucial. Beyond these economic consequences, it is the erosion of South Africa's international position that the sanctions reveal.

In fact, it is the coincidence between internal and external dynamics that leads all too often to overestimating the importance of external dynamics. The weight of external dynamics often deserves to be downplayed even more because the ability of the superpowers to lessen the scope of a conflict or to modify its direction may in no way indicate the ability to resolve it. The Eritrean conflict survived all of the evolutions of the East-West conflict. The reduction of its level of interiority did not necessarily mean its resolution. And what is true for Eritrea is a fortiori true for Angola or South Africa.

The Illusions of the Zero-Sum Game

Let us come back to the December 22, 1988, accord and an evaluation of its significance for the different protagonists. The Angolan government, like Cuba's, made a major concession: they both accepted a link between the presence of Havana's forces and those of South Africa's in Namibia. Even though Cuba never considered its presence in Angola definitive, it was not in charge of its withdrawal. It is in that sense that the New York accord forced Cuba into a retreat without fanfare. That being said, the symbolic defeat has been largely compensated for by a partial political victory. The immediate objective of Cuban intervention was to keep the Angolan regime in power. It has now been consolidated, even if it finds itself constrained to negotiate the terms of a division of power with UNITA.

The results of American policy are symmetrically ambiguous. On the face of it, the United States' diplomatic victory was complete. But appearances are deceptive. One year before the signing of the New York accords, the situation was at a complete impasse. The reversal of the situation underscores simply that in international politics the margin between failure and success is extremely narrow and often unexpected. American policy in southern Africa did not escape that rule. In truth, the plan initially drawn up by Chester Crocker was only loosely followed. From the outset, he was burdened by the concept of linkage, which he had never planned on. He later found himself forced to integrate into his efforts those economic sanctions he had once fought. Finally and above all, United States policy had to take into account two factors that were unpredictable from the start: the internal eruption in South Africa and changes in Soviet policy.

Collaboration with Moscow enabled Washington to accelerate the withdrawal of Cuban troops. But in doing so, the United States lost all ideological advantage. At the beginning of the eighties, getting Cuban troops to withdraw had a particular meaning: it meant rolling back the limits of the Soviet empire and calling into question the sacrosanct principle of irreversibility. But from the moment the Soviet Union relinquished that principle and opposed Cuban conservatism, the American success seemed limited. It is, again, for symmetrical reasons that the Soviet failure seems less obvious than is usually thought. To be sure, the ideological softening of the Soviet Union seems patent. But once Moscow questions its own past, the indices by which to interpret its policies are modified. In addition, the notion of failure or success is, in Africa, more a question of degree than of kind. On this continent there is no Korean success to oppose to a Vietnamese failure, no capitalist triumph or communist failure. None of the United States' African allies has truly kept its promises. Liberia's failure, the bloody turn taken by events in Somalia, and the politically disquieting developments in the Kenyan regime demonstrate to what extent American expectations can be disappointed in this part of the world. In fact, what the Soviet Union loses and has lost at the level of ideology has been perhaps regained on the more classic diplomatic-strategic terrain. Moreover, Moscow was careful to reinforce the Luanda regime militarily before pushing it along the road toward negotiations with UNITA. Even if it has changed considerably at the political level, and not only under external pressure, the 1975 Angolan regime is still in place. Furthermore, by opening the dialogue with Pretoria and ceasing to align itself with the more maximalist African positions, the Soviet Union is perhaps providing itself with the means to be present more than ever in southern Africa. By moving from the position of militant ally to that of arbiter, it converges with the United States position while simultaneously giving itself the means to compete with the United States on its own ground.

In evoking the most recent configuration of international relations in southern Africa, we have evoked an essential dimension of the dynamics between the superpowers in Africa. It stems from the non-univocal nature of relations between external actors and internal stakes. If Africa is a continent particularly permeable by external interference, it is far from conforming to external schemas. In this regard, the superpowers' ability to control regional tensions is only equal to their impotence in integrating Africa into a capitalist or communist matrix.

The purpose of this book is to show, in a historical perspective, how the dialectical relationship between the superpowers and African actors has evolved. For the most part, doing this means studying the diplomatic-strategic framework; but although it is essential to the analysis, it is not always the determining factor and at any rate not the only one. The importance of economic considerations led us to pay more attention to some aspects traditionally neglected by classic internationalist analyses, such as the economic and social impact of aid policies. The considerable importance on the African continent taken on by the Bretton Woods institutions naturally led us to focus on the direction of these new actors and on the importance of their mediation. The incredible decline of French influence in Africa, remarkably unrecognized in the United States, also claimed our attention.

This book was for the most part written in the mid-eighties. Only this introduction, the epilogue, and certain parts concerning economic issues and American aid are new to this edition. If I had to write it today, I would do it differently. That said, none of my major conclusions seems to me to have suffered the wear and tear of time.

Paris, October 7, 1989

Introduction to the French Edition

On a par with the "inscrutable East," perhaps, Africa[1] lends itself easily to normative approximations or a succession of commonplaces. A scarcely declared African crisis gives rise to spontaneous interpretations whose persistence owes a great deal to their sketchiness. Even where they differ in their definitions of the enemy ("tribalism," "communism," or "imperialism"), these reductive explanations implicitly converge toward the same rallying point: essentialism. Basically, whether seen as awash with tribalism or as tainted by communism, Africa emerges as a continent that willingly accepts simple and univocal explanations.

Such specious analyses, whose forms could be drawn in detail and whose martyrs could be enumerated, are linked to a network of causes and responsibilities amply shared.

Western colonialism has powerfully contributed to this imagery. The cultural stereotypes that it has applied and popularized insist on the infantilism of African tribes, their irresponsibility, and their pressing need for tutelage. Today still, the conflicts that run through African societies or their economic decay feed sordid explanations more easily than finely tuned analyses. These prejudices have in no way been mitigated by a "Third World vulgate" whose waves are still breaking along African coastlines. Thus, under the guise of wanting to denounce neocolonial domination, certain African authors always take cover in mechanistic analyses that deny African actors any piece of autonomy vis-à-vis their "foreign tutelage."[2] From this point of view, they join those who hunt out indisputable signs of allegiance with Moscow behind any Marxist reference.

In fact, the difficulty of thinking about Africa as an actor in its own right, regardless of external forces putting pressure on it, would not be so great were it not for the rudimentary level of our knowledge of African societies.[3]

This cloudiness gets even murkier as soon as one ventures to grasp these societies' mechanisms for entering into the international arena. Confronted with undeniable problems of empirical validation, such an attempt suffers from obvious methodological weaknesses.

The first such weakness arises from the excessively operational or pragmatic nature of inquiry in international relations, from the difficulty analysts seem to have in removing themselves from normative interpretations to the prospect of good reviews or serious censure. The strategies of different actors are more or less reduced to simple strategies of diplomatic maximization, as if instrumental rationality could explain everything. Measuring Soviet-Angolan ties only according to the volume of aid granted by the Soviet Union would lead to privileging diplomatic circumstance with all its risks (crisis, tensions or, conversely, a strengthening of relations), at the expense of more structural elements, such as the role of the Soviet Union in the internal legitimization of Angolan power.

The second problem stems largely from the choice of "objects" of international analysis. A study of relations between the superpowers and Africa will spontaneously turn to inter-state relations with the whole parade of declarations and negotiations. In placing the soldier and the diplomat at the center of the board, such a gameplan overestimates identifiable variables (diplomatic-strategic actors) and apparent or immediate stakes (Cuban presence), at the expense, perhaps, of the process of ideological dissemination exercised by non-state actors, of economic influences (the role of the IMF), or even of undeclared stakes (Franco-American competition).

This weakness seems all the more regrettable since almost everywhere in Africa one sees a shattering of state frameworks that could be targets of influence or sources of power. Indeed, none of these problems would be so acutely manifest if the dichotomy between internal and external fields were not so pronounced and if their respective analysts did not sometimes develop in such different theoretical contexts. Most of the Sovietologists' analyses of Soviet policy in Africa barely even bother with matching the elements that are at work in Moscow (the socialist orientation, for example) with their local expression or adaptation. On the other hand, internationalist Africanist research still only occupies a marginal position in the effort to renew this discipline.

Fifteen years after the decolonization of Portuguese-speaking Africa and the accompanying, marked arrival of the superpowers, the role of these two great powers in Africa is still noteworthy. In southern Africa American policy has been deeply involved in the processes of Namibian independence, as "political reconciliation" in Angola and Mozambique and "peaceful transition" in South Africa. In Angola and Mozambique, Soviet support remains as crucial as ten years ago. In fact, with greater or lesser intensity, the East-West dividing line in southern Africa crosses the entire continent. Given this, it does not seem so important to list its location as to understand the unstable and impure dialectic of the relations between regional stakes and external strategies. For in the zero-sum competition between the Soviets and the Americans, there is a whole series of shadings and interactions that, because of or in spite of the superpowers, contributes sometimes to exacerbation of that competition and other times to its devitalization. The case of South Africa is revealing in this respect. The persistence of the apartheid regime is an indisputable factor in East-West polarization. At the same time, South Africa's great power in the region inhibits the control external powers have on its actions. While modulating the intensity of East-West tensions, these same shadings and interactions sometimes end up displacing the center of gravity of what is at stake. Even though directed against the Soviet Union, American influence in Africa is perhaps competing still more with the presence of France.

This book offers only fragments of answers to all of these problems. But by putting Soviet-American relations in Africa since 1960 into historical perspective, it focuses on a double process: the integration of the superpowers into the African political arena and the capture of these actors in the East-West vise. Until 1975 this double process had a form both fragmented and discontinuous. For the most part, intervention by the superpowers answered a simple need: to deny the other access to any supposedly vacant area. On the African side, the mechanism of appeal to the superpowers answered a similarly modest need: to decrease their sources of dependency with an eye to maximizing diplomatic ties.

Since the 1975 Angolan crisis, the equation of relations between the superpowers and Africa has changed. Soviets and Americans no longer fight only over African space. They are rivals competing in part, at least, where organization is concerned. Moves made by African actors also have changed. They are motivated less by the desire to come up with an alternative to the old tutelary powers than by an attempt to take advantage of East-West divisions. This shift brings with it new significance: Soviet-American competition has ceased to be limited to the diplomatic-strategic realm. It now extends to the internal legitimation of African states as well as to economic dependence.

Given the evidence, this process is far from uniformly spread throughout the whole continent. It is also far from being expressed in identical terms by each of the superpowers. It simply brings about a new form of inquiry that no longer focuses on the unstable, or rather persistent, character of the superpowers' involvement in Africa, but rather on their ability to organize the three areas that constitute the African political scene (internal legitimation, diplomatic maximization, economic dependence) around their own global goals.

Alger-Vandoeuvres, August 1985

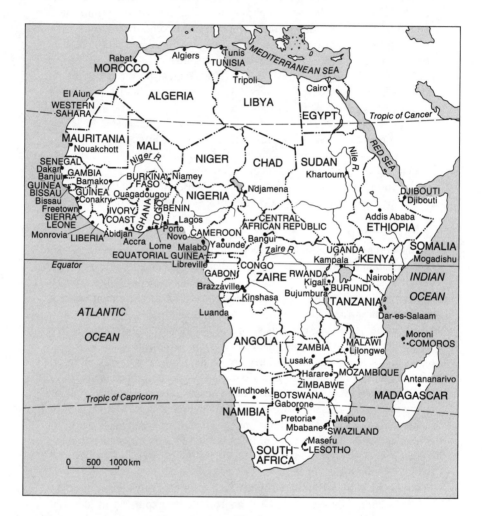

MOROCCO
Rabat
Algiers
Tunis
TUNISIA
MEDITERRANEAN SEA
Tripoli
Cairo
El Aiun
WESTERN SAHARA
ALGERIA
LIBYA
EGYPT
Tropic of Cancer
MAURITANIA
Nouakchott
MALI
NIGER
CHAD
SUDAN
RED SEA
Niger R.
Nile R.
Khartoum
SENEGAL
Dakar
Banjul
GAMBIA
Bamako
BURKINA
FASO
Niamey
GUINEA
BISSAU
Bissau
GUINEA
Conakry
Ouagadougou
NIGERIA
Ndjamena
DJIBOUTI
Djibouti
Freetown
SIERRA
LEONE
IVORY
COAST
GHANA
TOGO
BENIN
Lagos
CENTRAL
AFRICAN REPUBLIC
Addis Ababa
ETHIOPIA
Monrovia
LIBERIA
Abidjan
Accra
Porto
Novo
Lome
Malabo
CAMEROON
Yaounde
Bangui
Zaire R.
UGANDA
SOMALIA
EQUATORIAL GUINEA
Libreville
CONGO
Kampala
KENYA
Mogadishu
Equator
GABON
ZAIRE
RWANDA
Kigali
Nairobi
INDIAN
Brazzaville
Kinshasa
Bujumbura
BURUNDI
TANZANIA
OCEAN
Luanda
Dar-es-Salaam
ATLANTIC
OCEAN
ANGOLA
ZAMBIA
MALAWI
Lilongwe
Moroni
COMOROS
Lusaka
Harare
MOZAMBIQUE
Antananarivo
ZIMBABWE
Windhoek
BOTSWANA
Gaborone
MADAGASCAR
Tropic of Capricorn
NAMIBIA
Pretoria
Mbabane
Maputo
SWAZILAND
Maseru
LESOTHO
SOUTH
AFRICA
0   500   1000 km

1

The Trial of
Decolonization
(1960–1964)

The Legacy of History

The rapid decolonization of the African continent beginning at the end of the fifties brought about a major change in relations between the two great powers and Africa. While exempt from all colonial responsibilities in this part of the world, these very same powers were nevertheless not totally indifferent to its evolution.

The existence of a significant black minority on its own territory seems to structure the way the United States perceives Africa. Even before slavery had been abolished, southern United States groups for whom the presence of blacks was no longer deemed useful were establishing plans aimed at turning liberated slaves into "new American missionaries." This policy quickly took the form of renewed deportation of blacks and concluded with the "freedmen's" creation of the Republic of Liberia in 1847. Black Americans were also instrumental in evangelizing Africa at the end of the nineteenth century. In many respects, their action was regarded as fundamentally non-African, but it helped to coin the ideas of "pan-Africanism" and "cultural proximity" among limited groups of Black Americans and Africans.[1]

The historical relationship of Russia to Africa is at once older and more restricted. During the fifteenth century the first Russian explorer set foot on African soil, but not until 1723 with Peter the Great's project to create a road from India does one witness the birth of the idea of a Russian presence in Africa. In the nineteenth century the goal of the project was refined to preempt the unification of the Mediterranean British colonies with those of the Indian Ocean. Seen from this angle, choosing Ethiopia seems totally predictable since such a choice enabled Russia to secure stopovers for its traffic en route to the Pacific, an observation point on the road to India, as well as compensation for Turkish control of the Black Sea and the Mediterranean.[2] As a rival of European powers, czarist Russia mod-

1

estly attempted to play an anticolonial tune. At the time of Ethiopia's war with Italy (1895–96), Russia consented to giving the imperial Ethiopian regime medical aid and moral support—an act even reflected in Tolstoy.[3] Russia looked on with interest at the unraveling of the Boer War in southern Africa that pitted British power against Dutch "settlers." And there were, incidentally, no less than seventy works on the Transvaal war published in Russia between 1900 and 1905.[4]

Colonization of this continent caused America's attitude toward it to oscillate between interventionist inclinations and an already powerful isolationism. In 1884 the United States participated in the Berlin Conference but refused to sign its final accords.

Immediately following World War I President Wilson's politics suggested a bolder policy on the part of the United States—one clearly in favor of colonial emancipation. In fact, this policy primarily influenced an American pan-African movement, which made a top priority of decolonizing the continent as early as the 1919 Congress. This concern, it seems, was not shared by federal authorities. As a signatory of the Treaty of Saint-Germain-en-Laye in 1919, the United States found itself bound by the appended conventions about the future of German mandates. At the same time, the United States was also involved in controlling liquor and arms trading in Africa. But faced with congressional refusal to ratify the Versailles treaty and its attendant provisions, the United States requested a reorganization of the colonial pact. To this end, it negotiated a series of bilateral accords with each of the European powers granting it most-favored-nation status in the mandated territories.

It was Russia's October Revolution immediately after World War I that introduced the first break in colonial order. Although its ramifications were significantly muffled by the colonial powers and by the embryonic structure of African liberation movements, its historical impact on African decolonization seems undeniable. Indeed, as early as the Baku Congress, the Bolshevik regime chose a realist strategy of alliance with all anticolonial forces.

The Bolsheviks were excluded from Africa because European powers prohibited their presence; nevertheless they attempted to remain in direct contact with Africa. As early as 1921, they welcomed nationalist Africans to the University for Proletarians of the East—foremost among them Jomo Kenyatta, the future Kenyan head of state.[5] At the end of the twenties they designated George Padmore to head the African bureau of the Communist Internationale's trade union organization (PROFINTERN). Their intention was to improve their control of the pan-African movement. Soviet support, however, very quickly took the shape of a tutelage that the beginning of the Stalinist freeze helped to solidify. The injunctions given the South African communist party to reject any alliance with the white proletariat only led to its own weakening. The dogmatism inherent in its positions, the sharpness of its policy reversals, and the absolute priority accorded by the Soviet Union to the defense of its own national interests—all conspired in slowing down the search for some sort of Soviet-African solidarity.

After World War II the question of decolonization resurfaced in a new context. Having emerged a victor in the fight against Nazism, the United States in a graceful move called on Western powers to set dates as quickly as possible that would give colonial peoples the status of complete independence within a "future system of general security." [6] But faced with the demands of the Cold War and its Manichaean struggle, decolonization was relegated to the back burner. Instead, it seemed wiser at the time to give preference to interdependence (as opposed to independence), to the responsibilities of European powers, and to the defense of white minority interests. [7]

For example, having once declared itself in favor of Eritrean independence, the United States in 1950 asked the United Nations to adopt the principle of federal unification in Ethiopia. The source of this reversal is to be found in America's concern for maintaining a presence at the Kagnew Air Force Base in Eritrea. The Kagnew Air Force Base, which is integrated into a worldwide network stretching from the United States to the Philippines, offered a particular advantage in being located in a geographic zone distant from the magnetic poles where, therefore, the narrow range of daily variability reduces the number of frequency changes needed. [8]

In the global fight that the United States sought to wage against communist influence, it militated in favor of integrating Africa into the Western defense system. The United States naturally included Ethiopia in the constitution of a "Southern Tier" in the Middle East. At the Nairobi Conference in 1951 and at the Dakar Conference in 1954, the United States pressed for the insertion of Africa into NATO's defense sphere.

Stalinist Russia did not reap any benefits from this situation, a situation that nurtured anticolonial demands. The general air of Zhdanovism made it difficult to consider the young states' nationalism any other way than as the latest avatar of a vacillating imperialist system. The Soviet Union ordered communist parties to oppose the agreements that Burma, and then Indonesia, made for their independence. In Iran, the Soviet Union likened Mossadegh nationalism to a simple bourgeois maneuver, supported by the United States. Only at Stalin's death, and with the impetus of a peaceful, if timid, coexistence between the two superpowers, did the Soviet Union soften its position.

This evolution appeared clearly in February 1955 when Moscow officially took responsibility for the five principles (Panch Sila) of peaceful coexistence laid out in the Sino-Indian treaty of 1954. The same year, the highest Soviet leaders of the time, Khrushchev and Bulganin, traveled outside the socialist bloc for the first time. By taking political initiative in the Third World this way, the Soviet Union clearly demonstrated its willingness to support the Bandung spirit.

It was on the margins of the Soviet world and especially in the Middle East that the boldness of the Soviet view was most evident. Its April 1955 declaration on the Middle East followed shortly thereafter by the first Czechoslovakian arms sales to Egypt represented the major break in the Soviet Union's foreign policy since 1945.[9] A year later in February 1956 the Twentieth Congress of the Soviet Union's communist party (CPSU) empowered Khrushchev to specify three axes of Soviet policy in the Third World:

1. The choice of a "peaceful coexistence" policy justified by the irreversible reinforcement of the socialist camp and the emergence of a broad "peace zone" in the new, liberated countries;
2. The willingness of the Soviet Union to offer support for the economic development of these new states;
3. The recognition by the Soviet Union of the "national bourgeoisie" as principal vector in the antiimperialist struggle.

The desire for openness, which took the shape of an increased flow of exchange between the Soviet Union and the Third World, was essentially focused on the Middle East. Black Africa remained on the sidelines of the dynamic process. At Ghana's independence ceremonies in 1957, Moscow was represented by a single, disgraced minister, whereas the United States sent its vice president, Richard Nixon. The Soviet Union's errors with regard to Ghana up to 1960 stem from several factors. The Soviet Union obviously hesitated to get involved in a country where British influence seemed strong, or where antiimperialist fervor seemed weaker than in Cairo. In addition, the Soviet Union did not want to seem preoccupied by the influence that George Padmore had on Kwame Nkrumah. This father of pan-Africanism, who had been educated in part at Stalinist academies, had not only converted to militant anticommunism but also had become a fervent pro-Zionist. At the December 1958 Accra Conference the Soviet Union helplessly witnessed the triumph of George Padmore's ideas. It had counted on the influence of another pan-Africanist, W. E. B. Du Bois, to prevail on the question of the construction of African socialism. This limited example implicitly reveals the abiding dilemma of Khrushchevian diplomacy: faced with realities it did not control and did not necessarily understand, what then should have been the limits of Soviet ideological "tolerance"?

Although dealing with content far less formal than in the Soviet Union, the United States' adaptation to a changing world was no less real. In 1956 the first American congressional mission dispatched to Africa remarked that the United States was poorly prepared to deal with the new independent countries on that continent.[10] One year later, the vice president returned from his trip to Africa with a different impression. But it is important to note that he pleaded in favor of an African policy uninvolved with the tutelage of the European powers.

The Imprint of Developmentalism

Voluntarist optimism, so characteristic of American and Soviet behavior at the beginning of the sixties, cannot be reduced to John F. Kennedy's or Nikita Khrushchev's personal actions. Beyond the diplomatic-strategic framework, an understanding of the superpowers' politics in Africa requires taking into account the ideological field on which the rivalry was being fought.

All the same, while the close relationship of Soviet policy and Marxism is generally taken for granted (questionable as that might be), the interpretation of American policy as related to a developmentalist ideological underpinning is generally neglected. Soviet policy is supposed to rest upon a well-established corpus of doctrines; it is evaluated in terms of an adequate matching of intentions and actions. In contrast, American policy, presumably devoid of any teleological vision of the world, largely escapes such assessment.

If the contrasting "natures" of the Soviet and American regimes make it impossible to make sense of their conduct on the basis of criteria that are identical on all counts, the overestimation of ideology in one case and its underestimation in another are scarcely factors. Packenham's work has highlighted the strong vitality of the liberal ideology in American aid programs.[11] Badie's works recommend a rereading of the American political discourse on Africa throughout developmentalist literature.[12] As things stand, initial American and Soviet views of Africa largely stemmed from a Western vision of the world that imperatives of diplomatic-strategic rivalry could perhaps hide but never erase. As far as this goes, a comparative reading of American and Soviet Africanist work from the first half of the sixties proves to be informative. Both Americans and Soviets project an eminently ethnocentric vision onto the African continent. The Soviet vision emanated from the Western dimensions of Marx's thought; the United States' vision stemmed from a belief in the Western model.

Simple references such as "noncapitalist way" or "objective laws of historical development" are enough to define the evolutionist approach in Soviet thinking. In 1957 the Soviet Africanist Potekhin summarized Soviet thought on nation building rather well: "The process of forming a nation is currently happening very quickly. Nowadays, not only is Africa's political map changing, but so is its ethnic map: old ethnic diversity is becoming a thing of the past, making room for national communities." [13]

Observing that Africa assimilates the lessons of history quickly, Soviet Africanist research manages quite easily to insert its entire social dynamic into the inevitable confrontation between traditional and modern forces. By that standard, tribalism is transformed into the survival of the past at a time when "peoples are becoming conscious of the idea of a nation." [14] To be sure, the Soviets did not totally eliminate African "specificities." But "the absence of a bourgeoisie" or "the collective ownership of the land," far from constituting obstacles to national integration, were considered, in fact, to be catalysts of an accelerated move from feudalism to socialism. To support this reasoning, the Soviet Union endlessly offered the central Asian republics or Outer Mongolia as "one-size-fits-all" models of accelerated development. Far from being reducible to a mere exercise in propaganda, the valorization of the central Asian historical experience effectively enabled application of the isomorphic Soviet image of what it meant to become an African society.

American developmentalist actions were largely motivated by similar assumptions. Shils's work, which faithfully reflects the developmentalist thought of the early sixties, defines "Western representative democracy" as the political ideal to be reached by all human societies. La Palombara echoes him; he sets forth the Anglo-Saxon system as political standard for "good" and "bad" political development. To be sure, like their Soviet colleagues, American developmentalists note the specific conditions of the developing countries, but these are seen as anachronisms that the march of history will undo. Thus, far from encouraging recognition of the historicity of African nations, the partial acknowledgment of their "specificity" reinforced the relevance of "step-by-step" development in the eyes of developmentalists. Shils shows himself to be "disposed" to accept, in passing, the existence of "tutelary democracies" insofar as they "offer a more realistic settlement with the only slowly tractable realities of traditional societies." [15] In the same vein, Coleman's analyses of Ethiopia and Liberia argue in favor of the chances of "democratization" of these "supple oligarchies," given the historical evolution of Western societies. [16]

The similarity between Soviet and American courses of action does not end there. For the developmentalist school, political development is seen as an inherent process aimed at converting traditional allegiances into allegiance to the nation-state. The process of modernization that always underlies it becomes a zero-sum game between "modern" actors and "traditional" masses.

Thus, even when they aspired to projecting antithetical ideological models onto Africa, Soviets and Americans both relied on evolutionist political constructs that explain their initial optimism as well as their subsequent disappointments.

African Manifestations of Khrushchevian Voluntarism

Filling the Vacuum

Always seeking even the slightest advantage, Khrushchev's policies made it a top priority to exploit situations where old colonial powers seemed exhausted and expended. In this respect, Soviet behavior in French-speaking Africa stands in striking contrast to its behavior in English-speaking Africa. In francophone Africa, nearly all of the new states (with the exception of Guinea and Mali) remained bound to their old tutelary power and the Soviet presence there was modest. In anglophone Africa, on the other hand, as well as in the African Horn and in the former Belgian Congo (now Zaire), wherever the neocolonial influence of other European powers emerged less strongly, the Soviet Union was more easily able to take advantage of the tensions and conflicts between African states and Western powers.

The Soviet Union's first African experience, that with Guinea, in large part stimulated Nikita Khrushchev's initial activism. The sharpness of Guinea's rupture with France was hailed as a "decisive blow" leveled at colonialism, even though recurrences on the rest of the continent were not expected.[17] From February 1959 on, the Soviet Union offered to buy Guinean agricultural products that France no longer wanted. Thanks to an initial $35 million loan, Guinea was offered the opportunity to import Soviet equipment without laying out any cash. Furthermore, as of 1961 the number of socialist countries figuring in Guinea's foreign trade reached about thirty-five percent. By offering an economic alternative to isolation, the Soviet Union was also to emphasize the unmistakable radicalization. When in March 1960 Sékou Touré announced his country's withdrawal from the Franc Zone, a protocol was signed with the Soviet Union for various economic projects (a canning factory, a cement factory, harbor installations, sports complexes).[18]

The same month, Czechoslovakia delivered the first arms shipment to Guinea, which had received no response to its request for military aid from the United States in December 1958. That was all the Soviet Union needed to pour on the flattery and exaggerated optimism about the Guinean "revolution."[19] And the Soviet Union was quite naturally inclined to extend similar praise to other African states, most notably to Ghana.

In August 1960, while the United States was still hesitating about whether or not to contribute to the financing of the Akosombo Dam project, Nikita Khrushchev proposed to a Ghanaian delegation that the Soviets take the operation in hand. In the wake of the "Aswan events," he demonstrated his willingness to open a $40 million line of credit, while the Soviet press purposely played up Western delays.[20]

The Soviet Union's ability to take advantage of the tensions between

Western powers and African states should not blind us to the latter's adeptness at bringing out the East-West rivalry, at capitalizing on it, and at containing it, too. On this point, the example of eastern Africa (Ethiopia and Somalia) is very instructive.

At the beginning of the sixties, Kenya and Somalia gained their independence, but the situation was soured by the question of their borders with Ethiopia. Worried about Somali irredentism, the Ethiopian government insisted that the emancipation of the country be subordinated to the final delimitation of borders, as provided by the 1948 accord. In January 1959, moreover, Ethiopia did not have the support of the United States, which was endorsing the British Lennox-Boyd declaration on the territorial fusion of "British" and "Italian" Somalia. Threatened by the territory's new independence and by an absence of border guarantees, the Ethiopian emperor attempted to compensate in Moscow for Washington's failing support. He made it clear to the United States that the alliance that bound them was conditional and that the United States support of Somali positions would compel him to accept the Soviet offer.[21] At the end of 1959, when the emperor went to Moscow, the Soviets declared they were ready to take on the training of an imperial guard of ten thousand men and that the offer could ultimately be extended further to the whole of the Ethiopian army.[22] They consented to a $100 million credit for the building of a refinery in Eritrea and a technological institute.[23]

It is interesting to see, notably in light of American diplomatic archives, how much the United States was duped in this game—to the point of fearing a veritable reversal of alliances in the area. Still, a close reading of the archives suggests that the opportunities for Soviet intervention in Ethiopia were limited. The emperor, who had held it against the United States that it had not financed the Aswan dam, was above all afraid of Egypt's intentions. He did not fear Somalia so much as its possible use as an Egyptian base of attack.[24] One can therefore well imagine the difficulties that a long-standing anti-Arab Ethiopian attitude might have had in accommodating a Soviet Union whose privileged ally in the Middle East remained Egypt.

Upon his return from Moscow, the emperor did not delay in obtaining a secret military guarantee from the United States against any Somali attack and ignoring the opportunity for reinforcing cooperation with the Soviet Union. When Ethiopia fell in 1974, it had made use of less than half of the 1959 Soviet loan.

Although the Soviet Union had not been able to take advantage of the passing crisis between Ethiopia and the United States, it nonetheless remained interested in the region. But faced with regional conflicts between Ethiopia and Somalia on the one hand and between Somalia and Kenya on the other, the Soviet Union maintained a cautious attitude. In March 1963 the Soviet press referred to Somalia's desire to be unified as "natural," but that reading of the situation turns out to have been purely tactical. When Mogadishu (Somalia) broke its diplomatic ties with London, Moscow saw some advantage in taking its side this time.

As soon as the Soviet Union learned of the United States' rejection of a Somali request for an arms shipment, the Soviet Union offered its services through a third party, namely, Czechoslovakia. Mogadishu turned down the offer but made use of the Soviet proposition to benefit from Anglo-Italian military aid. Falling deeper into the abyss, Moscow was still far from establishing itself as a reconciler of diverging interests. Concerning the heart of the problem—the intangibility of borders—its position remained ambivalent. For the Soviet Union, the idea of putting colonial borders back into discussion seemed desirable, but actually doing so was quite difficult.[25]

In fact, one of the essential dimensions of Khrushchevian strategy involved making clear decisions about all of the conflicts between African countries and Western powers, but it also included abstaining from interfering in inter-African conflicts. In 1963 on the eve of Kenya's independence, Somalia received $10 million in military aid from the United States, the Federal Republic of Germany, and Italy, on the express condition that it turn down all other sources of supplies. At the same time, Mogadishu preferred to turn to Moscow, which, without any conditional rider, offered $22 million more. No sooner had the Soviet delegation left Mogadishu, where it had come to evaluate Somali needs, than it moved on to Ethiopia. It then proposed military aid to Ethiopia in excess of that granted to Somalia, in exchange for breaking its military ties with the United States.[26] The Soviet Union extended its play in this game of furtive alliances to Kenya, a country that was of interest to the Soviet Union even before its independence. As of 1960, it understood the benefits it could gain from division at the heart of the Kenyan African National Union (KANU). The Soviet Union was indeed eventually solicited by one of its leaders, Oginga Odinga, whose rival, Tom Mboya, was arranging multiple contracts with American groups. Oginga Odinga was in favor of dispossessing the whites of their land and africanizing the Kenyan economy. He wanted to be enthroned in Moscow as the "progressive leader." The Soviet Union responded to his expectations by opening the doors of its universities to three Kenyan students. By 1964 Kenyan nationals had become the best-represented African students in Soviet universities. Several months before Kenya's independence, anticipated for December 1964, Oginga Odinga obtained a Soviet promise of military assistance and economic aid amounting to $45 million. This included the financing of the Lumumba Institute, which trained KANU cadres and where in 1965 both the Odinga-Kenyatta conflict and the Soviet-American rivalry crystallized.

Rather paradoxically, the crisis in the Congo, considered the major crisis of decolonization, fails to demonstrate clearly how much the Soviets wished to prevent an American presence in Africa. But it does illustrate the "at-the-least-cost" strategy based fundamentally on avoiding any direct confrontation with the United States.

From the start, the Congo affair developed poorly for the Soviet Union. In a very assertive way, the United States, Belgium, and the United Nations all agreed to keep the Soviet Union at bay. The Soviet Union did not have a network of influence at its disposal in the area. Its main African allies, Ghana and Guinea, were geographically rather distant from the Congo.

Since the Soviet Union did not have the real means to influence the course of things, it used "tribunal diplomacy" to the hilt at the United Nations. But there, too, its room for maneuvering turned out to be cramped. In order to cover its inability to act, it advocated "maximalist" amendments to Western and Afro-Asiatic resolutions. Its commitment in the field was of the most modest sort, in spite of the anticommunist drama deliberately orchestrated by Patrice Lumumba's adversaries. At Lumumba's request, in July 1960 Khrushchev declared that he was ready to take "decisive measures to curtail aggression." [27] As a first step, Soviet logistical support consisted primarily of shipping food supplies and transporting Ghanaian contingents. At the end of August, this same support helped Patrice Lumumba transport government troops dispatched to regain control of the Kasaï province. But the fact that Congolese airports were closed to foreign aircraft—a measure taken by the United Nations Organization in the Congo (UNOC) specifically to prevent Soviet intervention—ruined the Soviet Union's chances. In fact, the specter of Soviet involvement facilitated the acceleration of Lumumba's eviction by Kasavubu and enhanced the intensification of the United States presence at the same time. Speaking at the United Nations, Khrushchev quickly drew lessons from the crisis. Although he denied having suffered a setback from the crisis, he did not show any desire to renew the challenge. For the Soviet Union, involvement in the Congo was over for the time being; but for the United States, it was all just beginning.

The Soviet Network

The Congo crisis demonstrated to the Soviet Union the weakness of its means and the necessity for reexamining its ambitions; but at the same time it gave the Soviets the option of taking advantage of the potential for diplomatic solidarity with African states.

From the outset the Congo crisis helped to strengthen Soviet-Guinean relations. Sékou Touré went to Moscow officially on the eve of the Fifteenth Session of the United Nations General Assembly in order to reconcile the two countries' positions. It was, however, with respect to its relations with Ghana that the Soviet Union most profited from the Congo crisis. Nkrumah's reserve vis-à-vis the superpowers compelled him to try to dissuade Lumumba from dealing with either one of them. In favor of the United Nations action, he did not share the initial criticisms that the Casablanca group had expressed. But this policy of rigorous equidistance could not be maintained. Nkrumah's bias against the Soviet Union was tempered as a result of his meeting with Khrushchev at the Fifteenth Session of the United Nations General Assembly. Six months later, Patrice Lumumba's assassination convinced Nkrumah that Westerners were "guilty" and that a rapprochement with the Soviet Union was now a necessity. Symbolically, Ghana invited Leonid Brezhnev to follow his stay in eastern Africa with a visit to Accra on the very day that Patrice Lumumba's death was officially disclosed.

The Soviet ability to seize upon the expectations of African states left disappointed by the West should not, however, be overestimated. A careful reading of Soviet newspapers of the early sixties rather clearly underlines the difficulties the Soviet Union experienced in understanding the coherence of African diplomatic strategies.[28] It was as if the Soviets were expecting their interlocutors to adhere to a tacit code of conduct formulated in the following terms: in exchange for a Soviet commitment to change its attitudes toward these states' domestic and foreign policies, the latter necessarily had to align themselves with the Soviet Union on the Congo question as well as on Berlin.[29] Now, the Soviet Union's daily diplomatic practice presented it with contradictory conduct. Its perception of Nigerian foreign policy is revealing: Moscow referred to it as an "incoherent policy"—as if Lagos's anti-Western activity (its break with France in 1961 following nuclear tests in Algeria, its refusal to join the Common Market, and its militant anticolonialism at the United Nations) were contradicted by an attachment to the West and a distrust of the Soviet Union.[30] Far from being inconsistent, however, Nigerian foreign policy is quite clearly intelligible. The hostile stance Nigeria took toward France was not based on any sort of anti-Western mystique but rather on a certain distrust of an actor whose influence in West Africa stood as an obstacle to regional ambitions. The sequence of events, and most notably the Biafran War, eventually confirmed the importance of this particular aspect of Nigerian-French relations.

Nonetheless, Soviet resentment remained strictly verbal. Beginning in 1962, Soviet overtures toward the more moderate parts of Africa were increased, even with the combined effects of temporary relaxation of African tensions (Algeria's independence put an end to rifts between the Casablanca and Brazzaville groups, there was a lull in the Congo crisis, and the Mauritanian affair was settled) and the vicissitudes of the Sino-Soviet conflict. For Moscow, it was a question of appearing to be a responsible power hostile to "exporting the revolution" or deepening intra-African rifts.[31] Soviet integration efforts in francophone Africa fully met such intentions. As early as 1960 at Yaoundé in Cameroon, where it had never really supported the Union des Populations du Cameroun (UPC), the Soviet Union unsuccessfully proposed establishing diplomatic relations. But two years later at the Ebolowa Congress, President Ahidjo, pushed by rallying *"upécistes,"* encouraged a slow opening toward the East.[32] The Soviet Union, which was then clearly playing the established governments' card, completely neglected revolutionary alternatives. In Niger it made an overture to the Hamani Diori regime, in spite of the support it had expressly granted to the Sawaba at the end of the fifties. Even with respect to the Stanleyville regime set up by Patrice Lumumba's successors to oppose the central Congo-Leopoldville regime, the Soviet Union demonstrated remarkable prudence. While recognizing it as the only legal government of the Congo-Leopoldville, the Soviet Union refrained from providing any direct aid. The speedy rally of Gizenga in Adoula (August 1961) dissipated Soviet embarrassment and the Soviets in turn reestablished diplomatic relations with Leopoldville in December 1961.

Even though its returns were not spectacular, this outreach policy provided the Soviet Union with results that are worth considering. In certain cases, as in that of Nigeria, the very act of being in touch with the Soviet Union contributed to attenuating the categorical anticommunism of African leaders. For some of them, this outreach revealed the advantages of a foreign policy more emancipated from their old tutelary powers.

American Direct Involvement

The analysis of American policies regarding Africa has always been trapped in a web of debatable clichés.

The first among them takes for granted America's lack of interest in Africa, by reason of the limited number of its direct interests, the moderate level of Soviet pressure, and especially the presence of Europe. Such an America-centered reading, however, fails to bring together the marginal nature of United States interests in Africa on the one hand and the sometimes decisive impact the United States has as a presence on that continent on the other hand. Thus, if it is indeed probable that, on the scale of America's world priorities in 1960, Ethiopia and Congo occupied but a small place, it remains no less true that within the scope of these two countries America's influence was central.

The second commonplace tends to overestimate the United States' potential influence in African independence, presumably because of its non-colonizing history. There, too, certain facts suggest that more caution might be beneficial. At the end of his mission, carried out in thirteen African countries after John F. Kennedy's election, Senator Church stressed that the image the United States projected was far from being uniformly good. Senator Gore, who followed a short time later, concluded similarly. He reported finding that among a good number of African leaders there was a lack of understanding of the interests of the United States in Africa and that in West Africa American policy was accused of being procolonialist.[33]

Thus, while John F. Kennedy's voluntarism did inscribe itself well in an optimistic, developmentalist view, it was also motivated by a concern for putting an end to the deterioration of America's image in Africa. This process, born of the United States' excessive identification with the interests of colonial powers, was aggravated by the ramifications of racial tensions in America.

However, in both African cases where an American policy of direct influence was carried out—that is to say, a policy that was not contingent upon European behavior—United States strategy was never preconceived.

In Ethiopia, where America's involvement dates back to 1952, the basis of American policy amounted to a defense of the status quo in order to retain privileged access to military facilities awarded by the emperor. Besides the Kagnew Air Base, where seven thousand American nationals were employed (of whom eight hundred were officers), the United States had in Ethiopia a military mission, a marine research center, and a NASA observation center.[34]

In December 1960, when the Imperial Guard tried to overthrow the emperor, who was away on a trip to Brazil, the United States had a hand in his regaining power; the Kagnew Air Force Base enabled loyalist officers to communicate with the emperor. And shortly after the failure of negotiations between the American ambassador and the rebels, the chief of the American military mission became actively involved in the counterattack by loyalist troops.[35]

For the American embassy in Addis Ababa, the lesson of the failed putsch was clear: without a policy of internal reform, the future of the imperial regime was in jeopardy. And, as if he were in doubt that any such reforms could be undertaken, the American ambassador proposed avoiding "excessive identification with those who might be considered reactionary forces" in the event of a new insurrection.[36] There was no followthrough to this policy of conditional support, which the Bowles Mission had reiterated in February 1962. Indeed, until the emperor's death, the United States policy in Ethiopia was limited to military aid that the Bowles Report evaluated as being far beyond what Ethiopian needs warranted.[37] Between 1962 and 1965 Ethiopia absorbed sixty percent of America's military aid to black African countries. This completely unconditional military aid remained considerably greater than economic assistance. Three sets of reasons can explain the surprising and atypical imbalance visible in American aid programs to Africa.

By honoring Ethiopia's requests for military aid, the United States thought it could guarantee its own access to military facilities. The emperor, in fact, understood American interests in his country so well that he continued to up his requests. In 1963 he presented a shopping list of $300 million worth of armaments, which was, however, turned down. In addition, by delivering arms that Washington knew full well were poorly maintained, the United States was clearly seeking the sympathy of an army that was the sole alternative to imperial power.[38] In 1961 the American embassy was counting on the imminence of the army's accession to power.

Finally, America's economic aid was small compared to its military effort because the emperor requested very little. The rare agricultural aid programs that were under way were thwarted by the interests of "feudal" landowners.[39] In this instance as in others, reference to American policy in Ethiopia as an "absence of policy" suggests how totally ambiguous everything was. As it stands in this particular case, American policy demonstrated less a lack of interest in Ethiopia than a refusal, or an inability, to think through ways of reconciling the preservation of direct interests with the process of modifying the social status quo.

In the Congo American policy took a different course. At the outset the United States did not have any interests to preserve in the country that was soon to become Zaire. At the very most, it would have liked to maintain its privileged right of access to this imposing country's cobalt and copper mines. At the Belgium-hosted Brussels Conference in January 1960, the territory's date of independence was set for June 30 of the same year. But even before then, the political landscape seemed riddled with powerful rifts. With the exception of Patrice Lumumba's *Mouvement National Congolais* (MNC), most Congolese movements relied heavily on tribal associations and allowed foreign advisers too great a role. That was the case with Kasavubu's Abako. It was above all the case with Conakat—directed by Moise Tshombe, shaped by American missionaries, and powerfully backed by the *Union minière du Haut-Katanga*. From the moment independence was proclaimed, the balance of forces emerged as unstable. Belgium, which only reluctantly accepted Patrice Lumumba's electoral victory and his appointment to the position of prime minister, was unable to resist the temptation to return to the *status ante*. Ten days after the Congo's independence, Belgium sent in armed forces to squelch a mutiny of the army of this nonetheless sovereign country. This Belgian action opened up the Pandora's box that propelled Congo's conflict into the international arena.

Poorly versed in African realities, the Eisenhower administration saw Europe's tutelage of the Congo as the best defense against a Soviet incursion. At the beginning of the summer of 1960, the influence of Africanists in the State Department was remarkably insignificant. It is revealing that the first American arrangements were made by the United States embassy in Brussels.[40] When the Belgian intervention was discredited, the United States cleverly played its United Nations card. United Nations troops in the Congo, headed by the American Cordier and half-financed by the United States, in many ways constituted the best defense against Soviet military intervention, the best "anticommunist umbrella." On this issue, American diplomatic archives speak eloquently: Kasavubu's overthrow of Lumumba in September 1960 was meticulously prepared by the leaders of the UNOC, the United States Ambassador, and the CIA.[41] When it inherited the Congo file in early 1961, the Kennedy administration was forced to recognize that eliminating Lumumba—an event in which Kennedy's Republican predecessors had had a hand—did not guarantee the country's stability. The Kennedy administration therefore understood that only a broadened government would enable a relaxing of tensions and a spoiling of the success enjoyed by the Lumumbist government set up in Stanleyville. So its choice was Cyrille Adoula, an old unionist linked to the AFL-CIO. On the face of it, American goals in the Congo tended to ensure the country's stability by being opposed as much to Tshombe's Katanga secession as to the Lumumbist government in Stanleyville. In fact, United States behavior departed from this position in principle. Considered procommunist, Gizenga, Lumumba's successor, seemed to the United States to be more menacing than Tshombe. As a result it tried to put into motion an Adoula-Tshombe rapprochement that would marginalize Gizenga.[42] Since it was the only Western power able to supplant Belgium's discredited involvement, the United States acquired a dominant position on the Congo's political gameboard.

The Department of State records: "We are making every effort to keep Gizenga isolated from potential domestic and foreign support. . . . We assist the central government with advice on economic and political matters, aided by the fact that our relations with the government are very close, far better than those enjoyed by any other power."[43]

At the same time, the United States was forced to admit, as was noted by Assistant Secretary of State G. Ball in December 1961, that in fact the central problem in the Congo was still the Katanga issue. Despite the strong resistance of both France and Belgium, the United States resolved to cross swords with Tshombe via the UNOC. The hardening of the American position compelled Tshombe to start planning. In December 1961 he signed the Kitona accords with Adoula, to be overseen by both the United Nations and the United States. But Tshombe's recognition of the Congo's "fundamental law" and therefore the central power's authority emerged as purely tactical. At the end of 1962 following lengthy negotiations between Leopoldville and the Katanga province, the two parties split without having reached an agreement. Worried about Adoula's power and the possibility of a Lumumbist or a military coup, Guillon, the American ambassador in Leopoldville, vigorously pleaded in favor of military intervention by the UNOC against Tshombe.[44] Bypassing reservations of the Defense Department and of the State Department's Bureau of European Affairs, John F. Kennedy decided in December 1962 to provide all necessary equipment to the UNOC to obtain the Katanga region's surrender by force.[45] The Katangan secession caved in with unexpected speed on January 4, 1963. Confirmed and comforted in its role as protector of the Congolese regime, the United States saw its influence grow with each new development of this endless crisis. The reinforcement of American positions in this country stemmed in large part from the decisive action of the American embassy in Leopoldville. It was the embassy primarily that told Washington what direction to take.

Again, consulting American diplomatic archives is instructive. They reveal clearly how much control over public life the United States had acquired in the Congo, as well as how much control it had over the selection of local actors. When a Lumumbist insurrection at Kivu led by P. Mulele erupted in 1964, the American embassy proposed a direct American intervention, given UNOC's reluctance and the Congolese army's inefficiency.[46] Without first consulting Congolese military officials, the American embassy took it upon itself to establish a list of matériel that Washington would need to send to the Congo. It was also incumbent on the American embassy to convince Adoula and Mobutu of the well-foundedness of an American military intervention.

> I believe both [Adoula and Mobutu] are ready to accept accrued US military aid, but both would hesitate to commit themselves ahead of time to a 140-man military mission or to sign formal agreements. They want help but each in his own way fears political consequences.[47]

But faced with the disadvantages of direct intervention, the United States brought up the idea of pan-African intervention. The weak response, however, that this proposal elicited caused the United States to turn to Belgium, which consented to deploy a contingent to support the Congolese air force. At the same time, the CIA was running a decisive operation against Mulele's forces hiding out at Bukava.

Give or take a little, the same scenario was reenacted in August 1964 when Mulelist forces captured Stanleyville to combat Tshombe's access to power in Leopoldville. But failing this time to overcome Belgium's reluctance, the United States dispatched some one hundred men to Leopoldville. Its official intervention was accompanied by a CIA operation against Mulelist forces, which involved five B-26 bombers piloted by Cuban exiles, a maintenance team, and seven hundred mercenaries.

Despite its impressive nature, all of this was not enough to thwart Mulelist forces. For this reason, when these same forces took expatriate Europeans hostage in 1964, the United States added logistical support to Belgium's military intervention.

The endless recurrence of creeping intervention offered only mitigated benefits for the United States. While the decisive influence the United States wielded in Congo-Leopoldville was confirmed, it is equally evident that the United States was unable to come up with stable political solutions. The failure of the Adoula operation and Tshombe's 1964 return to the political scene clearly signaled that there were limits to America's influence.

Since the eradication of communist influence was apparently insufficient to ensure stability on the African continent, the United States finally came around to tempering its initial optimism regarding its activities in Africa.

The Search for Credibility in Africa

From the beginning of the sixties, when African states obtained their various independences *en masse*, thereby modifying the balance of power in the United Nations, the United States understood that the United Nations was becoming the symbolic field of its indirect confrontation with the Soviet Union. The United States realized very quickly that its diplomatic credibility in Africa hinged on completing the process of decolonization of lusophone Africa and on the struggle against apartheid regimes.

The question of the Azores occupied a particularly crucial place in American-Portuguese relations. In 1963 seventy-five percent of military air traffic between the United States and Europe still used the Terceira base as a stopover. The logistical importance of this base, obvious in American intervention in Lebanon in 1958 and in Berlin in 1961, was confirmed at the time of the 1964 Stanleyville crisis. The United States, particularly worried about ensuring its control over the Atlantic, even considered setting up an Atlantic navigation-aid radar network along the Portuguese coast and on the island of Madeira. In context, the position of Portuguese ultracolonialists deserves note, especially since Angolan and Mozambican ports regularly welcomed American ships on rotation.

Although less significant, American military interests in the Republic of South Africa are worth noting. In September 1960 the United States opened a NASA communications base that was integrated into the Deep Space Instrumentation Facility (DSIF) network. Near Pretoria, it housed the last earth relay station for the Atlantic Missile Range Telemetry Network (AMRTN) missile telemetry. In Johannesburg, Capetown, and Durban, the airport infrastructures were suitable for American Air Force ballistic missile launch operations. Finally, South African ports enabled instrumentation ships to guide American ships that operated between the southern Atlantic and the Indian Ocean.[48] Given the magnitude of interests at stake, the American military was the first to react to the possible renewal of questions about United States relations with Lisbon and Pretoria. In a memo addressed to the Secretary of Defense in July 1963, the Joint Chiefs of Staff recommended not to give in to "blackmail" on the part of the African nations that would endanger United States' relations with Portugal and South Africa. But with the hypothesis that some concessions by black Africa would become inevitable, the Joint Chiefs of Staff proposed to "sacrifice" American interests in the Republic of South Africa to better preserve American interests in the Azores.[49] The disadvantages of a strategic retreat in the Republic of South Africa were perfectly avoidable. Even on an economic level, South Africa offered no vital interest at the time. A secret State Department report dated October 1963 estimated that there was not a single raw material coming from the Republic of South Africa that could be characterized as being of strategic importance for the American economy.[50] On the basis of these considerations, the Kennedy administration chose a middle course whose uniqueness was quite quickly blurred.

Having barely begun its term, the Kennedy administration gave the United Nations the impression that it wanted to comply with African demands. In April 1961 the United States supported Resolution 1603 calling upon Portugal to extend to its colonies the right of self-determination. In June of the same year the United States backed a Security Council resolution deploring Portuguese oppression in Angola. It was at this time that the *União de Populações de Angola* (UPA)—forerunner of the *Frente Nacional de Liberação de Angola* (FNLA), as we shall see shortly—began to receive the first secret infusion of American funds.

But the effects of this multilateral diplomatic action were largely canceled out by assurances given to Portugal on a bilateral level. As the expiration date of America's lease (December 1962) on the Azores neared, American anticolonialist ardor diminished. Aware of still having a trump card to play, Salazar's government refused to respond positively to a request for a lease renewal. It seemed satisfied to offer the United States a simple and traditional lease, renewable on a yearly basis. Overestimating the "power of the weak," whose limits had indeed been pointed out by an *ad hoc* committee,[51] the Kennedy administration gave up its policy of harassing the Portuguese colonial regime in early 1963. It compensated for the cut in bilateral military aid with a series of gifts (three war vessels and thirty T-37s) and with an increase in its economic aid.[52] Moreover, under the decisive influence of the United States Ambassador to Lisbon, Admiral Anderson, American-Portuguese military cooperation was maintained at the highest level.

In July 1963 John F. Kennedy drew lessons from the situation. In a memorandum, he asked the State Department to put an end to initiatives against Portugal at the United Nations and to displace its efforts onto the Republic of South Africa in order to preserve American credibility in black Africa. And to dodge more effectively the debate over sanctions against the Republic of South Africa—a debate African states would not fail to bring up during the United Nations General Assembly meeting in the fall of 1963—America's chief executive took the initiative of making a unilateral declaration ending the sale of arms to that country. But here, too, American diplomatic archives reveal the gap between a position of principle and its concrete expression. The list of arms that were subject to embargo was so restricted that it understandably led Pretoria to view the American decision as an extension of "the earlier policy of a partial embargo." [53] Such was also the opinion in the State Department where, with the exception of the Bureau of African Affairs, few high-ranking officials in positions of responsibility seemed ready to trigger a test of strength against Pretoria. For Secretary of State Dean Rusk, domestic South African policy, as condemnable as it was, was no worse than that of other "small African states whose domestic practices reflect different forms of totalitarianism." [54]

Ideological Control in Socialist Experiments

Both cautious and versatile, the Khrushchevian strategy of opening up toward "moderate" Africa was accompanied gradually by an effort to build privileged alliances. These steps, which concerned Guinea, Ghana, and Mali, were a response to a number of imperatives.

At the beginning of the sixties, the Soviet Union noted the blossoming of situations in the Third World whose diversity the Twentieth Congress of the Communist Party of the Soviet Union (CPSU) misjudged. Regarding Cuba, the Soviet Union showed its surprise at the ability of a nationalist movement (in which the Communist Party played only a small financial role) to radicalize itself and engage on a socialist path. For Khrushchev, the Cuban experience was all the more significant for having taken place in the general context of peaceful coexistence. However, whereas the Castro revolution led the Soviet Union to revise upward its revolutionary expectations in the Third World, the Iraqi experience prevented it from giving broad scope to this *aggiornamento*. Quite the contrary, the severe repression of Iraqi communists by the "national bourgeoisie" dissuaded the Soviet Union from idealizing its antiimperialist virtues.

Confronted both with contradictory political experiences and with ideological pressure from China, the Soviet Union opted for an intermediate path. It consecrated this middle road with the concept of "national democracy." When, in April 1961 at the Twenty-second Congress of the CPSU, the first roll of "national democracy" states was drawn up, three of the five states on that list were African: Guinea, Ghana, Mali, Cuba, and Indonesia. In many ways such overrepresentation of African states seemed surprising. While the selection of Guinea seemed dictated by the severity of the Franco-Guinean break and the accelerated enhancement of Soviet-Guinean relations, the choice of Ghana and Mali seemed less justified.

In April 1961 the Soviet Union's relations with Ghana and Mali were still limited. In 1959 the Ghanaian Convention People's Party (CPP), unlike the *Parti démocratique de Guinée* (PDG), was deemed by Moscow to be a party without popular foundation.[55] Perceptions of Mali were hardly any more favorable. Like Senghor's, Modibo Keita's socialism in 1960 attracted the derogatory label of "petit bourgeois."

To be sure, since the Congolese crisis and the dissolution of the Federation of Mali, Soviet diplomatic relations with these two states had been reinforced. But compared to the strength of Soviet-Egyptian or Soviet-Iraqi relations at the time, their importance was marginal. Is this to say that the selection of these two African clients from among the "national democracy" states was inspired solely by ideological considerations? Or that by such standards, Ghanaian socialism was judged "more serious" than Egyptian socialism? Nothing could be less sure. In fact, on the eve of the Twenty-second Congress, Khrushchev needed to offer the party and China evidence of the vitality of Soviet foreign policy and of the correctness of its initial views. At a time when Khrushchev was trying to reassure Third World communist parties and appease China, it seemed difficult to put forth states like Egypt and Iraq as models of "national democracy," since these countries had become masters of the repression of communism. Consequently, Moscow had no other choice than to enthrone African states whose principal characteristic was the lack of a communist party.

Having made this choice, the Soviet Union insisted on rationalizing it *a posteriori* by using a classic procedure to strengthen its ties with the governments and the parties of these states. As early as 1961, agreements were signed with the Sudanese Union of Mali and the Ghanaian CPP. In January 1962 Anastas Mikoyan traveled to Accra to applaud the desire of Ghanaian leaders to construct socialism—later privately confiding to them that he did not deem any of them to be truly socialist.[56]

The Soviet Union tried to add economic and commercial support to the ideological unction it wanted to offer its new allies. Between 1959 and 1964, Guinea, Ghana, and Mali received nearly half (44.5%) of the Soviet Union's aid commitments to black Africa. Taking into account not just the commitments but also the disbursements by Moscow, the portion of these three countries in the social aid program to Africa reached 74.5%. More than 80% of this aid comprised credits authorized at a rate of 2.5% annual interest and reimbursable over twelve years. This Soviet aid naturally helped its beneficiaries to increase imports of Soviet goods. That explains the noticeable and sometimes spectacular increase of the part played by socialist countries in the foreign trade figures of these states. Between 1959 and 1962 Guinean exports to the socialist camp rose from 16% to 33%. During the same period, the portion of its imports coming from the same countries rose from 9% to 38%.[57] The progress of exchange between Ghana and the Soviet Union was just as telling. Between 1961 and 1965 Ghana's trade with socialist countries increased from 4.7% to 26.3% in exports, and from 5.4% to 26.3% in imports.[58]

In the first half of the sixties, the Soviet Union thus became the privileged trade partner of at least two states (Guinea and Ghana). That, then, was indeed a distinctive characteristic of Soviet policy, if one realizes that since 1964 that country has never again been able to achieve a comparable trade position in Africa.

In retrospect, the Soviet Union seems to have been, for those three states, a partner in difficult times, a "crisis ally." Ghana, for example, found a favorable outlet for its cocoa production in its relations with the Soviet Union and other socialist countries. From December 1961 on, the Soviet Union committed itself to purchasing up to sixty thousand tons of cocoa per year over a period of five years, at a slightly higher price than that established by the world market.[59]

To win the favor of its new allies, the Soviet Union did not hesitate to make its aid more attractive. In December 1961 Khrushchev agreed to Nkrumah's request to take over half of the financing of Soviet assistance personnel—a cost that had initially been the responsibility of the Accra government.[60]

In the eyes of its African partners, Soviet economic support offered two important advantages, at least at first. Unlike Western powers, the Soviet Union "does not require knowing the details of the economic situation of the country before concluding any agreements."[61] Also, the Soviet Union would often append its name to projects whose doubtful economic profitability was largely compensated for by their symbolic effectiveness: hotels, airports, state farms, and the like.

The results of this activism appeared almost immediately. In Ghana Soviet support reinforced Nkrumah's hand in an economic project that was tightly state-controlled, as it simultaneously drew disproportionate Western hostility toward Ghana. But benefits to the Soviet Union were far from uniform. In December 1961 the eviction of its ambassador to Guinea resounded in Moscow like an alarm. As a first step, the Soviet Union tried to circumscribe the incident, if only to cover up the fragility of its "national democracy" honor roll. As a second step, the Soviet Union put into place, alongside its "appropriation" of political allies, a process of ideological control aimed at demonstrating that one is not "socialist at will." The Soviet Union determined to cast a vigilant eye on the use of the label "socialist" in order to maintain an essential correlation between the "choice of socialism" and the maintenance of privileged relations with the Soviet Union.

In May 1962 in Sofia, Khrushchev set the tone of this new adjustment by denouncing "national socialisms." A week later, in front of the Malian president being welcomed to Moscow, he reiterated his charge: "It would be wrong to think that it is sufficient to enunciate the slogan 'we are for socialism' and that we can then rest in the shadow of a tree waiting for things to fall into place on their own. We would like our Malian friends to see and to understand the complexity of the tasks that arise in the construction of a new society." [62]

Characterizing specific socialism as a sum of "petit bourgeois illusions," the Soviets naturally were eventually brought to reconsider their perception of nationalism. If the "antiimperialist" dimension remained uncontestable, its antisocialist potentialities became all the more clearly visible. [63]

Nonetheless, Soviet strictness about African socialist experiments never had concrete diplomatic expression. On a continent where it faced double pressure from the West and from China, the Soviet Union well understood that it had no armed option. The need to win over ideological clients therefore quickly took precedence over the need to control them. Whereas in May 1962 Khrushchev had refused to endorse the process of constructing socialism in Mali, six months later he deemed "the people of Mali, under the leadership of the Sudanese Union, able to eradicate, once and for all, all of the surviving aspects of colonialism and build a just, socialist society." [64]

This reversal, though not based on a concrete analysis of the African state in question, was nonetheless not purely arbitrary. When Khrushchev proposed the new thesis of "revolutionary democracy" to weaken China's higher ideological bid once more, it was in the Soviet Union's favor to adorn its allies with attributes of "radicalism."

Kennedy and the "Rollback"

To raise the banner of liberalism high, Kennedy conferred a sense of priority to the struggle against communist influence, even as he sought to modify its modalities. This objective, to which American diplomacy was geared, must nonetheless not allow us to forget the sometimes decisive contribution of nongovernmental American actors in this battle.

In Kenya, for instance, the origin of American influence lay largely in AFL-CIO activities and other nongovernmental agencies. From 1957 on, the Kenyan union leader Tom Mboya sized up all the material and political profit he could extricate from the "American connection." A reformist leader of liberal inspiration, he saw the possibility of ties with the United States as a way of shaking off the tutelage of Great Britain on his country, without damage to the essential, namely, anchoring Kenya in the "free world." With the support of the American business world, Mboya set up a program to finance Kenyan scholarship students' travel to the United States. The local reaction to this first "airlift" of students would be used by Mboya in the Kenyan political battle preceding independence. His second visit to the United States in 1959 enabled him to institutionalize his relations with nongovernmental United States organizations. The creation of the African American Students Foundation helped to cover not only the cost of students' travel but also their tuition and all of their expenses. In 1960 a third "airlift" was launched from Nairobi to New York, this time with the personal financial support of John F. Kennedy, then a candidate for president.[65] Predating the United States' diplomatic involvement in Kenya, Mboya's "pro-American" markings would weigh heavily in political rivalries within the KANU.

But the "big story" of anticommunist diplomacy for the United States in the early sixties was Ghana. Traumatized by the troublesome Aswan precedent, the Kennedy administration wanted to make its "dams diplomacy" a way of first containing Soviet influence and then rolling it back.

The idea of an American contribution to the financing of the Akosombo dam in Ghana had been raised by Nkrumah as early as 1958. Two years later the Eisenhower administration answered Ghana's request by tying a loan grant of $30 million to a definitive agreement between the government of Accra and the American company Volta Aluminum Company (VALCO). The truth is that the Eisenhower administration, already worried about a Soviet-Ghanaian rapprochement, had found therein a means of deferring the agreement. In spite of the subtly worded dispatches that he received at the American embassy in Accra in 1960, American Secretary of State Herter saw Ghana "turn towards the communist bloc." Under the moderating influence of the leaders of the Calhoun-Kaiser group that had always been interested in the Ghanaian project, John F. Kennedy returned to his Manichaean analysis of Nkrumah's policy. The Nkrumah-Kennedy meeting in March 1961 eased America's reluctance. In December 1961, after lengthy deliberation, the American government granted Ghana a loan of $55 million through Eximbank, bilateral aid of an equal amount, and an officially guaranteed private loan of $54 million.

Three factors stand out in America's decision. The first two are very well known and involve the political desire "to get a foothold in the Ghana-

Guinea-Mali camp" and to erase the deplorable image left by America's refusal to finance the Aswan dam. The third factor, less well studied, rests on the idea that American financing would reinforce pro-West elements of the Ghanaian regime while weakening Nkrumah's "precarious" position.[66] In September 1961 the Assistant Secretary of State for African Affairs, G. Mennen Williams, in fact received a confidential letter from the Ghanaian Minister, Gbedemah, informing him of his intention of overthrowing Nkrumah in October, in complicity with the army and police.[67]

Though modest in Ghana, benefits provided by "dams diplomacy" would be more readily visible in Guinea, the Soviet Union's other special ally. When Conakry asked Washington to finance the Konkouré dam in May 1961, Ambassador Attwood strongly supported the Guinean request. He saw in it the opportunity to reinforce Western influence and to create friction between Guinea and the Soviet Union.[68] Because interest in Guinea was secondary for the United States "establishment," the Kennedy administration, paradoxically, had no problem launching an aid program aimed specifically at financing a hydroelectric plant. Taking advantage of the reduction in Guinea's room for diplomatic maneuvering following the expulsion of the Soviet ambassador, the United States did not hesitate to give its involvement a markedly conditional twist. As early as January 1962, the American ambassador insisted that Sékou Touré appoint a "pro-West" Guinean coordinator to manage economic aid.[69] He also pushed Guinea to join the IMF again and to sign a Guinean-American agreement guaranteeing American investments. The need for Sékou Touré henceforth to be compliant was evidenced in 1962 when he declined an invitation by Fidel Castro to come to Havana after a visit to the United States. The Guinean refusal to allow Soviet military vessels to stop over en route to Cuba during the missile crisis was even more significant. Finally, when Conakry addressed a new request for aid to Washington in 1963, the United States formulated new demands: a reduction in Soviet presence, a halt to the program of Soviet aid to Guinean civil aviation, and the cancellation of the World Federation of Trade Unions conference scheduled to take place in Conakry, which amounted to giving Guinean unionists authorization to go to the United States.[70]

At a time when John F. Kennedy was resigned to "losing" Ghana in spite of G. Mennen Williams' exhortations to maintain an "aggressive and continuous presence," the United States found in Guinea useful compensation. This balance game became very clearly visible in bilateral aid programs for the two countries. Between 1962 and 1964 Ghana fell from the rank of number one to number eleven among beneficiaries of bilateral American aid to black Africa. Inversely, during this period, Guinea moved from seventh to second place.

The contrast between the United States' success in Guinea and its relative failure in Ghana is very revealing. It expresses the ability of an external actor to influence the political choices of an African partner as much as it does the latter's diplomatic "free will." In the final analysis, the more or less strong hostility manifested by the United States toward Nkrumah only moderately affected his political options. Thus, the limited results the United States gained from the Ghana experience stemmed less from its "clumsiness" than from its inability to effectively influence the Ghanaian regime's most important political decisions.

The evolution of American-Guinean relations between 1962 and 1963 was such that it does not necessarily contradict this evaluation of the situation. Washington's means of exerting pressure on Conakry acquired in a particular context turned out to be real but equally precarious. When Sékou Touré took steps to reactivate his relations with Moscow in the mid-sixties, the United States would not be able to dissuade him from doing so.

Thwarted Plans

The Impact of the Sino-Soviet Conflict

Nikita Khrushchev's foreign strategy was based on a marked duality: to persistently test the West's weak points in the Third World while simultaneously seeking global accommodation to the United States. Carried out sometimes deftly after 1956, these political gymnastics revealed their perilous nature at the time of the missile crisis in October 1962. Between its activism in the Third World and its slow quest for parity with the United States, the Soviet Union saw that it would have to choose. This choice seemed all the more crucial since it had to take into consideration the country of China, whose strategy revolved around a central objective: to "unmask" the Soviet Union by proving that its dialogue with the United States disqualified it, *ipso facto,* from speaking in the name of the Third World.

At the 1960 world conference of communist parties, both the Soviet Union and China apparently agreed on a common line of action. The national democracy thesis which sealed their agreement was indeed grounded in a compromise, since "while protecting the position of the national bourgeoisie, it seemed that the socialist deadline was being moved up." [71] Intended to preserve the apparent cohesion of the communist movement, this surface-level *entente* remained ephemeral. Always rejecting the existence of an intermediary state between "bourgeois domination" and "the dictatorship of the proletariat," China was hesitant to speak of "national democracy." From the end of the Moscow conference on, it was anxious to give its agreement with the Soviet Union a restrictive interpretation by emphasizing the concept of a "noncapitalist road to development." The struggle for a monopoly on ideology, which had taken many forms in Africa—to the point of becoming a major handicap for Soviet diplomacy on that continent—could nevertheless not be reduced to a mere ideological controversy. It hid diplomatic antagonisms that were quite real: the Sino-Soviet conflict in Africa had always been based on a persistent gap between an exacerbated ideological controversy and political practices that were similar in the final analysis.

Indeed, even though China berated the Soviet Union for compromising with "imperialism and its lackeys," China did not proceed any differently. In an effort to assure international recognition in preference to Taiwan, Peking did not hesitate to use minimalist language and practices culled from the repertoire of "coexistence between different social regimes." Its support of the Rwandi monarchy that fell in 1963 bore witness to this eloquently.

In fact, the African "revolutionary situations" that were indeed supported in Peking and ignored by Moscow were rather few in number. In Cameroon the People's Republic of China's support of the UPC was not confirmed until after Yaoundé's refusal to recognize it. And although Peking did not hesitate to encourage Mulele in Congo-Leopoldville, its support remained highly symbolic. That did not, however, stop China from denouncing the Soviet Union's passivity in both cases in order to enhance its own position. The ability to make allies of ideological radicalism and diplomatic pragmatism was well illustrated by Chou En Lai's famous African tour of December 1963 and January 1964.

Even as Chou En Lai declared at Mogadishu that Africa was "ripe for revolution," he seemed more worried about increasing diplomatic visibility for Peking, to set the pace, than about sounding the alarm of the antirevisionist crusade.

In fact the head of the Chinese government, who spoke, literally, of the "excellent revolutionary prospects for Africa," meant to give this evaluation only extremely limited concrete content.[72] Without yet admitting it publicly, the Chinese, as the Soviets, had gradually been led to recognize that because Africa's priority was to fight against colonialism, its contribution to the world revolution was limited for the time being.[73] In addition, the two central points of Sino-Soviet conflict (relations with the United States and the place of the national liberation movement in the world revolution) had little ramification in Africa during the beginning of the sixties. The Soviet-American collusion so decried by Peking was never fully experienced by African states. And concerning the two international events that China cited to demonstrate flagrant Soviet revisionism—the Cuban missile crisis and the signing of the nuclear nonproliferation treaty—the receptivity of African states to Chinese arguments remained purely a matter of protocol. Chou En Lai could hardly denounce the Soviet retreat from Cuba in a country like Guinea, which had expressly refused to let Soviet

**Table 1 Diplomatic Presence of the USSR
and the PRC in Black Africa**

Years	Independent States	Diplomatic Presence in African States	
		Soviet Union	People's Rep. of China
1960	22	9	5
1961	25	11	6
1962	28	15	7
1963	30	18	9
1964	31	22	13

Sources: Derived from information in C. McLane, *Soviet-African Relations* and A. Ogunsawo, *China's Policy in Africa.*

airplanes stop there en route to Havana. And although Nkrumah showed some enthusiasm for the Chinese revolutionary arguments, he vehemently refused to take part in the Sino-Soviet conflict. Moreover, he was far from total agreement with Peking. In 1964 he deplored the first Chinese nuclear explosion the same way he had criticized the revival of Soviet nuclear testing in the atmosphere in the preceding year.

Progressively becoming aware of the obstacles to its revolutionary proselytizing in Africa, China deftly made use of an anti-Soviet repertoire that was more appropriate to the African context. Peking never tired of denouncing the Soviet Union's arrangements with the United States. It tried to awaken the receptivity of the African states to its arguments by resorting to a racial argument: because it is "white," "European," and "developed," the Soviet Union, in contrast to China, would be unable to understand the problems posed to peoples of color in the underdeveloped world. China's wish to discredit any "natural alliance" between the Soviet Union and the Third World reflected a specific goal: that of excluding the Soviet Union from the Second Afro-Asian Conference. The various meetings of OSPAAAL therefore became the preferred field of confrontation between the Soviet Union and China. Until the Cuban missile crisis, conflicts between these two countries had remained discrete. The Soviet Union wanted to avoid irreparable damage, whereas China never gave up trying to make Moscow return to a "just way." In the aftermath of the Cuban missile crisis, Nikita Khrushchev gave priority to accommodation with the United States. Before the Supreme Soviet in 1962, he declared, without beating around the bush, that "the Cuban crisis had demonstrated once more that those who have held, or are holding, dogmatic positions represent [hereafter] the principal threat." [74]

The Chinese were quite clear about this situation. In February 1963 at the meeting of the OSPAAAL executive committee gathered at Moshi (Tanzania), they struck some sharp blows against the Soviet Union. In this manner Peking could gain the benefit of the precious support of the host

27

country and its chief of state, Julius Nyerere, who blasted Soviet policy with unequaled vigor: "Socialist countries . . . are now committing the same crimes as were committed by the capitalists before. On the international level they are now beginning to use wealth for capitalist purposes, that is, for the acquisition of power and prestige.[75]

Strengthened by this support, China stiffened its tone and endeavored to transform the conference into an accusatory session against Soviet policy, in the name of solidarity of peoples of color. Even if this offensive did not lead to an official, direct censure of its action, the Soviet Union was trapped. It reacted to the racial arguments advanced by China by hardening its ideological position. But at the same time its major preoccupation not to alienate any state, given the prospect of the Afro-Asian conference, forced it to use great diplomatic caution. To extricate itself from this dilemma, the Soviet Union in 1963 and 1964 worked according to two contradictory themes: that of hardening its ideological position to invalidate China's racial arguments; and that of diplomatic pragmatism to denounce "Maoist adventurism."

Ideological hardening, which quickly forces a situation from which there is no escape other than attack, was obvious from the end of 1963 with the development of the thesis of "revolutionary democracy." Devised to sanction the radicalization of "national democracies," this new terminology came six months after the signing of the nonproliferation treaty, during Chou En Lai's African tour. For Nikita Khrushchev, the revolutionary democrats were the leaders "who plead sincerely in favor of noncapitalist methods to regulate their national problems and express their determination to construct socialism." [76]

Without being communists, revolutionary democrats were thus judged apt to engage on a road that would bring them closer to scientific socialism. Unlike "national democracy," promoted to stop radical behaviors that the Twentieth Congress had not foreseen, the concept of "revolutionary democracy" approached some unrealized ideological intentions. For the Soviet Union, it was a matter of not being caught empty-handed by China. Among "revolutionary democracy states," African countries again occupied a privileged position. Among them were Ghana, Mali, and soon Congo-Brazzaville, along with Algeria and Egypt. With the exception of fallen Guinea, black Africa maintained a stable position among the Soviet Union's various ideological alliances. But, just as in 1960, when the concept of national democracy was forged, any evaluation of the concrete realities of these states was put aside in favor of their statements of socialist intent and of their partial diplomatic solidarity with the Soviet Union.

Alongside this effort of ideological legitimation, the Soviet Union tried to counteract China's desire to call a second Afro-Asian meeting before the second summit of the nonaligned planned for Cairo in 1964. For Peking, maintaining an Afro-Asian organization that would reflect the nonaligned movement was essential, for it was the only one that would enable Peking to participate while excluding the Soviet Union.

To obtain support from Africans whose numerical strength within the Afro-Asian movement was decisive, the Soviet Union and China vied for their amity. Sometimes within a week's interval, each would rush to make loans to the same key countries (Tanzania, Kenya, the Congo-Brazzaville). For these two powerful countries, however, the benefits of this competition were ultimately rather limited. On the question of Soviet participation at the Afro-Asian summit, China seemed to be in a favorable position for a while. In April 1964, while a final decision was still to be made on the question, the Soviet Union was excluded from the preliminary meeting for the conference. But the final decision a year later not to hold an Afro-Asian summit deprived China of a decisive victory. As it was, the growing spread of a nonaligned movement in which neither of the two communist powers was involved reflected the reluctance of Third World states to let themselves be drawn into an uncertain struggle.

Indeed, beyond its part in the controversy around Soviet participation in the Afro-Asian conference, China never really did manage to unleash "frank and massive support" for its positions. In fact, on the question of international disarmament and nonproliferation, the opposite happened. In August 1963 the Council of Foreign Ministers of the Organization for African Unity (OAU) proposed to member states that they sign a nonproliferation treaty. A month later, the OSPAAAL meeting clearly favored Soviet initiatives on the subject of disarmament and peaceful coexistence.

For the Soviet Union, the temporary consequence of its conflict with China was ambiguous. In the middle of the sixties no African state, with the exception perhaps of Tanzania, seemed to the Soviet Union to be won over by China's arguments. At the same time, the Soviet Union was forced to admit that all solicited African states had balked at being enlisted under the anti-Chinese banner. In addition, even if China was not actually able to spoil the Soviet Union's few diplomatic achievements in Africa, it nonetheless succeeded in constantly determining the grounds on which their confrontations would take place. China would have to wait ten years, for the harsh decolonization of Angola, to modify this delicate position to its own advantage.

The Limits of American Voluntarism

While Khrushchev's diplomacy was tied to a series of successive political reevaluations, John F. Kennedy's behavior can retrospectively be summed up as a succession of political and diplomatic arbitrations that were arduous to implement and uncertain in their consequences.

John F. Kennedy's plan had never been to reconsider the East-West structure of American diplomacy but rather to soften its rigidity. This shift was fed by a certain amount of political voluntarism and implied the confluence of three conditions: a partial recasting of international representations of America's bureaucracy; the identification of tangible African stakes for American power; and the ability of the United States to control African political space at least partially. In the mid-sixties, no significant change occurred at these three levels. In spite of the judicious inclinations of several ambassadors won over by a new African demeanor, the American establishment maintained its preference for European tutelage of Africa.

While G. Mennen Williams at the State Department could count on the President's confidence or on the support of liberal Democrats (Bowles, Ball, Stevenson, or Cleveland), he also had to take into account the territorial influence of the Bureau of European Affairs, as well as Secretary of State Dean Rusk's very poor receptivity to African affairs. Even within the liberal camp, anticommunism often took precedence over all other considerations. In spite of assurances offered to Robert Kennedy by Eduardo Modlane, a Mozambican leader educated in the United States, Washington refused to lend the least support to Frelimo.[77] Even a man like George Ball gave the impression of being rather sensitive to Antonio Salazar's reasoning about the risks of independence in Angola.[78] After the "Stanleyville affair," when Williams suggested offering financial support to Portuguese-speaking liberation movements, the idea fell on deaf ears.[79] Outside the State Department, the establishment's resistance was even more spontaneous. Williams, who spent most of his time convincing African leaders of the cogency of American policy, had at his disposal no support, not even a link to the heart of the legislative branch. Congressional sessions devoted to Africa were extremely rare, and the information given to representatives was fragmentary. The only active lobbies rallied those representatives favoring the Katanga secession or Portugal. As far as the black community was concerned—a community largely absorbed in the struggle for civil rights—its interest in Africa seems to have been essentially sporadic.

The initial policy conceived by John F. Kennedy died in 1963 with the publication of the Clay report on the "defense and security of the free world." This report, covering American bilateral aid programs all over the world, called for a "Cartierization" * of African aid.

Because the African continent fell under the realm of European responsibility, American aid programs there had to be reduced. American bilateral aid in Africa dropped from \$281 million in 1962 to \$219 million in 1964. In francophone Africa, for example, the United States limited its

---

* "Cartierization" refers to the arguments of conservative journalist Raymond Cartier that France should cut its losses by granting independence to its colonies.—Ed.

economic involvement to a symbolic sprinkling of funds. In 1964 United States aid to this group (with the exception of Guinea) did not exceed $30 million. Somalia, Kenya, and Tanganyika, originally courted by the United States, quickly suffered cutbacks in bilateral aid programs. The only countries to escape this fate were those without "legal tutelage," namely, countries such as the Congo-Leopoldville, Liberia, and Guinea, as well as the immensely populated ones like Nigeria. Because, as the Clay report indicates, Africa did not figure in the first perimeter of defense of the "free world," the United States had few reasons to consent to costly investments. As always in similar cases, the United States, unsure of benefiting from a bold policy in black Africa, opted for the preservation of its tangible interests by maintaining the status quo in their relations with Lisbon and Pretoria. This choice was all the easier to implement as the United States quickly recognized the difficulty it was having controlling its African allies and partners. At the time of the Stanleyville operation, the United States was unable to mobilize support from a single African actor. Quite the contrary, it was confronted with the determined hostility of those states that were most favorably disposed toward it, such as Guinea or Kenya. Even in countries where it had exercised direct influence, the United States recognized the limits of its influence. In Congo-Leopoldville, for example, the United States was unable to dissuade Adoula from recognizing the Angolan Revolutionary Government in Exile (GRAE) that was formed by the FNLA. In fact, the United States was gradually forced to admit that the political instability of African states was not reducible to a game of communist interference. Since national leaders were its only political interlocutors, the United States seems to have been singularly deprived of the means of achieving the real stakes in African society. To extricate itself from these chains, Williams suggested to American heads of diplomatic posts that they make a priority of broadening contacts with opposition forces.[80] The questioning of John Kennedy's original policy, already perceptible in mid-1962, increased with his death. His successor's slim interest in the Third World, the priority given to southeast Asia, and disappointments with Soviet policy would eventually reduce initial American expectations to naught. For the United States, Africa was not yet a "new frontier."

2

Africa Marginalized?
(1965–1974)

The two superpowers' initial involvement in Africa rested on the implicit assumption that neither one had any tangible interests in this part of the world; they could therefore intensify their rivalry there, without harming "peaceful coexistence" with each other. This dissociation, which even the Cuban crisis did not affect, only ended with the 1975 crisis in Angola. As a secondary site of Soviet-American competition, the African continent offered the potential for making only marginal gains.

In the mid-sixties, when Soviet-American optimism was ebbing, this general pattern foundered. While, as it seems, none of the decolonization crises blocked or delayed the building of *détente,* neither superpower managed to transform its diplomatic gains in Africa into influential global leverage. In this respect, the contrast between what the Soviets gained in Egypt after 1956 and in Ghana at the beginning of the decade is extremely revealing.

For Khrushchev's and Kennedy's successors, the modes of their involvement needed major correction, especially as the Soviet-American balance in the mid-sixties took a brand new shape. Although actively on a path of strategic parity with the United States, Soviet power had plateaued. The strain of its political, strategic, and financial constraints forced it to make a difficult decision between military parity with the United States and its own activism in the Third World. For the Brezhnev-Kossygin-Podgorny troika that overthrew Khrushchev in 1964, the dilution of Soviet influence in the Third World and the financial tricklings from it between 1956 and 1964 resulted in a slight loosening of Soviet control over Eastern Europe. The priority then lay in refocusing the Soviet Union's means, in restructuring the strict hierarchization of its international objectives at a time when the poor performance of its economy was leading it to increase its financial dealings.[1]

As for the United States, the mid-sixties revealed the inflexibility of its power. Even if the Cuban crisis had confirmed its provisional strategic superiority over the Soviet Union, the war in Vietnam unmasked its inability to identify its own security in the world order once and for all.[2] Because it was unable to be present in all areas of the Third World, the United States found that it, too, had to hierarchize its global objectives and relinquish some of its obligations to its Western allies. For Robert McNamara, the architect of United States policy in Vietnam, "there have been classic cases in which our deliberate nonaction was the wisest action of all."[3]

The readjustment of the superpowers' regional priorities, which would translate into significant disengagement in Africa, was unquestionably made easier by a noticeable evolution in Chinese policy.

For the United States, which was worried about China's influence because of its revolutionary potential and its ability to capture the support of African states at the United Nations, the African continent after 1965 no longer seemed to be the preferred ground for an anti-Chinese struggle. Between 1965 and 1968 a move toward recognizing the People's Republic of China had suffered a real setback. States like Ghana, Burundi, the Central African Republic, and Dahomey went so far as to break ties with Peking following changes in leadership. This weakening of China's diplomatic position was evident in the United Nations as the number of countries in favor of its membership dropped between 1965 and 1968 from forty-seven to forty-four. Inversely, unfavorable votes were up to fifty-eight in 1968, as against forty-seven just three years earlier. Because it was entangled in its cultural revolution, Peking considerably reduced its diplomatic activity. The number of Chinese delegations sent to Africa dropped from sixty in 1964 to twelve in 1968. During the same period, the number of African delegations dispatched to China fell from ninety-one to twelve.[4]

Even if the Soviet Union did not perceive China as a danger in the same terms as the United States did, it could only congratulate itself on Peking's mishaps in Africa. The blow received by China at the 1965 Afro-Asian conference marked the end of the first phase of the Sino-Soviet conflict, as well as the geographical relocation of that conflict to Asia. Moreover, unlike Nikita Khrushchev, who had lost interest in southeast Asia because "race and geography favored China," his successors realized that the Vietnamese conflict offered the possibility of containing Chinese ambitions without simultaneously neglecting the possibilities of reaching some agreement with China.

These parallel interests, which led both Soviets and Americans to modify and limit their African expectations after 1965, did not solely hinge on the restructuring of their priorities worldwide. The superpowers' apparent marginalization of Africa stemmed in large part from the failure of their strategies for integration of African states into their global objectives.

A majority of African states deliberately remained on the margins of the three main confrontations during the early sixties: the two East-West crises in Berlin and in Cuba and the Sino-Soviet rivalry. To the extent that Western powers seemed in no hurry to reach a compromise between their *de facto* support of white domination and the support of African demands, African states demonstrated little eagerness to respond to Western appeals. At the same time, their awareness of the marginal role the Soviet Union was playing in accelerating the process of decolonization hardly encouraged them to choose the "other side." Such a pragmatic vision of international order explains their virtual lack of receptivity to the Sino-Soviet conflict. Since it had no bearing on any of their diplomatic demands, African states saw only slight advantage in taking sides.

The fact remains that beyond the reduction in aid commitments, the modalities of a Soviet-American retreat often seemed easier to conceptualize than to achieve. Even when each superpower tried to leave African soil, it could not, from one day to the next, extricate itself from the acquired political responsibilities in those countries where it was present. Neither could it disregard Africa's permeability by other influences or issues in which its interests were more directly involved (in the Middle East and the Indian Ocean). Finally, the very idea of retreat had very different connotations for the United States and for the Soviet Union. For the Soviet Union, the idea was to freeze all its large-scale political ambitions in favor of affirming its presence as just a "power like other powers." For the United States, temporary renunciation of any significant benefit in Africa was accompanied by a constant preoccupation: preventing its retreat from Africa from enhancing the harmful power of the Soviet Union or of African states. From then on, "the redistribution of the burden" with Europe, far from taking on the shape of a pure and simple retreat, was in fact a transformation into indirect control over the old continent's gameboard.

The USSR: A Presence without Influence

Fragile Alliances

It was precisely when the redefinition of its global priorities forced it to observe more and more parsimony that the Soviet Union was confronted with increasing appeals from its troubled allies.

Faced with the economic incompetence and diplomatic isolation of his regime during the mid-sixties, Nkrumah asked the Soviet Union to increase its cocoa purchases, to guarantee cash payment, and to refinance the Ghanaian debt. In January 1965 Accra elicited from Moscow a commitment of an annual purchase of one hundred and fifty thousand tons of cocoa per year but was unable to obtain satisfaction on the principle of partial payment in cash.[5] Thus, while prompting Nkrumah to emphasize productive economic projects rather than social programs in the future, the Soviet Union did not seem at all willing to save a Ghanaian economy that was adrift. Neither did the Soviet Union balk at the end of 1965 at reducing the number of consultants assigned to Ghanaian state firms.[6] This change appears very clearly in Soviet writings. While emphasizing that Ghana had gone "beyond the stage of state capitalism," the Soviets stressed the fact that it was far from having accomplished "the serious technical and economic tasks of developing productive forces."[7] In addition, the Soviet press, while suggesting that the Ghanaian government resort to foreign capital and foreign aid to accomplish them, implicitly expressed the Soviet Union's unavailability to take on such responsibilities.[8]

In fact, the only sector in which the Soviet Union maintained its presence was that of national and army security. During the year in which the Soviet Union specifically limited its economic presence, it also dispatched a dozen advisers charged with reorganizing the presidential guard for Nkrumah, who was increasingly worried about his own personal security.[9] Evidently, assurances Nkrumah received from Washington in March 1964 about the absence of CIA involvement in Ghana did not fully reassure the Accra government.[10]

With respect to Mali, the other "revolutionary democracy" confronting a serious economic crisis, the Soviet desire to disengage was just as clear.

In May–June 1966, a delegation from Mali went to Moscow to obtain increased economic support. The fact that the joint communiqué emphasized the "problems" confronting Mali rather than the "achievements of its revolution" demonstrates well how, on the Soviet side, disenchantment had replaced optimism.[11] Meanwhile, measures adopted by the Soviet Union "to contribute to the reinforcement of Mali's economic independence" scarcely seemed to have had any effect. In December 1966 Modibo Keita, who had made Mali's exit from the Franc Zone a symbol of national independence, announced the upcoming reintegration of his country into this monetary union dominated by France.

Very quickly, the ideological categories honored under Khrushchev suffered a significant loss of meaning. "Revolutionary democracy" was hardly mentioned anymore; instead it was simply the "noncapitalist path." In 1967 *Izvestia* would even call the "revolutionary-reformist" split in Africa artificial.[12]

Added to this ideological pessimism was an anxiety regarding the collective capacity of African states to speed up the process of decolonization. The Soviet Union therefore was surprised at Africa's passivity vis-à-vis the Unilateral Declaration of Independence (UDI) in Rhodesia by the white majority government.[13] Having observed grudgingly that only ten countries had taken the risk of breaking diplomatic relations with London, Moscow was stunned to see the OAU turn to Great Britain for a solution to the problem.[14]

The small amount of credit it had provisionally allotted to Africa logically led the Soviet Union to react with restraint to the failure of its political allies: Odinga in 1965, Nkrumah in 1966, and Modibo Keita in 1968. Nkrumah returned to Moscow after having been overthrown while he was in China. In spite of the expulsion of all of its advisers from Accra, the Soviet Union did not seem prepared to allow for the least distortion of "state realism." In fewer than forty-eight hours the Soviet Union placed the fallen Ghanaian leader on a plane to Conakry. A short time later it recognized the new regime, while the Soviet press carefully avoided reporting on Nkrumah's calls for insurrection from Conakry. Meanwhile the Ghanaian leader's fall from power left untouched the broad economic cooperation previously established between the two countries. Those projects solely financed by the Soviet Union were quickly frozen; but the extensive and, for each party, commercially profitable cooperative programs were spared. On the political level, however, one could not hear any echoes of the Soviet Union's moderation among the new Ghanaian leaders.

While legitimating their newly acquired power through rejection of Nkrumah's politics, these leaders understood that denouncing Soviet "agitation" was a convenient way of attracting Western financial resources. Thus, in March 1967, as expelled Soviet experts were preparing to return to Accra, the Soviet Union stood accused of bringing arms into Ghana. In October of the same year, Soviet trawlers were stopped and inspected and their crews arrested. Faced with the prolongation of their detention, the Soviet Union suspended its oil deliveries as a first step. On 16 February 1968 the Tass news agency announced the upcoming visit of one of the Soviet Union's naval units to Conakry. Ten days later, as a Soviet warship neared Ghanaian waters, the Soviet trawlers' captains were symbolically convicted before being released. Despite the coincidence of these two events, it would seem that the lightness of the charges and the care taken not to uselessly compromise favorable commercial relations with the Soviet Union influenced the Ghanaian decision more than Soviet military intimidation did.[15]

In fact, the Soviet Union noticed that the hostility toward it on the part of some African actors stemmed more from the severity of internal tensions in these countries than from a deliberate wish to get the Soviet Union out of Africa. The deterioration of Soviet-Kenyan relations as early as the end of 1964 is very revealing on this point. As soon as the internal political debate in Kenya became polarized around agrarian problems, fears of communist danger could only be related to fears of loss of land.[16] Taking advantage of Odinga's ties with the Soviet Union, his adversaries naturally found a means of getting at him through the weakening of the Soviet position in Kenya. A few days after Jomo Kenyatta's refusal to accept a delivery of Soviet arms, Tom Mboya made public his famous document "African Socialism and Its Application to Kenyan Planning." This manifesto, which favors foreign economic interests, rejects Odinga's positions on nationalization, on the repossession of the white colonizers' land, and on compulsory planning. The following day, the government also decided to take control of the Lumumba Institute that had been managed until then by KANU.[17] This institute, built by the Soviet Union and inaugurated in March 1965, had symbolized Odinga's power. Its "normalization" followed by its closing were signs of the political failure of KANU's left wing.[18] At the end of 1965, Jomo Kenyatta asserted that his country was now finally truly anchored in the West.

The Soviet Union was quick to draw conclusions from these African disappointments, for which it was in fact only slightly responsible. Less than two months after Nkrumah's fall, at the Twenty-second Congress of the Soviet Union's Communist Party, a disapproving eye was cast upon "noncapitalist" experiments. The misfit between excessive voluntarism "from above" and weak mobilization "from below" was deemed responsible for the failure of the reforms that were undertaken.[19] Just as the United States became aware that "communist plots" were not at the root of all of Africa's conflicts, the Soviet Union recognized, symmetrically, that imperialist adventures did not explain all evils.[20]

Furtive Alliances

Because Africa no longer lent itself to any grand design, and because the aggiornamento of its foreign priorities hardly caused it to move in that direction, the Soviet Union opted for a modest action profile starting in 1965. Although breaking with Khrushchevian optimism, the new course of Soviet policy continued the past on one essential point: the diplomatic affirmation of the Soviet Union as no more than a "power like other powers." This effort, made easier by Africa's weak potential for revolution, led it to tighten its diplomatic relations with the Central African Republic in 1965, with Upper Volta and the Ivory Coast in 1967, and with Niger in 1971. The Soviet Union no longer appeared to be a dangerous power, even to the most anticommunist states of francophone Africa.[21] The evolution of its relations with Chad and Zaire in this regard is very revealing.

In Chad the Soviet Union seemed rather uninterested in the insurrection movement of the *Front de Libération nationale du Tchad* (Frolinat), created by Ibrahim Abacha in the Middle East in 1966. It even thought more and more favorably of the Tombalbaye regime, to the point of congratulating itself in 1972 on the annihilation of "the armed movement of the northern rebels" who were, after all, supported by French troops.[22]

In truth, as soon as a state no longer manifested any declared hostility toward it, the Soviet Union did not fail to make a show of its diplomatic receptivity and political leniency. All that was needed, for example, was for the Mobutu regime to express its desire to renew relations with the socialist camp in 1966 and "mobutism," described a year earlier as "a horrible combination of military adventurism" and accused of "an absence of political principles,"[23] would not be held up to public obloquy again. The Soviet Union excelled at playing this game of circumstantial alliances and furtive connections.

In East Africa, for example, the Soviet Union sought to move nearer to Uganda as soon as its chances in Kenya seemed compromised. In July 1965 it proposed aid to Kampala for formation of a Ugandan air force. Obote, the head of the Ugandan government, found this offer much to his liking. He saw Soviet backing as precious support, given London's backing of the Baganda oligarchy.

This policy of presence, which arms shipments increasingly came to symbolize, nevertheless more and more clearly precluded any economic concessions. The financial conditions placed on Soviet loans seemed, indeed, to be so draconian that a good number of its African partners preferred to pass them up. The $12 million Soviet loan granted to Uganda in 1966 included the local costs of Soviet assistance; that is to say, it included the expenses of Soviet technicians as well as the training of Ugandan cadres in the Soviet Union. Now, although the agreement called for disbursement over a twelve-year period, the repayment of this loan was to begin with the initial delivery of Soviet equipment, in other words, before the first signs of profit from the project. On top of that, the contingent nature of the loan imposed the obligation of obtaining goods from the Soviet Union that Uganda produced itself.[24] The 1966 renegotiation of a loan awarded to Kenya two years earlier by the Soviet Union encountered similar obstacles. The Kenyans, declaring themselves unable to guarantee the sale of Soviet goods in their country, requested conversion of contingent aid into a looser loan. The Soviet refusal to meet this demand led to a *de facto* cancellation of Soviet credits, with the exception of two projects whose local costs were covered by Soviet sugar imports and of a hospital that had been built free of charge as a favor.[25]

In fact, during this whole period the only important example of economic cooperation undertaken by the Soviet Union revolved around the value to it of the Kindia bauxite mines in Guinea. In exchange for financing the project, the Soviet Union would receive two and a half tons of bauxite per year. This agreement was implemented in December 1970: it enabled Guinea to exploit its bauxite without spending cash; and it offered the

Soviet Union the advantage of being able to make a long-term plan for stocking bauxite, the only raw material it really lacked.

Present in Africa but not influential, Soviet policy saw no spectacular activity for nearly ten years. The only exception was perhaps its limited military involvement in the Nigerian civil war.

On the eve of Ironsi's coup in January 1966 that accelerated the decomposition of the Nigerian federation, the Soviet Union was still only somewhat involved in the country. It was satisfied to oblige the Nationalist Socialist Workers and Farmers Party (NSWFP) with small favors, particularly by participating in its December 1965 meeting. The Nigerian leaders still harbored a deep mistrust of Moscow despite the tentative development of bilateral Soviet-Nigerian relations. In reality, when it signed a 1966 cultural cooperation agreement with the Soviet Union, the Nigerian government appeared primarily worried about having exclusive control over the sending of scholarship recipients to socialist countries.

When Ironsi acceded to power, the Soviet Union showed prudent optimism. It saw his arrival at the helm of the Federation as a progressive step, hostile to the northern Hausa oligarchy backed by Great Britain.[26] Through what they saw as a struggle between the "modernist South" and the "traditional North," the Soviets perceived signs of a cloaked rivalry between the British and Americans.[27] When Gowon in turn overthrew Ironsi six months later, Moscow interpreted this new putsch as the North's revenge.[28] This negative evaluation of the Nigerian crisis was short-lived. As Western backing of Ibo leader Ojukwu became increasingly obvious, Moscow tended to take the military government's point of view. But this subtle support remained tainted with ambiguity. Facing the extraordinary fluidity of power relations within the Federation, the Soviet Union did not see any advantage in adopting a clearer position. This was the case especially since Ibo opposition to Hausa "feudalism" led the Soviet Union to cast a favorable eye upon Ibo demands: "the development of nationalism or of tribal consciousness is in itself a positive phenomenon that can in no way satisfy imperialists. . . . That is why the development of national consciousness, even when it takes place within large tribes, represents . . . a progressive phenomenon."[29]

This veiled support of the Ibos, which Nigerian students in the Soviet Union detected until the advent of the civil war in May 1967, led Soviet diplomacy to avoid alienating any side's sympathies. Thus, when Soviet delegations came to Lagos in January and March 1967 to discuss the ways and means for granting of credit, they expressed a desire to meet on Ibo soil. In April 1967 a Hungarian delegation's insistence on building a hospital in Enugu, in the heart of Ibo country, arose out of a desire to reach out to Ojukwu.[30]

With the collapse of the Federation and the beginning of the civil war in May 1967, the ambiguity of the Soviet diplomatic position dissipated. In a country firmly in the Western camp, the Soviet Union was all too happy to be able to respond to the solicitations of a military regime looking for arms.

Faced with British and American refusals to meet Nigeria's need for bombers, General Gowon turned to Moscow as early as July 1967. A month later, under the guise of a cultural accord, the Soviet Union committed itself to delivering twenty MiG-15 fighters and six Czech L-29 planes within a short amount of time. It dispatched an additional one hundred thirty military advisers responsible for their assembly and maintenance. Out of a sense of independence, Nigeria insisted on paying for the arms in cash. It was only later, when the financial burden became too heavy, that Nigeria accepted an exchange of arms for cocoa.[31]

Retrospectively, compared to the Soviet interventions in Angola and Ethiopia, Soviet involvement in the Nigerian civil war exhibited two peculiarities.

The Soviet Union was unsuccessful in attaching its commitment to an axis of specific diplomatic and ideological polarization as much because of the reluctance of its provisional ally as because of the particular nature of the Nigerian situation. Despite the increasing hostility that the Nigerian government would develop toward the Western powers, it was scrupulously careful not to displace its diplomacy's center of gravity. At the very most, Soviet support made clear to Nigeria what interest it could have in pursuing a more balanced foreign policy henceforth.

For its part, while the Soviet Union sought to profit from its recent presence in Nigeria to improve its position (increased cocoa purchases, more scholarships granted to Nigerian students, and the political and financial support of the two left wing groups, the SWAFP and the NTUC [Nigeria Trade Union Congress]), it was also careful throughout the civil war to avoid an irreparable rupture with Biafra. In spite of the Soviet Union's declared opposition to secession, it continued, revealingly, not to condemn the Ibo cause. In October 1968 it was noted in *Izvestia* that "the Ibo people, more than other nationalities in Nigeria, has acquired characteristics that bring it close to the concept of a nation."[32] The fact that the Soviet Union kept in secret touch with Biafra until the summer of 1969 confirms this interpretation.

In spite of the indirect influence that it exerted on international perceptions of Nigeria, the Soviet Union's military involvement did not affect the military outcome of the conflict. The promptness of the Soviet Union's first armament deliveries were largely canceled out by the logistical difficulties of the Federation army, its poor qualifications, as well as delays in shipping the Soviet instruction manuals.[33] As it stands, for most observers of the conflict, the military impact of the Nigerian bombings by Soviet aircraft was marginal.[34]

"Creeping Globalism" in East Africa

Although it had ceased to believe in the "brilliant future" of socialism in Africa, the Soviet Union still was not exactly disinterested in this continent's future. At a time when it was trying to attain strategic parity with the United States, it had to ponder ways of integrating Africa into its global agenda. Given this proposition, the Soviet Union concentrated its interests on the African East and did so for two essential reasons. Because Moscow paid special attention to the Middle East and especially to Egypt, it could not appear to be indifferent to Egypt's regional environment. By the same token, from the middle of the sixties onward, the Soviet Union appeared to be worried about securing some anchorages in the Indian Ocean at a time when the United States was deploying its Polaris missiles there for the first time. Under the decisive influence of Admiral Gorchkhov, the Soviet Union thus sought to endow itself with a "balanced fleet," that is to say, a fleet capable of handling both civil and military, nuclear and conventional operations with ease.[35] The complementarity of the Soviet Union's political and strategic interests in the region caused it to develop a particular interest in two states: Sudan and Somalia.

The Soviet Union largely interpreted the evolution of Sudanese politics as an outgrowth of its Egyptian policies. Jaafar el-Nimeiry acceded to power in 1969, with the intention of making his country the "Cuba of the Arab world." The Soviet Union saw in this the confirmation of the process of radicalization of the Arab world that followed on the 1967 defeat.[36] However, conflict quickly opposed the Soviet Union to the Sudanese Communist Party, placing it back into a context more Arab than African.

While Moscow reinforced the Khartoum regime with arms deliveries, the Sudanese Communist Party (SCP) hesitated as to which line of action to take. A minority faction favoring political cohabitation with Nimeiry stood opposed to a Central Committee that was hostile to any participationist attitude. To carry weight in the internal debates of the SCP, the Central Committee did not hesitate to send a confidential letter in October 1970 giving a detailed account of the advantages of a participationist line of action.[37] Although carrying a veiled threat, this letter in no way disarmed SCP Secretary-General Mahjoub's hostility. Making a pretext of the persistent opposition of the communists toward his regime, Nimeiry quickly excluded them from the "leadership of the revolution." While reproaching the Khartoum regime for its repression of communists, the Soviet Union was itself even more severe toward these same communists. The confidential memorandum of the talks held in Damascus in May 1971 between the Syrian Communist Party and the Soviet Union's Communist Party summarizes the Soviet point of view rather well: "Mahjoub's position is not comprehensible. . . . We are doing our utmost to improve the climate between the Party and the regime. . . . It is the Sudanese Com-

41

munist Party's duty to help Nimeiry without dragging behind him nor moving faster than he does. Nimeiry has told us 'I want to build socialism.' " [38]

But once again the Soviet Union displayed its inability to play the role of arbiter decisively in a given country's domestic political game. When communist officers attempted a show of strength in July 1971 against the head of state, there was no indication that the Soviet Union had been previously informed of their intentions. Nevertheless, that did not stop the Soviets first from endorsing the communists' accession to power, in spite of having thus far denounced their intransigence, and then sharply retracting everything immediately upon the failure of the putsch. [39]

Saved by Colonel Qaddafi, who had had the airplane carrying the political leaders of the putsch stopped and searched, General Nimeiry unleashed a brutal repression of the communists and accused the Soviet Union of "complicity."

For Moscow the worsening of relations with Khartoum rang like a warning bell for its entire Middle Eastern strategy. A year later, the expulsion of its military advisers out of Egypt confirmed the ebbing of its status, established as far back as 1956 and enhanced after 1967.

To limit the damage from setbacks in Egypt and Sudan, the Soviet Union attempted, in a customary diplomatic move, to find regional retreat positions by assiduously courting Somalia and Uganda. Barely three months after the failure of the communist putsch in Khartoum, Moscow drew up a positive balance sheet of the political situation in Uganda, even though it had clearly disapproved of Colonel Idi Amin Dada's ascent to power in January 1971. [40]

Soviet outreach was even more noticeable with regard to Somalia's military regime, whose advent to power the Soviet Union had hailed in 1969. In November 1971 Moscow welcomed its head of state, Siad Barre, to whom it granted a loan of $19 million. It also canceled an $8 million debt and deferred by five years the repayment of loans agreed upon in 1961. Three months later in February 1972, the Soviet Defense Minister, Marshal Grechko, paid his first visit to black Africa in Mogadishu. In exchange for substantial military aid ($120 million between 1972 and 1974), the Soviets obtained authorization to use the port of Berbera to counter American reinforcements at Diego Garcia. Cumulatively, the Soviets established barracks there for fifteen hundred troops, a communications center between Moscow and the squadron in the Indian Ocean, an area for stocking fuel, and a runway to be used by TU-95 reconnaissance aircraft. Very quickly, the base at Berbera came to occupy an essential place in the Soviet Union's naval strategy for the Indian Ocean. Soviet naval stopovers in Somalia climbed from eleven in 1973 to ninety-seven in 1976, of a total of one hundred fifty-three stopovers in the entire Indian Ocean. [41]

On a more modest scale, the Soviet Union found that its increasing arms deliveries were a critical instrument to find a way into Uganda. At the very time that its own advisers were being thrown out of Egypt, Moscow welcomed the first Ugandan military delegation of Idi Amin's regime. A year later, in November 1973, it began to send a considerable quantity of military matériel to Kampala, including two squadrons of MiG-17s and MiG-21s and approximately one hundred heavy tanks.[42] It dispatched three hundred on-site advisers and trained two hundred Ugandan military cadres in the Soviet Union.

Despite the ideological justifications the Soviet Union brought to its relations with the Mogadishu and Kampala regimes, notably through the positive reevaluation of the role of the African militaries,[43] the Soviet Union's regional behavior largely followed immediate geostrategic imperatives. This perspective in the short term naturally led the Soviet Union to neglect the use that its circumstantial allies were making of its arms. By making Uganda the principal military power in East Africa, the Soviet Union contributed significantly to stimulating the war ambitions of Uganda's head of state as well as to feeding Tanzanian fears. By overarming Somalia, it also facilitated the reactivation of the Somali irredentist project. Finally, the Soviet Union imposed on Kenya, threatened by two overarmed neighbors (Somalia and Uganda), an arms race in which the United States would be invited to participate.

An Ambiguous Neglect

Rather than ambiguity, one should speak of ambivalence to characterize American behavior beginning in the middle of the sixties.

Indeed, the priority accorded the global dialogue with the Soviet Union led the United States to favor maintaining the status quo in peripheral regions and to give its African policy two directions. One approach was to force the old tutelary powers to ensure Western control wherever American interests were limited *and* there was a low probability of political upheavals that would affect the global Soviet-American balance. The other was to directly reinforce the strength of regional actors where the risk of severe tensions seemed potentially more significant and where American interests appeared more immediately vulnerable. The first approach coincided more or less with the outline of tropical Africa, while the other mapped itself out perfectly on white-dominated southern Africa.

Such differentiated behavior has rarely ever been so clear. Steps taken by the Johnson administration were, for example, far less consistent than those taken by the Nixon administration. In addition, the morally reprehensible character of any declared support of white minority regimes forced the American executive branch to opt for discrete measures rather than overt behavior, lateral initiatives rather than direct and massive support. Moreover, the multiple conflicts that permeated the United States executive sometimes undermined the effectiveness of covert measures. Finally, the apparent disinterest of the United States nevertheless did not negate the necessity of sometimes keeping a vigilant eye on the behavior of European mediators.

Sharing the Burden

The idea that the United States devolve a part of its global responsibilities to the old European powers is more complex than it appears.

Far from being a matter of political resignation, pure and simple, redistribution of the burden implies the existence of American control over its allies on two levels at least: (1) guiding and orienting the action of the old tutelary powers so that direct American involvement in Africa would never be required; and (2) taking care that European behavior not do any harm to the global coherence of American interests.

In addition, the division of labor required the implied meeting of at least two conditions: the willingness of the old tutelary powers to effectively ensure that role, and the consent of African actors to ratify such arrangements. Now, if one looks a bit more closely, the idea of redistributing the burden in Africa between the United States and Europe between 1965 and 1974 actually turns out in many cases to have been improper, incomplete, and imperfect.

In large part, the redistributing of the burden, underwritten by the concept of a "devolution of responsibilities," does not apply to the African context well. In the middle of the sixties European intercessors continued to play major roles. In Rhodesia (the UDI crisis) as in Nigeria (the civil war), it was not therefore so much the "redistribution of the burden" that characterized American policy, given its weak initial commitments in those two countries, so much as a refusal to respond to the expectations of the African actors. In Rhodesia the white minority regime solicited the help of the United States in order to better counteract London, whereas in Nigeria the federal government tried to capture the interest of the country it deemed its privileged diplomatic partner. This difference in perspective seems essential for, in both of these cases, America's apparent disinterest was accompanied by a sometimes vigilant control of British behavior.

In Rhodesia, for example, the United States clearly rejected Ian Smith's overtures. On the eve of the Unilateral Declaration of Independence (UDI), President Johnson sent him a secret message entreating him to renounce his undertaking and to keep dialogue alive with London.[44] Having failed in this effort, the United States refrained from engaging itself further. By hiding behind British responsibility, Washington thought it could deflect ahead of time the African states' entreaties to get tougher against white dissidence. In addition, confronting a pusillanimous Great Britain, the United States helped formulate and limit British efforts to resolve the crisis every time the idea of a military action arose.[45] Fearing a request for logistical support, the United States indirectly encouraged British passivity, despite hostility in principle to UDI.

Besides being improper as a characterization of situations in which the United States had been hitherto rather absent, the "redistribution of the burden" seems also to have been very incomplete.

In the Indian Ocean, for example, the devolution of American responsibilities to Great Britain coincided poorly with England's stated desire to remove itself from all positions east of the Suez Canal. On top of this, the increasing strategic interest of the United States in this region of the world (deployment at the end of 1964 of American Polaris A-3 missiles) was such that it favored replacement rather than an American retreat. As early as December 1966, an Anglo-American agreement put the whole of the British Indian Overseas Territories (BIOT) at the joint disposal of both governments for a period of fifty years.

Less than a year later, the closing of the Suez Canal accentuated American interest in the region because of the impact on the tankers' route between the Gulf and the consumer markets and because of the reinforcement of the Soviet Union's naval presence. In 1970, when Soviet naval development in terms of naval stopovers was equal to America's, the United States came up with the idea of endowing itself with a permanent communications center at Diego Garcia. In 1974 an Anglo-American agreement extending the one signed in 1972 provided for the installation of an American base on that atoll for very-low-frequency communications integrated into the OMEGA communications system for the guidance of nuclear missiles.[46] The same year, the Soviet Union signed a friendship and cooperation treaty with Somalia, confirming the importance the Indian Ocean had taken on and would have henceforth in the rivalry between the two big superpowers.

Both improper and incomplete, "redistribution of the burden" is also imperfect, as revealed during the Nigerian civil war because of Great Britain's hesitation and above all because of Nigeria's categorical refusal to accept this sharing of tutelage. This second point, which highlights the ability of actors to set up, consent to, or else to interfere with a possible "division of labor," deserves a bit more of our attention.

The determined refusal of Nigeria to ratify the principle of British "responsibility" stemmed in large part from the ideological, psychological, and diplomatic perceptions of the Nigerian elite.

Being the most important country in Africa, Nigeria had always perceived the United States as the only true international partner of equal stature. To this perception one must add its fascination with the American model of a federal government that could only have been enhanced by the Nigerian elite's longstanding attendance of American universities. A poll taken of Nigerian members of parliament between 1963 and 1965 shows that for sixty-nine percent the United States was considered their country's privileged partner.[47] These perceptions set up expectations on which the first Nigerian redevelopment plan (1962–68) depended. The important role this plan assigned to foreign financing was based on a very optimistic estimate of American involvement. The relative importance of bilateral American aid to Nigeria and the presence of American assistance personnel within the central planning organs quickly ensured that the United States had effective control over the process of using public funds set aside for the Nigerian plan.[48] That potential influence fixed Nigeria in the Western camp; however, this never translated into any spectacular diplomatic activity.

To be sure, American diplomacy regularly solicited the support of Nigeria during the Congo crisis; and it also supported Nigeria's regional action vis-à-vis Nkrumah. But this support remained insufficient in the eyes of the successive Nigerian leaders. From the United States, they expected recognition of their privileged place in Africa, open support that would help them in their *tête-à-tête* with Great Britain, and unswerving endorsement of the territorial unity of the Nigerian federation.[49]

With the beginning of the civil war, Nigerian pressure on the United States increased. But as long as American diplomacy sought only to turn things over to Great Britain, the entire Nigerian gameplan was to reject the principle and the modalities of such British "mediation" before taking, in the face of failure, any calculated anti-American stance.

The steps taken by the American ambassador to Lagos and the consul to Enugu to dissuade Ojukwu from doing anything irreparable, several days before the beginning of the secession, appeared to Lagos to bode well for the future. But Washington's refusal to satisfy a symbolic demand for armaments made at the outbreak of hostilities sowed the seeds of Nigerian-American misunderstanding. This distrust quickly turned into hostility when the head of American diplomacy clumsily characterized Nigeria as a "country under British responsibility." At a time when Biafra had acquired American B-26 bombers from Portugal, the Lagos government was tempted to interpret American behavior as duplicitous.

In reality, American policy appeared ambiguous for reasons that stem more from the functioning of the American system than from the vicissitudes of the Nigerian conflict.

The White House, only marginally interested in this crisis, did not give the Department of State any firm instructions as to what line of action to take. The latter therefore found it possible to remain the sole master of operations of American policy on Nigeria. J. Palmer, head of the Bureau of African Affairs, was regarded as being very much in favor of the Nigerian federal government's cause.[50] He was, for example, opposed to any American political mediation in the conflict.

Nonetheless, beneath the weight of powerful media campaigns deploring the malnutrition of Biafran children, and in light of the interest that certain public figures had in gaining solidarity with Biafra in the context of an election, the White House accepted partial reevaluation of its position. In December 1968, the White House decided to sell eight long-range aircraft to a Catholic rescue organization in Biafra, at a laughable price.[51]

In fact, the excessive dramatization surrounding Biafra stemmed from a political manipulation that a March 1969 CIA report admits straightforwardly: "In an effort to obtain sympathy for its cause, Biafra encouraged numerous foreign observers to visit refugee areas where conditions were worst. . . . It seems reasonable to assume that most Biafran farmers and their families were not starving."[52]

In the pro-Biafran propaganda effort, the role of Catholic missions became a determining factor, as is described by public relations firms that were working for the Biafran authorities, as well as by Ibo students who were the majority of the Nigerian community in the United States. Already disappointed with how long it took Washington to close its consulate's doors in Enugu in Biafran territory, the Nigerian government allowed its exasperation to explode when the United States invoked "humanitarian motives" to justify its support of the International Red Cross Committee. At a time when international opinion had discovered the Vietnamese massacres at My Lai, this American argument seemed rather unbelievable.

Richard Nixon's arrival to power in January 1969 did not improve efforts to clarify American-Nigerian relations. The White House, determined to counterbalance the pro-Nigerian influence of the State Department, relied on the National Security Council (NSC) to formulate its Nigerian policy. It held the State Department in such suspicion that it dispatched a CIA mission to Nigeria to verify the truth of the American embassy's analyses in Lagos.[53] Richard Nixon's choice of a special coordinator for humanitarian aid outside the State Department came out of a similar preoccupation. Partially discharged from its responsibilities, the State Department, which understood Lagos's hostility to humanitarian aid to Biafra, did not hesitate to thwart the White House's actions every chance it got.

The bureaucratic quarrels on America's African policy, particularly striking under the Johnson administration, would slowly be blurred under Nixon's Republican mandate. The undeniable coherence with which Nixon would imprint American foreign policy would surface most particularly in southern Africa, which would have the privilege of having the "Nixon doctrine" applied to it.

Regional Dynamics and American Strategy in Southern Africa

In the double context of the Watergate debacle and Portuguese decolonization, the Nixon administration's African policy, thus far ignored, was radically reinterpreted. The revelation by the American press of an official document, the NSSM-39,[54] indicating the broad outline of an American policy in southern Africa, made an *a posteriori* rationalization of American conduct easy to the point of caricature.[55] In fact, the value of this document resides less in its intrinsic content than in the illumination it offers of American decision-making processes.

In 1969, the year this document was created, eighty-five other studies of equal importance were also made. In October 1971 the number of these studies reached one hundred and thirty-eight, of which only four were relevant to Africa.[56] If the importance of the NSSM-39 as a political document deserves to be taken in context, its bureaucratic significance seems more serious. It marked the end of the Department of State's influence over the determination of America's African policy.[57]

At the beginning of the summer of 1968, the Department of State laid down the broad outline of the United States' policy in southern Africa. Nine months later, an internal document presented three alternatives on the issue. Proposed by the State Department as the working draft for the preparation of NSSM-39, this text was contested by the National Security Council and by the Pentagon, who were both concerned with keeping their hands free to formulate a new policy.[58] Within the interdepartmental group responsible for composing the NSSM-39 document, the divergence between the Department of State and the White House was visible very early on, so much so that it caused a six-month delay in the drafting of the final version.[59] The line separating the different groups seemed relatively clear: while the White House and the Pentagon deemed a maintenance of the dialogue with the white regimes essential, the Department of State was preoccupied primarily with African demands. But faced with the White House's desire to regain control of American policy, the State Department's opposition rapidly took the form of rear-guard action. Adopted in 1970, the second option in the NSSM-39 developed three ideas:

1. that the white presence in southern Africa was a durable phenomenon that violence would not alter;
2. that only dialogue would enable the United States to convince white regimes of gradual and peaceful change in southern Africa;

3. that the interests of the United States resided in a peaceful rapprochement between black and white regimes.

Although lacking in originality, this definition of American strategy did offer the advantage of being coherent. At a time when the United States was having to take into account its inability to have direct control over an international universe, even when that area was reduced to the noncommunist world, the United States needed to rely on some privileged ally to play the role of go-between or police officer.[60] This policy, which S. Hoffman has called "less cost primacy," implied a retreat from regions of secondary interest, a decrease in direct military operations, and an increase in covert operations.[61]

With respect to Africa, the formulation of the Nixon doctrine did not introduce any noticeable change in American behavior. Nevertheless, the discontinuity noticeable during the mid-sixties was extended in one important respect: the need for ambiguous arbitrage between American interests in black Africa and in white Africa was now denied. Accompanying a reduction in the flow of exchange, communications, and economic transfers with black Africa, the United States would no longer hesitate to reinforce an insecure white presence in southern Africa.

The shift of America's African policy in a direction more overtly favorable to the status quo in southern Africa came naturally from several factors. But fundamentally it stemmed from an image of Africa as a minor actor, marginal in the international system, whose political entropy was too strong for it to represent any real "nuisance value" in the global balance. In American reasoning, this understanding was enhanced by a decisive factor: the perception of disinterest in Africa on the part of the Soviet Union.[62] In 1972 Richard Nixon indicated that Africa resists any involvement in international conflicts and controversies. In 1973 an American congressional mission sent to assess Moscow's African policy drew a moderate picture, stating that Soviet aid to liberation movements was limited to the sole necessity for maintaining open lines of communication, and that even when this support took the form of military aid or training programs, it hardly helped anyone mount significant operations.[63]

For Washington, if there was indeed a communist design in Africa, it followed from commercial considerations rather than a desire for political infiltration.[64] The moderation inspired by America's perception of the Soviet Union's gameplan in Africa demonstrated the modesty of the Soviet Union's progress in this part of the world. But the serenity displayed by Washington can be explained by another important factor: the strengthening of the white bias in southern Africa around South Africa.

South Africa's pretension to hegemony. Far from disturbing the regional status quo in southern Africa, the 1966 independence of the former British High Commission Territories (Botswana, Lesotho, Swaziland) accentuated the regional hegemony of the Republic of South Africa. For these territories, rise to political sovereignty did not diminish their political vulnerability vis-à-vis Pretoria. In 1971 two hundred and twenty thousand nationals of these three states, out of a population of two million, worked in the Republic of South Africa. Concerned with establishing its regional hegemony while acknowledging its poorer neighbors' accession to sovereignty, Pretoria revived the idea of a regional sphere of coprosperity in 1966. In 1968 it instituted a fund for economic cooperation. By granting loans at low interest rates, the Republic of South Africa discovered a way to augment its exports and keep its neighbors more effectively under its domination. But South Africa's effort went far beyond the narrow limits of the former British High Command Territories. It extended as far as Zambia, whose break with Rhodesia in the aftermath of the UDI forced it to engage in yet more commerce with Pretoria. Between 1967 and 1973 the Republic of South Africa brought itself up to the rank of second largest supplier to Zambia and Mozambique. Between 1967 and 1973 the Republic of South Africa's share in Mozambican foreign trade increased from 2.35% to 12.25%. And considering South African exports to Mozambique alone, this trend was even more obvious: 15.3% in 1973 versus 3.2% in 1969.[65]

It is, however, the project of a hydroelectric complex in Cabora Bassa (Mozambique) that symbolizes and best expresses Mozambique's increasing integration into South Africa's sphere, while also reflecting its growing economic autonomy with respect to the Portuguese mother country. Two-thirds financed by the Republic of South Africa, the dam was primarily intended to supply electricity to the Transvaal Province. The financing agreement signed in 1969 was also supposed to have facilitated the settlement of a million people in Mozambique. Far from being isolated, South Africa's regional actions extended that same year to Angola. A hydroelectric plant on the Cunene river was planned to supply energy to Angolan mines in Cassinga and to irrigate the entire Namibian Ovamboland. Although economic in nature, these projects obviously had an eminently political significance. By engaging in such projects of long-term cooperation, the Republic of South Africa and Portugal demonstrated their desire not merely to freeze at the status quo but to consolidate it.

Pretoria even managed to reap certain benefits from the Rhodesian secession. The United Nations vote for sanctions against the rebel colony strengthened Pretoria's presence in that country, even though the entire period before the UDI had been marked by Salisbury's deliberate care to limit its dependence upon its powerful southern neighbor.[66] The Republic of South Africa's share in Rhodesia's foreign trade increased from 16% on the eve of the UDI to 38% five years later.[67]

Hardly any time elapsed before the commercial consequences of this strategy became visible. From $10 million in 1965, South Africa's trade surplus vis-à-vis Africa grew to $132.4 million five years later. In addition, by stressing its neighbors' dependence on itself, the Republic of South Africa contributed to defusing the slightest desire to fight.

The coherence of South Africa's regional actions at the end of the sixties seemed all the more confirmed as its repercussions began to register in the rest of Africa. These repercussions surfaced in April 1969 with the publication of the *Lusaka Manifesto* by nine eastern and central African governments.[68] Without renouncing its basic opposition to white domination in southern Africa, the manifesto insisted on the moral and nonracial nature of African demands. It also restated its preference for peaceful solutions. With regard to Portugal, the manifesto remained respectful of its international alliances and committed itself to taking into consideration the rights of its nationals once the Portuguese-speaking countries' independence was attained. Finally, it implicitly emphasized the political independence of southern African liberation movements with regard to socialist countries.[69]

While sticking stubbornly to its intransigent positions, the Republic of South Africa was cleverly trying to take advantage of these overtures in order to find a political opening in the region. In 1970 Prime Minister Vorster took his first trip into black Africa, in Malawi. The same year, Pretoria found that Madagascar and Mauritius were receptive interlocutors. The next year, it was the Ivory Coast that preached in favor of dialogue with Pretoria. The Ivory Coast was followed by the other members of the Council of the Entente, and also by Ghana, Uganda, and Gabon. At the ministerial conference of the OAU at the end of 1971, while twenty-eight states displayed determined hostility to any dialogue with Pretoria, ten others declared themselves in favor of such a dialogue.

The progress in Africa of the idea of a dialogue with Pretoria could only comfort the Nixon administration in its own convictions. It was also natural for the administration to accentuate an underestimation of the collective diplomatic influence of black Africa, just when the United States' own interests, most notably its economic interests, were prospering in southern Africa.

The strengthening of America's economic presence. America's economic presence, concomitantly with the development of South Africa's regional influence, achieved remarkable progress during the first part of the seventies. It was all the more noticeable as America's economic penetration into black Africa set the pace.[70] Whereas, immediately following the independence of African countries, the increase in American investment in the rest of Africa largely surpassed that of investments in the Republic of South Africa, this relationship was reversed from 1970 on. For American investors, the dichotomy between southern Africa and the rest of Africa seemed particularly pronounced: the former offered political stability and economic profitability, whereas the latter, agitated in political convulsions, still allowed the threat of nationalization to loom.

51

**Table 2   American Economic Involvement in Africa 1970–1975
(Base 100 : 1970)**

	1	2	3	4	5	6	7	8	9
1970	100	100	100	100	100	100	100	100	100
1974						2,547.7	209.6		
1975	115	182	120.4	168.5	158.6			1,618.6	167

KEY:
1. Increase of American investments in **all of Africa.**
2. Increase of American investments in the **Republic of South Africa** (RSA).
3. Increase in American investments in **Portuguese Africa.**
4. Increase in the share of American investments in **white Africa** in relation to total American investments in Africa.
5. Increase in the share of American investments in the **Republic of South Africa** in relation to total American investments in Africa.
6. Increase in payments made by **Gulf Oil** to the provincial Angolan government.
7. Increase of the United States share in Angolan exports.
8. American trade exchange balance with **Subsaharan Africa** (excluding RSA).
9. American trade exchange balance with the **Republic of South Africa.**

   It was in the exploitation of Angolan oil in Cabinda that the development of America's economic presence was most spectacularly visible at the beginning of the seventies. Being in possession of a research license since 1954, the American company Gulf Oil began to exploit and commercialize Angolan oil in 1968. Starting at 1.4 million tons in 1968, production reached 9 million tons in 1974. Under the double effect of increased production and the evolution in the global market, oil exploitation in Cabinda endowed the Portuguese colony with a spectacular surplus of resources. From $0.3 million in 1968, oil fees paid by Gulf Oil to local colonial authorities reached $400 million on the eve of the "carnation revolution."[71] It seems that Gulf Oil's economic involvement in Angola did not arise from any preconceived political plan. Nonetheless, the imposition of Gulf's involvement by colonial authorities made it one of the principal contributors to their war effort. Beginning in 1972, the date at which Gulf Oil's payments showed a noticeable increase, the Portuguese war budget in Angola grew in comparable proportions. The contribution of the "Angolan province" to the Portuguese military budget in Angola increased from an annual average of seventeen percent between 1968 and 1971, to thirty-three percent in 1972.[72] Thus, Gulf Oil backed sixty percent of the Portuguese war effort in Angola on the eve of decolonization.[73]
   The dynamics of American investment in southern Africa extended into the commercial level where, in spite of the cancellation of Eximbank loans in 1964, the Republic of South Africa appeared to offer a particularly flourishing export market. American operators were thus able to benefit from the support of the Private Export Funding Corporation (PEFCO), established in 1970 through the initiative of American banks and Eximbank to support efforts to win foreign markets with the use of credit. In 1974, ten

percent of PEFCO's commitments was assigned to the export of American products to the Republic of South Africa.[74]

Despite their noteworthy progress, American interests in southern Africa remained marginal on the global scale. For that reason, any mechanistic interpretation of American policy in the region does not really seem credible. The real differences that opposed Gulf Oil and Henry Kissinger on the issue of Angola at the time of the Portuguese decolonization do, at any rate, make a deterministic interpretation of American diplomatic behavior impossible. Nonetheless, the real prosperity of American economic interests would without question make it easier to support white regimes, as the Nixon administration was advocating.

Taking sides. The desire of the Nixon administration to break with the ambiguous and clumsy behavior of its Democratic predecessors vis-à-vis problems in southern Africa took a deliberate shape from the start.

As early as March 1969, President Nixon expressed his desire to put an end to the political harassment directed at Portugal for its African policy.[75] Judging that Portugal's contribution was essential to the stability of the African continent, Washington tried to rehabilitate Lisbon within the Atlantic community. In June 1970 the American secretary of state left for Lisbon to make the normalization of American-Portuguese relations official. A year later the North Atlantic Council met in the Portuguese capital, symbolically, for the first time since 1952.

This political rehabilitation was buttressed by diplomatic support that Portugal's international isolation up to then rendered all the more significant. In 1970 the United States opposed the United Nations resolution requesting that the international community put a stop to all military support of Portugal. The same year, the United States abstained from voting on the resolution condemning Portugal for its attack on Guinea. In December 1971 it rejected a resolution advocating immediate independence for Portuguese colonies. Finally in 1972 it fended off two resolutions, one concerning the incompatibility of colonial wars with the United Nations Charter and the other, the representation of African liberation movements.

To emphasize United States alignment with its colonial policy, Portugal did not fail to play its traditional trump card: American access to the Azores base. In March 1971 the head of the Portuguese government demanded the signing of a new agreement with the United States to put an end to the principle of tacit annual renewal, adopted in 1962. For Lisbon, the aim of this operation was clear: to test the United States political will to sustain its presence in Africa overtly. Is that to say that Portugal found itself endowed with the "power of the weak," leaving Washington no other alternative than to take the side, unconditionally, of Lisbon's colonial flag? Nothing seems less sure.

Despite appearances, the Portuguese position at the beginning of the seventies seems to have been extremely precarious. In Europe its diplomatic isolation was growing more severe. The arrival of the Social Democrats to power in Bonn in 1968 damaged the Portuguese-German military alliance. In a context where Portugal's maintenance of its presence in Africa depended on American support, it is difficult to gauge what advantage authorities in Lisbon might have seen in initiating a battle of wills with Washington. In addition, the strategic value of the Azores base as a stopover for aircraft, an antisubmarine patrol base, and a communications base had diminished by the end of the sixties. Atlantic surveillance functions could henceforth be easily accomplished from the Rota base in Spain and from the sonar station at Palomares in the Canary Islands. Even the need for layover facilities at the Terceira base decreased in light of the growing range of large cargo planes. The percentage of military air traffic between the United States on the one hand and Europe and the Middle East on the other dropped from seventy-five percent in 1963 to twenty percent in 1968.

In fact, everything suggests that Lisbon's "blackmail" of Washington in March 1971 on the future of the American presence in the Azores was deliberately exaggerated in order to cover the Nixon administration in the face of the reluctance of Congress and the recriminations by African states. The significant economic and military support granted by the United States attendant with the signing of accords on the lease of the Azores in December 1971 confirms the partially feigned nature of Portugal's blackmail, as well as the deliberate nature of American support in Portugal.

During 1971 and 1972 alone, American bilateral economic aid to Lisbon represented fifty percent of the aid package to that country between 1962 and 1975. On the military level, American support was even more obvious. Between 1969 and 1973 the United States welcomed five hundred Portuguese officers for training, notably in two pivotal areas of the colonial wars: the air force and antiguerrilla warfare. In addition, under the Nixon administration, Lisbon, like Pretoria, benefited from a relaxation of American control over products in the so-called gray zone, that is to say, those products that could be put to two different uses: civil and military. The relaxing of American sanctions and controls was most significant in the areas of aviation and telecommunications. Between 1969 and 1972 seventy-seven planes and helicopters were thus sold to colonial provinces of Angola and Mozambique.[76] During the same period, the sales of air matériel to Pretoria reached $218 million, as against only $92 million between 1965 and 1968.[77]

In all respects, the evolution of America's position with regard to the Rhodesian conflict confirmed the increasing indulgence by the United States of white regimes. Even if, officially, the United States attitude did not change at all at the advent of the Nixon administration, many signs aimed at Salisbury allow one to detect a greater receptivity to the white regime's arguments.[78] When, in 1970, the possibility of a proclamation of a Republic of Rhodesia became known, the White House favored maintaining the United States consulate in Salisbury. The State Department's appreciation of the situation was completely different. In its eyes, maintaining the consulate would needlessly isolate the United States in Africa.

Faced with the prospect of a conservative victory at the next election, the American administration preferred to buy some time. A secret message from Mr. Heath to President Nixon let it be understood that the British position would be relaxed if there were a conservative victory.[79] But the acceleration of events in Rhodesia and the unilateral proclamation of the Republic in March 1970 quickly rendered this position untenable. In a very curt note addressed to the American ambassador, the British foreign minister demanded that Washington put an end to its consular presence in Salisbury, failing which Great Britain would remove its jurisdiction by a letter of *exequatur*. Because keeping the consulate would force it to recognize Ian Smith's government officially, the United States resigned itself to closing its consular doors on March 17, 1970.

Closing the consulate in Salisbury nonetheless did no harm to American-Rhodesian relations. The White House person responsible for African affairs, R. Morris, established regular contact with the representative of the Rhodesian Information Office (RIO) as early as 1969. In 1972, after the RIO closed in Canberra, Washington became the only place where Rhodesia had overseas representation other than Portugal and the Republic of South Africa. The RIO's influence proved to be essential for the defense of the Rhodesian cause, especially when the question of supplies of Rhodesian chromium came up before Congress.

Within Congress, a Senate pressure group, made up of southern representatives favoring white regimes and heavily underwritten by American companies that imported Rhodesian chromium, attempted in March 1971 to legalize American violation of the United Nations embargo against Rhodesia. Presented before the Senate Committee on Foreign Affairs, this resolution was rejected. But without giving up on its aim, the pro-Rhodesian group changed its tactics. It no longer invoked support of a white regime in order to obtain a lifting of the embargo; instead it argued for the need to receive Rhodesian chromium in order to reduce American dependence on Soviet chromium. This tactic proved to be quite shrewd. In presenting his proposal for an amendment to the Military Procurement Act, Senator Byrd displaced the debate from the Committee on Foreign Affairs (more sensitive to the pressures of international opinion) to the Armed Services Committee (especially receptive to the East-West conflict). After favorable votes in both the House and the Senate, the Byrd amendment authorizing the import of Rhodesian chromium was enacted in January 1972. This vote, which the administration later conceded in 1975 to have offered the Salisbury regime considerable moral and psychological support,[80] nonetheless did not diminish America's dependence on the Soviet market. Several years later, the Department of State would admit that its imports of Soviet chromium had hardly changed between 1972 and 1975.[81]

The Byrd amendment vote was officially criticized by the executive branch of the American government. But this position in principle does not withstand analysis. At no time did the White House use its influence to discourage congressional action. To the contrary, the White House's congressional liaison, MacGregor, seemed a strong partisan for dialogue with white regimes. In November 1972 he even embarked on an unofficial, personal trip to Salisbury.[82] Moreover, when somewhat later several senators thought that they could cancel the Byrd amendment, the support they had thoroughly expected from the White House never materialized.[83]

The limits of coherence. There is no doubt that America's conduct in Africa, as conceived by the Nixon-Kissinger administration, seemed undeniably consistent. It was congruent with the global objectives assigned to American diplomacy. Washington's approach to Africa was not out of line with anything within the current African context marked by the strengthening of white hegemony and the lifelessness of African counterstrategies.

Very quickly, however, limitations to this design emerged: it overestimated the ability of white regimes to impose themselves durably; and, symmetrically, it neglected the ability of African countries to resist them at least partially.

In spite of its outrageous regional influence, the Republic of South Africa did not manage to accomplish its plan for construction of a sphere of regional coprosperity. The long-awaited breakthrough in the region never came. The very idea of a dialogue with the apartheid regime vanished as fast as it had been born. As early as the end of 1972, the Ivory Coast had resumed its original position. Madagascar, which had followed in step, also abandoned its stance as soon as the military gained power in 1972. Even the lethargy of liberation movements, which had seemed so worrisome during the end of the sixties, now seemed less pronounced. In July 1973 Frelimo estimated that it was powerful enough to tackle colonial village groups, the *aldeamentos,* to the point of forcing Lisbon to skim troops from its Angolan contingent.

In Guinea-Bissau, the combativeness of the *Partido Africano pela Independença da Guinea-Bissau e das islhas do Cabo Verde* (PAIGC) proved to be just as remarkable. The PAIGC was the only liberation movement to truly succeed in fully controlling liberated zones; and in September 1973 it quickly declared the unilateral independence of the territory.

These evolving factors were in turn indisputably reinforced by a movement toward African political radicalization from which the intensification of Arab-African relations was not exactly removed. These relations influenced American-African relations negatively to the extent that they revealed the existence of a Washington-Lisbon-Tel Aviv axis. In this regard, the American Air Force's utilization of the Azores for layovers during the October (1973) War facilitated the games of identity that were constantly denounced by Arab diplomats in sub-Saharan Africa. In addition, the success of OPEC in 1973, largely seen as an Arab achievement, increased the pace of nationalization and efforts at cartellization in black Africa.

Asked by the Senate in 1973 about the direction of his policies in Africa, Henry Kissinger made it clear that reevaluating United States policies in this region was the order of the day.[84] But in his eyes nothing justified the least hurry. So in 1973, when the Department of State was preparing to renegotiate the American-Angolan agreements on the Azores that would expire in December 1974, Henry Kissinger asked that Portuguese demands be most generously fulfilled. To this end he ordered the Bureau of European Affairs to keep the Bureau of African Affairs at a distance.[85]

The "carnation revolution" in Lisbon neither shattered Henry Kissinger's convictions nor did it destroy his personal disaffection with African problems. In September 1974 he only grudgingly engaged in discussion with the Nigerian foreign minister. The failure of the interview only confirmed for him the rather unflattering opinion he had of African leaders.

His attitude made no dent in the desire of the Bureau of African Affairs under David Easum to take advantage of the transition toward independence in Portuguese-speaking Africa to make some initiatives. In Mozambique the Assistant Secretary for African Affairs declared himself ready to consider the economic demands of the future independent government. In Lusaka he indicated, remarkably, that American influence in the region favored change in southern Africa, not continuation.[86]

Very quickly, however, the autonomy of the Bureau of African Affairs ran up against Henry Kissinger's hostility. The latter insisted that American aid to Angola and Mozambique be channeled through Lisbon. He also censured the bold declarations of Easum in Lusaka. Suspected of wanting to instill a new direction in United States African policy, the head of the Bureau of African Affairs was dismissed in December 1974 upon his return from southern Africa. The choice of his successor proved to be disastrous: in naming M. Davis, who had been ambassador to Chile at the time of Allende's fall from power, the Secretary of State worsened the psychological divorce between the United States and Africa.

To be sure, Henry Kissinger's selection reflected his interest in affording himself a less troublesome assistant—a deputy whose lack of familiarity with the African dossier would make it easier for him to recede into the background. But in the eyes of Africans, this nomination could only be interpreted as an American desire to extend its policy of destabilization in Latin America to the African continent.[87] The unleashing of the Angolan crisis several months later would not disarm African suspicions.

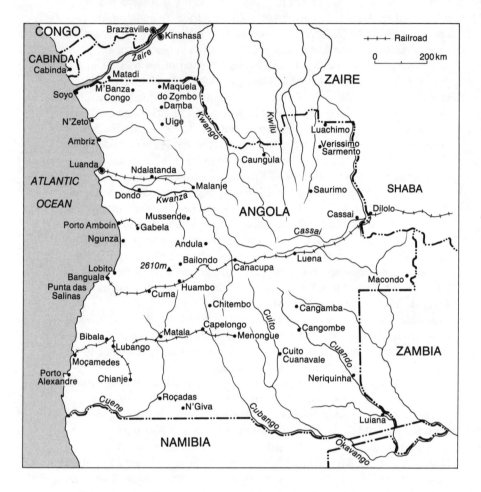

3

The Angolan Crisis

Given the broad scope of its consequences in intra-African relations and given the recurrence of external intervention in Africa, the Angolan crisis does indeed constitute a line of fracture in relations between the great powers and Africa. In itself, just as much as in what it reveals, this conflict deserves to be studied closely.

The Angolan Crisis

There is no doubt that the internationalization of the Angolan crisis hinged on the importance of the regional context and more generally on the constraints of Soviet-American antagonism. But it also indisputably had sources in the historical division of the Angolan nationalist movement— a division which can only be elucidated if Angolan society and its relation to colonization are set in historical perspective.[1]

The Original Weaknesses of Angolan Nationalism

On the eve of the nationalist insurrection of 1961, Angolan society was riddled with profound rifts. These conflicts, which the nationalist struggle would never be able to overcome, stemmed above all from ethnic divisions that were sharply molded by Portuguese colonization.

Of the three large groups that constituted Angola in the early sixties, it was the Bakongo group that had the most particular characteristics. Almost exclusively rural, it was poorly integrated into colonial society. At the same time, it was the group that suffered the most during the fifties from the policy of land dispossession undertaken by the colonizing Portuguese. Keeping very much to themselves, and tightly held together by a very strong ethnic character, the Bakongo had very little to do with colonial society. Limited schooling meant their ranks had only a small number of *assimilados,* the Portuguese equivalent of the French "évolués nords-

59

africains." This sense of exclusion from colonial society was indisputably heightened by the vitality of Protestantism, which, unlike Portuguese Catholicism, encouraged African social practices rather than Western ones.

Even though it rested on a relatively coherent social structure, Bakongo society was nevertheless not homogeneous. It sustained significant immigration from the Belgian Congo, from which its contribution to the emergence of a Bakongo nationalist movement would come. Compared to the Bakongo group living in Angola, emigrés from the Congo had two distinct characteristics: they were urban and they enjoyed a relatively high level of education. This emigré elite, socialized within the tight circle of Bakongo society, stirred up parochialism, exacerbated the antiwhite nature of nationalistic demands, and held in deep suspicion the urban world of the *assimilados* and half-castes, precisely the world where the *Movimiento Popular de Liberação de Angola* (MPLA) would seek part of its support. The 1957 creation of the *União das Populaçoes do Norte de Angola* (UPNA) expressed the regional and ethnic nature of the Bakongo claim well. According to J. Marcum, it was apparently under the influence of G. Houser, in charge of the American Committee on Africa (a Methodist association), that UPNA accepted in 1958 nominal abandonment of particularism in order to set itself up as a nationalist movement known by the acronym UPA (*União das Populaçoes de Angola*).[2] Given the evidence, this change of name proved to be insufficient. Despite numerous efforts toward "nationalizing" itself, the UPA, which would give way to the FNLA (*Frente Nacional de Liberaçao de Angola*) in 1962, would nonetheless remain deeply marked throughout the nationalist struggle by its regional identification.

The second large ethnic group in Angola, the Mbundu, were considerably different from the Bakongo. Of all the Angolan populations, the Mbundu were the most profoundly integrated into the system of colonial domination. Their secular cohabitation with the colonizer naturally helped racial mixing. It also enhanced *assimilaçao* (assimilation) in the cities and principally in Luanda. Compared to that of the Bakongo, the cultural integration of the Mbundu was relatively strong. Although they were subjected to the majority influence of the Catholic church, they could not help being influenced by American Methodists, too. It is with their backing that A. Neto managed his first trip to the United States. It was also with their assistance that nationalist Angolan students threatened by the Salazarist repression in Portugal managed to escape to Franco's Spain without running the risk of being turned over to authorities in Lisbon.

At the heart of the Mbundu, it was the former *assimilados* out of the former multiracial colonial bourgeoisie who created an impulse in the cities for a nationalist movement and who gave birth to the MPLA. They did nonetheless share a common trait with the founders of the FNLA—a weak spot that the unraveling of the nationalist battle would keep recalling: they were emigré elites that were marginal to their groups of origin. While open to Marxist ideas, the founding kernel of the MPLA should nonetheless not be understood as an outgrowth of the Portuguese communist party. The 1955 creation of the Angolan communist party, ultimately melded into the MPLA, was a response to a nationalist demand that Portuguese communists were still reluctant to bury. But the nationalism these men exalted coincided rather poorly with the one that the Bakongo advocated. Rather than "africanity," they advocated an "angolity" whose racial mix would be one of its characteristic components.

Between these two-large ethnic groups, whose quarrels the nationalistic battle would crystallize, were the Ovimbundu, whose specific political character can be seen today in UNITA battles.

Of the three important Angolan ethnic groups, the Ovimbundu group was by far the most integrated into colonial society. But because it was fragmented and dispersed by migrant work, the Ovimbundu had no oppositional strength at their disposal. This reality probably accounts for their belated entry into the war of liberation.

Beyond its ethnic diversity, what characterized Angolan society even more on the eve of the nationalist insurrection was the absence of bridges or areas of intersection between all these different groups. The principal intersections of national socialization, such as cities and schools, fulfilled their function poorly in a rural country afflicted with an impressive rate of illiteracy.

The segmentation of Angolan society, aggravated by fragile representation by the leaders of the two nationalist movements (FNLA, MPLA), ultimately took its toll on the fight for liberation. It would make of the mobilization of external support an imperative and determining factor.

Mobilizing Foreign Support (1961–1974)

In February and March 1961 following the initial uprising in Luanda, the various movements took steps to increase their backing from the outside. Early in 1961 Holden Roberto made his third trip to New York City to plead the nationalist cause, just as the Security Council of the United Nations was debating the issue. Reassured by the United States vote in favor of the March 1961 resolution that called on Portugal to implement self-determination for the Angolan territory, Holden Roberto turned to the Kennedy administration. Using the CIA as an intermediary, President Kennedy consented to awarding him financial assistance in the amount of $1 million per year. To equal the aid the UPA was receiving from the United States, and in order to refute the communistic image that his movement was attracting, the president of the MPLA, Mario de Andrade, also traveled to the United States, in December 1961. One year later, his successor, A. Neto, made the same cross-Atlantic trip, accompanied by the American Methodist minister Rev. Dodge. At the end of his visit, the Department of State advised the American Embassy in Leopoldville not to upset the MPLA's turn toward the West and not to choose between the two movements.[3] But this apparent neutrality was belied from the start by the CIA's exclusive support of the UPA.

The conditions and the chronology of Soviet support of the MPLA remain essentially unknown. One can nonetheless surmise that the warm message of support that Khrushchev addressed to the MPLA in March 1961 in response to a request for aid marked the beginning of Soviet involvement.[4]

Very quickly identified with the two great powers, these two principal Angolan movements during the mid-sixties suffered the reversal of simultaneous withdrawal. As early as December 1962, Roberto sized up the limits of United States anticolonialist temerity at the United Nations. In a letter addressed to the American chief executive in December 1962, the UPA leader requested a meeting to obtain clarification on the rumors of a suspension of CIA aid to his movement.[5] In March 1962 when the FNLA established the GRAE, even Roberto encountered hostility from the United States. G. Mennen Williams immediately went to Leopoldville to dissuade Adoula from recognizing this government in exile, but his effort was in vain.

Faced with America's increased reluctance to support him Roberto tried to diversify his sources of support. In December 1963 in Nairobi he met with Chinese diplomatic chief, Marshal Zhen Yi, who promised to come to his aid. But because the Adoula and then the Tshombe governments refused to allow the transit of Chinese materials through Congolese territory, Chinese support was temporarily reduced to its simplest expression.

Nonetheless, for a number of years yet the FNLA would be compensating for its meager military performance with an increasing diplomatic audience. It would also take advantage of the difficulties of an MPLA shaken by profound internal struggles. In July 1963 the GRAE, backed by Congo-Leopoldville and also by Algeria and Tunisia, was recognized officially and exclusively by the OAU. This decision contributed to isolating the MPLA even more.

Although having a laudatory appreciation of the MPLA and its political program (africanization of the administration, state control of foreign trade, industrialization, agrarian reform), the Soviet Union was also forced in its own turn to recognize the FNLA.[6]

Deprived of support from the Soviet Union, which seems to have suspended all aid at the end of 1963,[7] the MPLA saw no other alternative than to turn to Cuba. The Castro regime, having assured the training of Angolan cadres on Cuban territory since 1961, dispatched a medical mission to the MPLA as early as 1962.[8] Thus, from the mid-sixties on, the landscape of the internationalization of the conflict seemed partially set: the Soviet Union and Cuba standing beside the MPLA, the United States and China at the side of the FNLA. But in between then and the time of Portuguese decolonization, power relations among the different movements never ceased to shift.

In 1964 the FNLA was shaken by the departure of J. Savimbi. Two years later, he created a third nationalist movement, UNITA. His defection weakened the FNLA, under increasing pressure from Congo-Leopoldville to refuse aid from China.[9] In July 1964 the OAU summit in Cairo reconsidered its initial position of exclusive support for the GRAE. A year after that, the Committee on Liberation of the OAU agreed to give the MPLA a third of the funds that had been intended for Angola.[10]

This decision led to the timid withdrawal of Soviet support from the MPLA. In 1964 the Soviet Union for the first time welcomed Neto through the intermediary of Alvaro Cunhal, the leader of the Portuguese Communist Party. In the Soviet press the MPLA would hereafter be presented not only as an anticolonialist movement but also as a force intent on "propagating the idea of socialism."[11] Soviet aid between 1961 and 1974 was to reach $63 million.[12] But on a strictly military level, Soviet backing seems in fact to have been quite modest. While visiting the MPLA underground in 1970, B. Davidson was struck by the small number and poor state of the arms that were in the hands of the guerrillas.[13] The meagerness of Soviet support pushed Neto to attempt in July 1971 to renew ties with China. Indeed, its privileged support of the FNLA did not mean that China was not wooing rival movements. It is true that in the meantime the FNLA's military ineffectiveness led the OAU to retract its recognition of the GRAE. Made more obvious by the reduction in CIA aid, which had dropped to $10,000 per year in 1969, this situation divided the FNLA to the point of making it a simple appendage of the Zairian government. In April 1972 it was Zairian forces that saved Roberto from a mutiny at the Kinkuzu base, located in Kinshasa's suburbs. Also, several months later, one thousand Zairian soldiers penetrated Angola to attempt an on-site reinforcement of the FNLA's weakened structure.

Progressively becoming the tutelary power of this movement, the president of Zaire used the international position of his country to attract outside support to help the FNLA. At the time of his visit to Peking in 1973, he obtained a promise from the Chinese to come to the assistance of Roberto's movement.[14] In the meantime, with the backing of J. Nyerere, the Zairian chief of state gave priority during the summer of 1973 to the rehabilitation of the FNLA within the OAU.[15]

While the FNLA slowly resurfaced, with decisive support from Zaire, the MPLA moved deeper into crisis. In February 1972, Chipenda, the eastern front commander, became a dissident against Neto's power and thus sparked active revolt. This power struggle, conducted against a backdrop of racial conflicts (the "black base" of the MPLA reproaching the *mestiços* for monopolizing power), shook up the MPLA to the point of forcing Neto to abandon the leadership of the movement temporarily. He would, moreover, have to wait until September 1974 to fully reestablish his authority.

Faithful to the prudent line it had not abandoned up to then, the Soviet Union judged it useless to prolong its support of a movement so deeply divided. From 1972 on, in the context of détente with the United States, it reduced its aid to the MPLA significantly. For a while, the Soviet Union even decided to offer its favors to the Chipenda faction. But in December 1973 the Soviet Union welcomed Neto to convince him to work for unity but also to warn him about Chipenda's plans to assassinate him.[16] As it waited in the meantime, it decided to halt all support of the movement at the beginning of 1974.

On the eve of Portuguese decolonization, the profound dissension within the Angolan nationalist movement, accentuated by its feeble combativeness, already seemed to bring on considerable tension. To survive and to have some authority facing the competition, each movement was forced to mobilize support from sources outside of Angola. This dependence upon external actors would become increasingly clear as the decolonization movement in lusophone Africa accelerated.

On the Eve of the Alvor Accords (April 1974–January 1975)

The Portuguese revolution of April 25, 1974, did not immediately or drastically alter the course of events in Angola. While the new Portuguese leaders were committed to the idea of a political solution, they preferred acquiring independence in stages. Moreover, in May 1974 Portugal excluded any immediate possibility of total independence.[17] Confronted with political ferment in Angola, authorities in Lisbon relieved the military governor of his duties in July 1974 and replaced him with Vice Admiral Coutinho, who became one of the MPLA's best allies in Luanda.

China was the first foreign power to react to the events of April 25, 1974. At the end of May a military mission, one hundred twelve men strong, arrived in Kinshasa with plans to train five thousand fighters for the FNLA. In conformity with the agreements to back this movement made in December 1973, this support was augmented by logistical aid assessed at four hundred fifty tons of armament.[18] In the fall of 1974 the FNLA likewise began to benefit once more from CIA aid—as of that moment, the CIA was intent on launching a secret operation in Angola. Meanwhile, Portugal under General Spinola was sketching the broad outline of a solution. He informed President Nixon about it at a meeting in the Azores in June 1974. On September 15 a crucial secret meeting took place in Cape Verde. Present there were Mobutu, Spinola, and Roberto. For Portugal the issue was finding a common ground of agreement with the FNLA, in order to deal with Neto's MPLA.

Soviet aid to the MPLA, which had been completely suspended at the beginning of 1974, did not really start again until the month of October. Shipments of Soviet arms, initially worth some $6 million, were channeled through the OAU's Committee on African Liberation. Neto's reorganization of the MPLA, together with the fear of a Sino-American alliance, to a great extent explain the Soviet renewal of aid. In November 1974 the Soviet journal *New Times* expressed concern over the coincidence of Washington's and Peking's interests in Angola.[19] One can probably add to these two concerns the point of view of the Portuguese Communist Party (PCP), whose leader, A. Cunhal, was in Moscow in October 1974.[20] The fact that, at the same moment, Angola had learned of a plot by the extreme right wing—itself a consequence of the radicalization of the Portuguese regime—underscores once and for all the strong connection between the Portuguese situation and Angolan decolonization. Given the pessimistic Soviet perception of the Angolan liberation movement's revolutionary potential at this time,[21] the Soviet Union seemed to believe, or hope, that a solution could be found that would benefit the MPLA, with the help of a "revolutionary" Portugal.

Within the American executive branch, the diffusion of power and the conflicts among different centers of authority made it difficult to elaborate coherent policy. At the Department of State, the Bureau of African Affairs was kept at bay concerning Henry Kissinger's Angolan project. The African bureau of the CIA, for its part, enjoyed considerable autonomy. At the end of the summer of 1974, the renewal of payments to the FNLA took place without the knowledge of the American consulate in Luanda. For that reason, the consulate believed that the perceptible increase of the movement's resources had come from the financial support of the white planters of northern Angola.[22]

CIA activity in Angola, which had been largely autonomous until the end of 1974, would nonetheless be placed under the direct authority of Henry Kissinger starting in January 1975. But even if the Secretary of State took on direction of these operations at that time, he was careful not to associate them with the Department of State. It would only be on December 31, 1975, once the MPLA's victory became irreversible, that American ambassadors located in Africa would be seriously informed of the reality of United States involvement.[23]

The Transition Phase

In the very first days of January 1975, representatives of the three Angolan movements meeting in Kenya agreed on a common platform. On January 15 at Alvor in Portugal, the three movements signed an agreement with Portuguese authorities setting November 11 as the formal date of independence of Angola. In anticipation of this event, a high commission, much like a cabinet, composed of representatives from the three movements was made responsible for organizing and readying the elections for a constituent assembly.

Given the depth of inter-Angolan conflicts and their exacerbation by external powers, this agreement was quickly emptied of all significance. Within the MPLA, Neto reinforced his position in February 1975 by eliminating the dissident faction of Chipenda who, with his two thousand members, would swell the ranks of the FNLA. At the beginning of 1975, power relations between the various movements still worked to the advantage of the FNLA; but the domination by the MPLA in Luanda deprived the FNLA of a strategic position. Thus, the CIA's payment of $300,000 to the FNLA in January 1975 was made to help it reach its primary objective: to dislodge the MPLA from the capital city before the pivotal date of November 11, 1975.

Conscious of the danger that awaited it, the MPLA appealed once again to Moscow for some backing. With this in mind, it received the first official Soviet delegation headed by Dzasokhov, the executive secretary of the Soviet committee for the organization of Afro-Soviet solidarity.[24] In March 1975, while FNLA forces were preparing to launch an offensive from Caxito against Luanda, the Soviets launched their first military airlift. During the month of March alone, between twenty-five and thirty round-trips were thus flown to Brazzaville.[25] From there, military matériel was transferred by train to Pointe Noire, then by truck to Cabinda, and finally by ship along the Angolan coast. In April 1975 the Soviets may even have unloaded some one hundred fifty tons of armaments right in the port of Luanda, thanks to certain Portuguese officers.[26] The importance of the Soviet Union's military support between March and July of 1975 has been subject to extremely contradictory evaluations. For Henry Kissinger, these deliveries marked the beginning of the internationalization of the conflict. On the other hand, according to John Stockwell, former head of the CIA's Angolan operation, the Soviet aid did nothing but counterbalance the powerful Zairian support of the FNLA at the time of the February offensive.[27] This interpretation seems confirmed by the urgent steps the MPLA took to obtain arms and direct military aid from Cuba.[28] From the end of the spring, a contingent of two hundred thirty Cubans worked aside the MPLA. But its participation in combat, notably in the battles in Caxito in May of 1975, seems arguable.

Whatever the case, Soviet and Cuban aid enabled the MPLA to regain the advantage very quickly. At the beginning of the summer, the FNLA was dislodged from the suburbs of Luanda. In the rest of the country, the MPLA controlled twelve of the fifteen provinces. The Soviet Union therefore regained confidence. The MPLA alone was credited with having a truly national plan. Its rivals were discredited as "tribalist" (FNLA) or as "conciliatory toward foreign interests" (UNITA). But although temporarily reassured, Moscow still feared the possibility of a right wing military putsch in Angola that would interfere with the Portuguese revolution.[29]

The Internationalization of the Conflict (October 1975 – February 1976)

Beginning in the fall, the declared involvement of foreign powers bestowed a new dimension on the Angolan conflict. But this involvement had two distinct chronological phases. The sole goal in the first phase was to gain control of the Angolan capital before November 11. In the absence of an organized transition, legitimate political power in an independent Angola would devolve to whomever could ensure effective power, beginning with control of the capital.

At the beginning of October, a contingent of seventy Cubans landed south of Luanda. A short time later, an American ship unloaded a large lot of armaments in Matadi (Zaire) that was intended for the FNLA. In the field, there was increasing collaboration between South Africa's BOSS (Bureau of State Security)[30] and the CIA.[31] On October 22 a South African column, at least one thousand men strong and backed by fifty tanks, penetrated into Angola.[32] For the South African troops supplementing the Portuguese military dissidents of the Portuguese Liberation Army (ELP), the objective was clear: to help UNITA and the FNLA recapture territory conceded to the MPLA since the month of May and to dislodge it from the capital before November 11, 1975. While a first group was in charge of recapturing all of the cities of the Angolan coast and moving up toward Luanda, a second group moved toward the east. Coordinated in the south with UNITA, South African intervention was also precisely coordinated with that of the FNLA. The day South African troops launched their offensive, the FNLA set off a massive attack on Luanda. In the field, the numerical relation of the forces was as follows: there were eight thousand MPLA members backed by approximately two thousand Cubans, opposing thirteen thousand FNLA and UNITA fighters backed by three thousand Zairians and three thousand South Africans. The progress of Pretoria's troops quickly became dizzying. The first column took Moçamedes on October 28, Benguela on November 5, and Lobito on November 7.

Facing the collapse of its position, the MPLA thought of proclaiming unilateral independence. During the week preceding official independence, six hundred fifty Cuban soldiers arrived in Luanda with the imperative mission of holding the capital until November 11. At the same moment, the Soviet Union unloaded a large shipment of heavy, effective materials. By contrast, American arms delivered to the adversary camp proved not to be very effective. They had been taken from World War II stock so that their origins could be more easily concealed.[33]

Overnight, from November 10 to 11, while FNLA troops were camped out fifteen kilometers from Luanda, Portuguese authorities officially withdrew from Angola. The MPLA, controlling Luanda, succeeded them proclaiming the birth of the Popular Republic of Angola.

From this moment, the nature of internationalization of the conflict changed. Having the symbolic characteristic of sovereignty (the effective control of the capital), the MPLA seemed to be in a better position to justify foreign support in the name of defending its sovereignty. Such was the interpretation the Soviet Union immediately espoused in insisting on an "authorized declaration" to the effect that "in the present circumstances, all aid to the MPLA is aid to an independent Angola."[34] As a matter of fact, a week after the proclamation of independence, the first Soviet military advisers arrived in Luanda.

At the same time, no less than seventy air shuttles were carried out between Cuba and Angola, with stopovers first in Barbados, then in Guyana, and finally in the Azores. Subjected to the diplomatic pressure of the United States, the governments of Barbados, Guyana, and Portugal had shut down their respective airports to the transfer of Cuban equipment. This inconvenience was nonetheless rapidly circumvented by direct recourse to Soviet logistics, on the heels of the American Congress' vote on the Tunney amendment. Because the executive branch of the American government now found itself deprived of the means to prolong its Angolan commitment, the Soviet Union was taking few risks in exposing its involvement directly. Sending nine thousand Cuban fighters in the space of two and a half months did have a decisive influence on the course of the conflict. Once the progress of the FNLA toward Luanda had been halted, in the days following the proclamation of independence, Cuban forces turned around and moved back toward the south to focus on South African forces. On November 27 the Republic of South Africa, whose troops were then located approximately one hundred kilometers from the capital, officially acknowledged its participation in the conflict. But in appealing to Western powers for relief, Pretoria implicitly set limits on its own commitment. On the same day, a grant of $7 million to the anti-MPLA coalition exhausted the CIA's secret funds.[35] To prolong its action the American government now had to appeal to Congress for official backing.

The shrinking options available to the MPLA's adversaries were unquestionably stressed further by the mobilization of African actors, who until then had been the impotent witnesses of a crisis of international proportions. Nigeria's recognition of the Luanda regime as early as November 25 prefigured the toppling of African diplomatic strategies. From an initially reserved position the majority of African countries moved to a different approach to the situation. Henceforth, South Africa's intervention would serve as generic explanation for the internationalization of the conflict. It led to the relegation of inter-Angolan conflicts to the background and to *ipso facto* legitimation of Soviet-Cuban intervention.

In this respect, the evolution of the Nigerian position seems typical. The official attitude of prudence in the face of inter-Angolan rifts in fact covered up deep dissension within governing powers in Nigeria. The head of Nigerian diplomacy, J. Garba, hid his support of the FNLA poorly. For that reason, in the immediate aftermath of November 11, the movement did not hesitate to count Nigeria among those states in favor of its cause. The Nigerian head of state, however, Murtallah Mohamed, seemed more to favor the tenets of the MPLA, notably because of his profound mistrust of Western states. Furthermore, South Africa's intervention provided the occasion, or the pretext, for rushing to the rescue of the new regime in Luanda by giving it $20-million in aid.

On December 9 the conflict reached its culmination with the "Battle of Bridge 14" between Cuban and South African forces. This confrontation had paradoxical effects on the conflict. On one hand, it confirmed the superiority of the Republic of South Africa vis-à-vis the Cuban forces that were, it seems, only saved from rout by airborne intervention. On the other, it placed before Pretoria a simple alternative: to intervene even more extensively to kick Cuba out of Angola or to prompt Cuba's withdrawal in the face of an increasingly untenable political situation.

China was the first to react to the consequences of the new situation. As early as December 24 its military mission officially left Zaire, deeming its mission in support of the FNLA to have been completed. Moreover, having found itself one of Pretoria's allies, China decided to pull out in a hurry.

Thus, to the extent that support for the anti-MPLA coalition had fallen away, Moscow and Havana reinforced their commitment. As early as December the Soviet press, until then rather silent on the unraveling of military operations, noted that the fighting was taking a turn in favor of the MPLA.[36]

In mid-December Angolan-Cuban forces took the offensive again in the north, to push the FNLA back toward the border with Zaire once and for all. On December 28 Pretoria effectively began its retreat. On February 8 Huambo's capture marked the end of the "Second War of Liberation." Three days later, the OAU admitted into its ranks the Popular Republic of Angola. On February 22 the Lisbon government established diplomatic relations with Luanda.

But Who Started It?

Ascertaining the responsibility of the various actors in the internationalization of the Angolan conflict is not a matter simply of demanding truth. It is an integral part of a debate in which each actor implicated has tried to legitimate its own activity and discredit the legitimacy of its adversaries.

But all of the actors overestimate the coherence of their adversaries' intervention and underestimate that of their own. Thus, in order to attribute the responsibility for internationalization to the Soviet Union, the United States deliberately ignored the fact that Cuba's action was autonomous from the Soviet Union, while it simultaneously underestimated the coincidence of its own interests with those of Zaire and the Republic of South Africa.

The American thesis, as Henry Kissinger articulated it immediately after the crisis, can be summarized in the following arguments. Before the MPLA decided to impose itself militarily with Soviet backing, the United States held to a position of strict neutrality in the conflict. The United States maintained good relations with all of the movements, including the MPLA. It was the Soviet-Cuban intervention that was responsible for the modification of internal power relations and that was at the root of America's counterinvolvement.[37]

On two central points, namely initial neutrality and the purely reactive character of America's involvement, the American thesis fails to stand up to analysis. American support of the FNLA dates from 1961. Even if it remained rather modest for a long time, its political significance never changed. For the United States, the issue was always finding an anticommunist alternative to Portuguese colonization and reinforcing the regional position of its principal ally, Zaire. On the question of whether the United States could have initially supported the MPLA, moreover, one of Henry Kissinger's aides answers clearly: "I don't see how that could have happened since the MPLA was created out of the Portuguese communist party."[38] And if, in fact, the United States did communicate with the MPLA through its consulate in Luanda, the consulate played no part in the formation of American policies in Angola. Quite the contrary, its opinions were systematically ignored.

The second part of the argument, devoted to the purely reactive character of American involvement, is even more specious. To date the beginning of the escalation of Soviet arms shipments to the MPLA from March 1975 is to deliberately ignore the entire prior process of internationalization to which the United States indirectly consented. For a long time the United States believed in an agreement toward independence negotiated between Portugal and the FNLA with the support of Zaire. In addition, as long as Zaire (later supported by China) seemed ready to impose a solution favoring the FNLA, its own involvement was deemed superfluous. The complementarity of American-Zairian interests was explicitly recognized by the CIA. In July 1975 its request for assistance for the FNLA and UNITA was justified specifically by Zairian deficiencies.[39] Omission of the role of America's allies in the process of internationalization leads naturally to the obscuring of South Africa's essential responsibility in the conflict. Even when the United States carefully avoided any official consultation with Pretoria during the whole crisis, the collaboration in the field between the CIA and BOSS suffered no ambiguity. American arms intended for UNITA were unloaded in Kinshasa to be forwarded to the south of Angola by South African vehicles.[40] Can one say, all the same, that the United States encouraged or approved the direct and massive intervention of Pretoria in the conflict beginning in October 1975? To that question, South African Prime Minister Vorster offered an answer that has become famous: "If you say that of your own accord, I will not call you a liar."[41]

In fact, it seems established now that the United States was aware of South African preparations. The close collaboration between the CIA and BOSS, and the presence of the CIA in Angola, make it impossible to think that these preparations could have been carried out without American knowledge. As far as determining whether Henry Kissinger encouraged them, one can offer the following interpretation: given the diplomatic risks at stake, the head of American diplomacy had no interest in giving formal consent to the Republic of South Africa's intervention. At the slightest sign of tension between these two countries, South Africa would have immediately made public the secret approval of the United States and would have put America in a difficult position. At the same time, it seems reasonable to think that the reduction of American options in the conflict (Zaire's exhaustion, the FNLA's incompetence, China's retreat, the increase in Soviet-Cuban involvement) led Henry Kissinger to avoid discouraging South Africa's undertaking. His refusal to condemn it explicitly proves the point well.

Because of the obscurity the Soviet Union maintains on the chronology of its involvement, critical analysis of its actions presents quite a few problems. In truth, the only unofficial non-Western version of the Angolan crisis is reconstructed for us by Gabriel Garcia Marquez in his story on the "Carlotta Operation."[42] This version stresses two points strongly contested by the United States: Cuba's total independence with respect to the Soviet Union and the precedence of the South African intervention. Intended more to convince than to explain, the Cuban version of the Carlotta Operation is far from answering all of the questions raised about Cuba's involvement in Angola.

In the first place, the justification of Cuban intervention exclusively in relation to South Africa's intervention is hardly satisfactory. Cuban support of the MPLA goes back to the middle of the sixties. In addition, its involvement followed a logic of extraversion, analyzed later, whose bases and manifestations go well beyond Africa. Even if South African intervention unquestionably amplified Cuba's, the principle of its intervention existed earlier. In an account of the Angolan civil war, a Polish journalist mentions the presence of Cuban military advisers in Luanda and southern Angola in October 1975, a month before the official declaration of independence.[43] The breadth of this intervention, moreover, makes one doubt the credibility of Garcia Marquez' thesis on the improvised character of Cuban action. From the end of August 1975, the principle of military intervention seems to have been a given, probably because of the Portuguese refusal to involve more new troops in Angola. Furthermore, at the end of August the head of Cuban diplomacy stressed that "actions of nonaligned states meant to safeguard Angola's independence and territorial integrity are imperative and must be agreed to in any way possible." [44]

As to the question of Soviet-Cuban relations, Garcia Marquez' argument seems quite imprecise. It is limited to a reminder that Cuban intervention was carried out totally independently and was communicated to the Soviet Union after the fact. There again, the plea obscures the analysis. That Cuba had taken the initiative to intervene in Angola, and that it had itself convinced the Soviet Union to support it, are hardly disputable claims. As things stand, the history and the logic of Cuban policies largely argue in favor of this point of view. On the other hand, the argument presented by Garcia Marquez fails to recall that, without the Soviet Union's financial and logistical support, Cuba never could have carried out an operation of such magnitude. Even when, at the end of December 1975, Cuban forces were deployed by specifically Cuban logistical means, Cuban soldiers arrived in Brazzaville to find substantial matériel provided directly by the Soviet Union. Starting in January 1976, moreover, half of the Cuban expedition was deployed by Soviet planes. Fidel Castro was later to confirm this information by indicating that "the Soviet Union participated in our efforts when imperialism had cut off practically all our air access routes in Africa." [45]

For the Soviet Union, whose involvement became more defined as global constraints weighing on it were alleviated, the Angolan crisis had three meanings. In Angola, it was a reminder that the Soviet Union was, like Cuba, entitled to a share in the MPLA triumph. It demonstrated to certain Africans that its support of "just causes" was vital and efficient. And it forced the United States to admit, for a while, that its accession to strategic parity and its pursuit of global dialogue with the Soviet Union had no bearing on its desire to carry out a truly regional policy in Africa.

Although the Angolan crisis came to an end for the time being, its impact on the structure of Soviet-American relations in Africa was only beginning.

The Implications of the Conflict

Until the crisis in Angola, the involvement of the superpowers in Africa rested on 'a double framework of rigid compartmentalization—involving partition between the regional level of superpower intervention and the global level of their confrontation, and a similar partition between the different loci of involvement in the African political scene. The 1960 crisis in the Congo had no effect whatsoever on the 1963 signing of accords between the Soviet Union and the United States on nuclear testing. The Nigerian crisis had even less effect on the initiation of a nuclear nonproliferation treaty. On the other hand, the crisis in Angola, followed shortly thereafter by the Shaba and Ethiopian crises, contributed to the United States' raising the question of compatibility between the global and regional levels of Soviet policy. From that point of view, the crisis in Angola served as an excellent testing ground for America's theory of linkage.

The idea behind linkage as advocated by Henry Kissinger called for setting up a network of interdependence between the East and the West meant to encourage "interaction of behaviors, interdependence of interests and interpenetration of societies." [46] By conceding the Soviet Union's access to strategic parity, the United States attempted to convert the Soviet Union into a comanager of the international system constrained by its new responsibilities to temper its planetary ambitions. Trying to make the Soviet Union a "sated superpower," Washington strove to fit it into a straitjacket that would constrain it permanently and force it to balance the costs of new involvement in the Third World with the increasing benefits it would cull from restraint. [47]

It was on the basis of this general scheme that America's Angolan policy was initially articulated in January 1975. Henry Kissinger, confident of the solidity of a set up he thought would constrain the Soviet Union, did not expect the Soviets to run needless risks in Angola. For that reason, contrary to what he would later declare, the head of American diplomacy did not interpret the delivery of Soviet arms to the MPLA in March 1975 as the beginning of a Soviet escalation of the conflict. If such had been his interpretation at the time, it would be difficult to understand why he would not have sent Moscow some warning. [48]

In fact, if Henry Kissinger did activate the linkage lever at this time, it was for one essential reason: having decided as early as January to support the FNLA secretly, Washington had no immediate interest in broaching the Angolan question with Moscow. On the other hand, once the operation had been launched and once the FNLA's position had been redressed, the United States could attribute the responsibility for escalation more easily to the Soviet Union by bringing linkage into play in cases where the situation would hypothetically turn to the advantage of the MPLA.

This plan's success nevertheless implied that the power relations between the superpowers in Africa would be defined independently of any regional constraint. It postulated an absence of regional action likely to interfere in the conflict between the superpowers to one or the other's clear advantage.

Now, by not opposing itself clearly to the Republic of South Africa's entrance into the conflict, the United States was underestimating the negative polar reaction that such an action could create among African states that were divided up to then. The United States overlooked in Angola, as it had in Ethiopia, the opportunity for the Soviet Union to protect itself behind the legitimate problematics of inter-African relations (the intangibility of borders and the hostility to the apartheid regime) so that its own view would prevail and an American response would be preempted.

The United States drew two major conclusions from this crisis. The first follows from the unprecedented nature of Soviet-Cuban military intervention and from the inability of the United States to counteract it. The second stems from the potential for interference and harm by African actors in the global game. The first suggested the necessity for the United States to compete, even imperfectly, with the Soviet Union on its own territory. The second presupposes coopting African expectations so as to render Soviet assistance unnecessary.

But while the Angolan crisis revealed to the United States the compelling need to reexamine the terms of its balance between global goals and regional interests, the crisis offered the Soviet Union a totally different interpretation. Having noted the difficulty with which the United States organized counterfire, and not just because of the hostility of Congress, the Soviet Union perceived that African territory was likely to offer some benefits while simultaneously sparing the Soviet Union any need for drastic choices between its own global objectives and its regional interests. Much to the contrary, American impotence and African tolerance led it to have a regional policy that it could carry out protected from global dialogue. The Soviet Union saw this partition as all the easier and more favorable because its gains in influence came at the cost of material and human investment that, while locally decisive, had only secondary significance at the global level.

But the Soviet Union's renewal of interest in Africa did not end there. By coupling its emergence in strategic areas (southern Africa, the African Horn) with "legitimate identification" (the struggle against racial domination, the preservation of the intangibility of borders, the defense of revolutionary conquests), the Soviet Union established or reestablished balance between its strategic imperatives and its obligations as an ideocratic power. In this respect, the objective identification of China with the Republic of South Africa and with the United States during the Angolan crisis contributed decisively to the reversal of the terms of the Sino-Soviet conflict in Africa. There again the existence of a caesura seems unquestionable.

While the Angolan crisis revealed active integration of the African system into the East-West framework, it also abolished traditional separations between sites of superpower intervention in the African political domain.

For the most part, the actions of the two large superpowers had thus far been limited to diplomatic-strategic areas. From this point on, the two superpowers strengthened their involvement on that plane but also became participants in the process of legitimation of certain African powers or in the restructuring of their dependency relations. The new arrangement of Soviet-American involvement did not seem to exhibit any uniform character. In addition, American and Soviet modes of intervention seemed quite different. Schematically, the specificity of Soviet policy was rooted in the Soviet ability to fit the framework of power legitimation closely to the more traditional areas of diplomatic-strategic action, while leaving intact the framework of economic dependence.

American policy proceeded differently. It attacked the diplomatic-strategic field directly and more frankly by deploying its managerial abilities in inter-African conflicts. It also worked more consciously and perhaps more voluntaristically at linking the first level of intervention to the preservation of direct economic interests whose relative importance it had discovered. Although articulated in a more diffuse manner and, at any rate, far less explicitly than the Soviet Union's, American participation in the legitimation of certain African powers cannot be ignored. Through the trail it managed to blaze for certain African actors to gain access to the distribution of international financial institutions' resources, the United States interfered indirectly with the selection and choices of certain ruling elites. Had not the benefit of the "confidence of financial institutions" become, in Kenya and in the Ivory Coast, a factor that was as significant as the "ideological confidence" placed by Moscow in this or another Angolan or Ethiopian leader? Moreover, did not the coincidence of political interests between the United States and Nigeria between 1976 and 1980 open up the potential for Nigerian identification with the American power, only undermined up to then by Washington's "blunders"? For these reasons, the abolition of the framework of compartmentalization between the global dimension and the regional dimension, as well as between the different sites of involvement in the African political arena, conferred a henceforth structural character upon the action of the superpowers.

Cuba in Africa

The intervention of Cuban troops in Angola emphasizes the caesura prompted by the decolonization crisis because of its unprecedented magnitude and the influence Cuba exercised not only on Soviet-American relations but also on the whole set of international relations in Africa.

But because Africa was only one particular place, and perhaps only a temporary setting in Soviet-Cuban relations, an interpretation of Cuba's

African policy and of Cuba's ties to Soviet behavior calls for a historical perspective on relations between Havana and Moscow.

The strategy of political extraversion that Cuba pursued more of less to its benefit from the beginning of the sixties came less from a sense of messianic mission than from an exigency imposed by its political and economic asphyxiation by the United States. Lacking the ability to confront its principal adversary directly, the Cuban regime tried to weaken it and to play upon its weakest point: the Third World. From this vantage point, any external action was conceived of as an instrument of domestic consolidation of the Castro regime.

In the aftermath of the 1961 Bay of Pigs crisis, Havana no longer believed in the possibility of a *modus vivendi* with Washington. Trapped in a hostile regional environment, it saw three principal advantages to an alliance with Moscow: "Soviet arms to defend the island against conventional attack, a 'nuclear umbrella' to deter full-scale US intervention, and economic assistance to rescue an economy . . . dependent on the US." [49]

In this initial stage of internal consolidation, the Cuban policy of extraversion remained quite modest. It was limited to sending a battalion to Algeria at the time of the Desert War (1963), a military mission to Nkrumah, and a medical team to the MPLA. But from the mid-sixties on, the profile of Cuban diplomacy changed. Disappointed by Khrushchev's "fall back" during the October 1962 missile crisis, Cuba initiated a rapprochement with Peking as the Sino-Soviet schism was taking shape. With its own means, Cuba attempted to rekindle the antiimperialist flame, out of concern about the excessive pragmatism of the Soviet Union, and its endeavors to reach an agreement with the United States. It was in the midst of the revolutionary ferment in Colombia, Guatemala, and Bolivia that it therefore thought it had found an excellent setting for its indirect confrontation with the United States. This setting was extended to Africa when Che Guevara took charge of two hundred Cuban fighters in April 1965. At the side of Gaston Soumaliot's forces, Che tried to overthrow the pro-American regime in Congo-Leopoldville. This Cuban strategy of planetary confrontation with the United States culminated at the OSPAAL conference held in Havana in January 1966. As the American threat in Southeast Asia became more clear, Fidel Castro could neither understand nor admit exacerbation of the Sino-Soviet rivalry. "As long as we have to deal with imperialism, it is ridiculous to argue whether we are dealing with greyhounds or boxers, or if it is made of paper or iron." [50] Allusion to the "paper tiger" (Mao Tse-tung) and to "his atomic teeth" (Khrushchev) was quite obvious.

The Cuban political intransigence, marked by a double mistrust of the two centers of communism, extended naturally to the internal level with the denunciation in January 1968 of a "microfaction" of the Partido Socialista Popular (PSP) headed by A. Escalante. The Soviet Union, which until then had tried to minimize its disagreements with Fidel Castro, reacted by suspending its oil deliveries throughout the first half of 1968. Cuba then found itself in the very peculiar situation of being subject to triple sanctions: by the United States from 1960, by China from 1965, and finally by the Soviet Union.

This strategic impasse, underscored in the Guevera disappointments in Africa and in Bolivia, made a redefinition of Cuban policy on a more realistic basis indispensable. The signal of this readjustment was Cuba's support of the Soviet invasion of Czechoslovakia.[51]

From that moment on, the hierarchy of Cuban objectives was clearly revised. Henceforth, the issue for Cuba was less to seek the means of singling itself out with respect to a Soviet policy judged fearful than to assure itself a favorable position within the socialist camp. Its membership in the COMECON from 1972 on ensured impressive economic advantages for Cuba (refinancing its debt, new credit, Soviet purchase of Cuban nickel and sugar at higher rates than in the world's market, oil deliveries at preferential prices). In its efforts toward integration into the socialist camp, military cooperation was not neglected. Soviet military assistance endowed Cuba with a battle corps of more than three hundred thousand men whose effectiveness would soon be tested by combined Soviet-Cuban exercises. Their usefulness would be revealed clearly in the effectiveness of Soviet-Cuban coordination in Ethiopia in 1977.

In reality, Cuba's presence in Africa raised the issues of its direct influence on Soviet-American relations, of its effect on Soviet-Cuban relations, and of its "mediational" function in Soviet-African relations.

Cuba and Soviet-American relations. After the intervention of Cuban troops in Angola, American administrations since then have, to a greater or lesser extent, tried to place the source of the African flames ignited by Cuba in Moscow. Without necessarily underestimating the advantages that Havana itself gained by its intervention in improving its position within the socialist camp, the United States remained preoccupied with the benefits derived only by Moscow, since Cuban intervention could not have taken place without the backing of the Soviet Union. But the clarity of this reasoning did not contribute to any resolution of the United States' difficulty in finding an appropriate response.

Even if the United States perceived Cuba as an actor strictly subordinate to the Soviet Union, it would probably never have managed to associate Cuban intervention with Soviet intervention, pure and simple. In the perception of the leaders as in that of public opinion, the involvement of twenty thousand Cuban soldiers could not have the same repercussions as the parachuting of twenty thousand Soviet soldiers. This difference seems all the more fundamental because Cuban involvement was so completely unprecedented for American decisionmakers. In their eyes, Cuban interventionism gave Soviet policy a flexibility hitherto unknown—a flexibility vis-à-vis the United States confirmed by its hesitation in formulating an appropriate response in Africa, and a flexibility, too, vis-à-vis African actors who were generally better disposed toward Cuba than toward the Soviet Union.

Although objections can be raised about this interpretation on the grounds that it underestimates Cuba's persuasive powers over the Soviet Union and belittles Cuba's own role, this interpretation seems nonetheless undeniable on one point: in Angola as in Ethiopia, the Soviet Union sought directly to profit from Cuban intervention. In Angola as in Ethiopia, it was the Soviet Union that fully assumed the function of leader on the roster of socialist countries.

In the two great African crises that gave rise to Cuban involvement (Angola and Ethiopia), and in the crisis in which Cuba's involvement has been presumed (Shaba), the United States oscillated between counterinvolvement, linkage, and preventive action.

In Angola, Kissinger's desire to escalate was thwarted by the Tunney Amendment. In Shaba, Brzezinski's desire to loosen American policy from the constraints of the Clark Amendment, in order to penalize Angola, ran up against opposition by the Senate.[52] When the Reagan administration began the operation again in 1981, Congress' hostility was just as vigorous.[53] Even Brzezinski's recommendation to ready naval units for departure to Somalia to counter Soviet-Cuban involvement in Ogaden were not followed. As long as Cuban troops did not cross the internationally recognized borders of Somalia, the United States had no way to justify possible counterinvolvement.

During the entire second Shaba crisis, the drafting of an appropriate response was complicated by differences in assessment of actual Cuban responsibility. Cuban mismanagement pointed out by France, as well as by Brzezinski in the United States, was at the same time disputed by Vance, Young, and McHenry.[54]

In fact, linkage, understood as global penalization of the Soviet Union for Cuban intervention in Africa, had been envisaged but never implemented. Despite some solemn warnings directed at the Soviet Union, by Henry Kissinger on the subject of Angola and by Brzezinski on the subject of Ethiopia, the ratification of the SALT 2 accords was never blocked by African crises, even if the latter did contribute to complicating exchanges between the Soviet Union and the United States. Serious establishment of a system of linkage presupposed a consensus among the politicians, the implicit backing of public opinion, and significant support from African actors in the dispute with Moscow. No American power could ever achieve that coherence. Congress' African policy oscillated eternally between two poles of concern: isolationism on the one hand and, on the other hand, an anticommunism that led it to penalizing all Soviet allies (especially at the time of the vote on the foreign aid budget). The American executive branch consistently suffered from this duality, all the more strongly because it was itself rife with dissension. The Carter administration's attitude on the question of recognizing the Angolan government highlights this situation clearly. Because it kept a powerful Cuban expeditionary corps on its territory, the Angolan government could not be officially recognized by the United States. To establish diplomatic relations with it would have been the equivalent of denying Cuba's presence. But this position did not in any way stop this same administration from carrying on a privileged dialogue with Luanda on all of the problems of southern Africa.

To extricate itself from these contradictions, the Reagan administration tried to rethink the linkage problem in a more concrete manner. By trying to relate its diplomatic efforts in Namibia to the retreat of Cuban forces stationed in Angola, the Reagan administration laid out the terms of regionalized globalism. But this effort was far from achieving conclusive results.

Africa in Soviet-Cuban relations. Africa, hotbed of tensions between the two great superpowers, was also a stake in Soviet-Cuban relations. For Cuba the direction of its African activism was clear: it was part of an increasing strategy of extraversion that enabled it to become indispensable to the socialist camp while avoiding being used, as in 1962, as a bargaining chip in a Soviet-American planetary agreement.[55]

From that perspective, the intervention in Angola takes on critical importance. The Castro regime had managed to achieve its first important victory over the United States on this particular territory. Having undergone a transformation in Ethiopia two years later, Cuba was able through this effort to rise to the rank of "mini-superpower." In Africa and in the Third World, the crises in Angola and in Ethiopia powerfully contributed to rehabilitating a "Castro ideology" whose weak areas had been exposed in Latin American disappointments at the end of the sixties. From then on Cuba appeared no longer just a revolutionary power but also a military power capable of consolidating the political authority or the borders of its allies. Cuba thereby managed to restore solid diplomatic capital, which was reinforced by its accession to the presidency of a group of nonaligned countries in 1979. For Fidel Castro, the benefit of his African interventions was all the more tangible in being accompanied by massive Soviet economic support.

Signed in February 1976, the first long-term commercial agreement between Cuba and the Soviet Union capped the strategy of maximization of

Cuban interests; and it demonstrated the exceptionally favorable treatment the Soviet Union accorded its Caribbean ally. By heavily subsidizing Cuban sugar and nickel and by delivering oil at a rate that was very clearly below that of other socialist countries, the Soviet Union enabled Cuba to overcome the limitations on oil and the drop in the flow of raw materials. For the Soviet Union the economic sacrifice was considerable. In 1978 the total volume of aid in the form of grants and subsidies for oil, sugar, and nickel had reached a record level of $2.9 billion, the equivalent of a fifth of the Cuban GNP.[56]

This substantial economic aid, to which one can add the restoration of Cuban military strength lost during the African campaigns, seems not to have been regarded as pure loss. To the extent that it emphasized the many forms of its support of the Cuban regime, the Soviet Union tended to make Cuba's entrenchment in the socialist camp irreversible. By subsidizing Cuban sugar and by prompting other socialist countries to supply themselves through Cuba, the Soviet Union contributed heavily to sealing Cuba's fate as a single-product country.[57]

On the political level, the integration of Cuba into the world of socialist countries was accompanied by an institutionalization of the Cuban regime. In December 1975, in the midst of the Angolan expedition, the first congress of the Cuban communist party was held in Havana. The establishment of formal structures taken from the functional Soviet model led to a noticeable reform in Cuban leadership positions. Since 1975 these positions had mostly been awarded to leaders of the PSP (pro-Soviet communist party before 1959) such as Blas Roca, Arnaldo Milian, or Isidoro Malmierca, the head of Cuban diplomacy. Even though it should not be overestimated, the emergence since 1975 of personalities in favor of the Soviet Union cannot be ignored. It should even less be ignored as Cuban diplomacy found itself thereafter constrained to espouse, officially at least, all the diplomatic positions of the Soviet Union.

In this regard, the Cuban reversal concerning Eritrea and its support of the Soviet invasion of Afghanistan posed problems. At the United Nations this lockstep diplomacy deprived Cuba of a seat on the Security Council. Within the nonaligned group Havana managed to contain opposition to its behavior but not to disarm it. Thus, all commitments of fidelity to the Soviet Union symmetrically diminished Cuba's position as a nonaligned country.[58]

Cuba in Soviet-African relations. On the African scale, Soviet-Cuban relations raise an essential question: that of the correlation of their respective interests and the eventual coordination of their means. On the face of it, Soviet and Cuban presences were strongly correlated at the military level. Soviet military presence in Africa represented approximately ten percent of the Cuban military presence.

But beyond these generalities, an appreciation of Cuban influence in Africa and of its coordination with Soviet policy can only be gleaned from concrete situations: those where Cuba enjoyed historical influence from before 1975, those where its presence seemed to be rather more tributary of Soviet strategy, and those, finally, where its interests were limited and it was confined to purely instrumental tasks.

The historical presence of Cuba in Africa is most visible in states having emerged from a liberation war (Angola, Guinea-Bissau) or from a marked rupture with colonial order (Guinea). In various states, to which one can add the Congo, ties with Havana had been established independently of Moscow. In certain cases, like that of Guinea, it was even a temporary scuffle with the Soviet Union that motivated the appeal to Cuba.

This historical dimension is critical, for in Africa it influenced a specific perception of Cuba that was largely independent from African perception of the Soviet Union. In Angola and Guinea-Bissau there is no doubt that this perception was enhanced by the racial mixing in Cuban society. Having gained independence, these states also took into account the Castro experience to reconcile the practice of resolute nationalism with a privileged alliance with the socialist camp.

In all of these states, Cuba's contribution has always been significant, even if the actual measure of its influence is difficult to evaluate. In 1970 it was Cuban troops that saved the Guinean regime from crumbling at the time of the invasion led by Portugal. In Angola the same troops assured the MPLA of its victory and continue to look after its consolidation even today. In the Congo it was also Cuban forces that helped current leaders depose Yombi-Opango in 1979.

The case of the Congo is interesting because it highlights both Cuba's direct participation in internal political dealings and the limits of its influence. The fact that certain factions of the Congolese regime could prevail upon Cuba for direct support to organize a palace revolution confirms the crucial nature of its aid as well as the interest Cuba had in the political decisions made by African leaders. In this case, the political-military guarantees given to the Congo from the middle of the sixties had been opened up to include involvement in internal conflicts, even though the guarantees had originally been confined to the external security of the country. At the same time, nothing seemed to indicate that Cuba had the political power for any permanent involvement in the Congo that could mold major political choices. The fits and starts experienced by that country did not at all seem to have been timed with Cuban intervention. The same thing can be said about Guinea-Bissau, where the overthrow of the regime in 1980 occurred against the will of Havana.

These particular historical situations inevitably influenced the articulation of Soviet-Cuban-African relations. In most of these states, differentiation in the perceptions of the Soviet Union and of Cuba was more pronounced than, for example, in Ethiopia. Thus, a crisis of confidence between the Soviet Union and the Congo would have had but a minor impact on the Congo's ties with Cuba.

In all of these states, Cuba probably tried to guard its own influence jealously and contain possible Soviet encroachment. Its support of Neto against Alves—who tried to overthrow him with, it seems, the tacit approval of Moscow—demonstrates the reality of Soviet-Cuban conflicts well. But these differences in perception should not be exaggerated. In this case, Alves' "pro-Soviet" profile and Neto's "pro-Cuban" profile do not seem to have been so clear-cut. The hurried recall of Cuba's ambassador to Luanda immediately after the failure of Alves' putsch suggests that the role Cuba played in the crisis must be interpreted with far more nuance.[59]

For the Soviet Union the necessity of respecting possible Cuban precedence was not necessarily harmful to its interests. In countries where the Soviet Union did not succeed in overcoming the mistrust of the leaders, Cuba could act as intermediary. In its presence, Cuba served above all as a political retaining wall able to prevent any disillusionment with the Soviet Union from leading to too sharp a change of course toward the West.

This sort of function, which Cuba took on to a certain degree in the Congo and in Guinea, should nevertheless not be overestimated. In its relations with the Soviet Union, Angola had no recourse to mediation by Havana. Furthermore, the Cuban presence, whose merits have often been praised, should not be idealized.[60]

The second case covers those situations in which Cuba intervened to give the Soviet position primary support. In Ethiopia, where Cuba enjoyed no traditional influence and where, apparently, the Soviet Union was more directly involved, the balancing of its interests with those of the Soviet Union was more difficult to achieve. In this respect, it is difficult to believe that its change of heart on the Somali question stemmed from a simple position of principle, especially if one is aware of the explicit and solemn support that Cuba had given Somali irredentist arguments in 1972. Had Siad Barre's Somali regime changed to the point of being subject to public obloquy after having been praised two years earlier at the Cuban communist party congress?

The third and last type of Cuban presence brings together very disparate situations where generally limited Cuban action had an essentially instrumental character. In many countries (Benin, Sierra Leone, and Equatorial Guinea until 1979), Cuba took on the function (on a military level) of praetorian guard, whose competence was recognized and whose presence was perceived with less fear than that of the Soviet Union. In these particular situations Cuba played a role that is comparable to that increasingly played by North Korea. The most significant case was perhaps that in

Equatorial Guinea under the now-fallen Macias Nguema. Under this regime, which decimated a quarter of its population, Cuban presence was not in response to a single ideological consideration. It simply expressed a certain political opportunism, a wish to have a presence in a Spanish-speaking African country. It also probably came from a request made by the Soviet Union, which found it somehow advantageous to reinforce an African regime that had given it very substantial fishing rights.

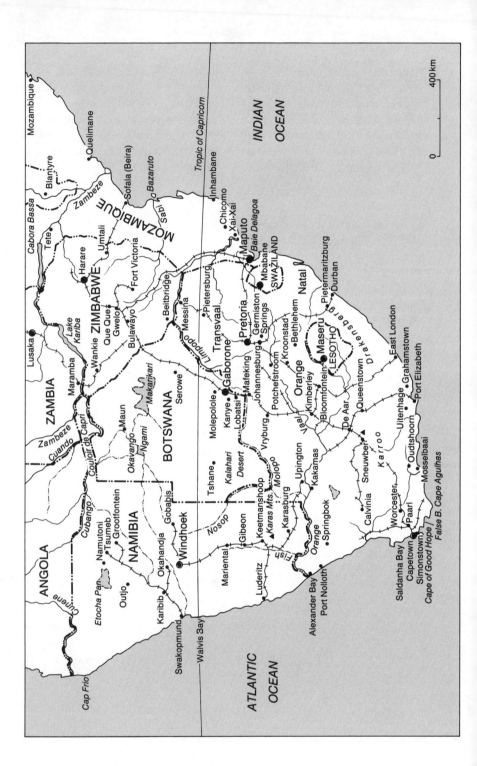

4

The United States: A Reluctant Ally

The United States and Southern Africa

Constraints and Perceptions

merican policy toward southern Africa, and especially toward the Republic of South Africa, has oscillated between the two poles defined by its ambitions and its limitations. Although its weight in the international system and the multiracial character of American society have helped the United States influence the choices made in this area of Africa, the United States' poor understanding of its real interests in southern Africa and its sensitivity to certain constraints have led it to quite timid behavior. Since 1975 the consequences of this ambiguity could be felt in its choices. The regional strategy of the United States followed a tortuous course in which the ambition to play a unique role in South Africa seemed to struggle with the fear of having only limited influence.

Short of thinking that American policy can be summarized as a simple set of genuflections before the "military-industrial complex," identification of its determinants is no easy task. There is no doubt that the difficulty is accentuated by the profusion of arguments in a confused mix of technical and economic assessments (of sanctions or economic dependence) and political interpretations. In fact, the United States' perception of the Republic of South Africa has been based on an unstable combination of perceptions and constraints. The former inevitably hark back to a set of American ideological values on the broadest scale. The latter more specifically reflect American interests directly at stake in South Africa. The relationship between these two distinct factors is not unidirectional. An abrupt deterioration of access to South African minerals must have influenced the political perceptions of the executive branch of the United States government. But at the same time the way in which perceptions are organized will always give the perception of constraints undeniable flexibility. The identifications by two different actors of the same constraint can easily lead to two different behaviors. In America's perception of South Africa, three factors seemed to occupy an essential position: the perceptions that the American elite leadership had about change in South Africa; the influence of public opinion; and the United States' economic dependence and strategic vulnerability in southern Africa.

Perceptions of "Change"

The specifics of the dominant elite's perceptions and the autonomy of its actions are difficult to apprehend. Nonetheless its maneuvering space was not negligible, since it is often more removed from strictly economic considerations than one might think.[1] All the same, the stability of American interests in the Republic of South Africa in recent years did not stop inconsistencies from emerging in perceptions of South African realities. It seems fair to think "that within the very broad limits, America's vital economic and strategic interests set few serious constraints on the development of policy toward southern Africa."[2]

In fact, perceptions of South Africa, like the whole of international relations, are inscribed in a system of perceptions whose character is essentially ideological, as polls taken in Congress as well as in the business world amply attest.[3]

The relative autonomy of ideological considerations with respect to tangible economic interests, for example, evidently could not save political decision-makers. The Kissinger image of the Republic of South Africa was more based on a bipolar model in which the power of South Africa was opposed to the fragility of black states, than on a concrete assessment of the cost of an economic break with Pretoria. The perceptible lack of interest the former head of American diplomacy also displayed toward Nigeria when the latter climbed to the rank of second major United States oil supplier underscores the fact that an economic rationale did not always guide the acts and gestures of American diplomacy—far from it.

It was precisely by rejecting this excessively bipolar view of the world, or by coming into contact with civil rights struggles, that the designers of African policy in the Carter administration generally forged their weapons.[4] Their understanding of Africa in general, and of the Republic of South Africa in particular, very plausibly caused them to privilege endogenous factors rather than geostrategic determinants in their analysis. But this as yet untested view of Africa nonetheless failed to avoid certain ambiguities. Because Andrew Young was a prisoner of his personal experience, he demonstrated an immoderate propensity for projecting the realities of the Deep South onto South Africa, in order to valorize pacifist strategies and discredit recourse to violence. Paradoxically, his perception of change in the Republic of South Africa seems to have been permeated with values of "triumphant liberalism" to a greater extent than his Republican predecessors' was. His *pro domo* plea for the "revolutionary virtues" of capitalism made him think that apartheid would not long resist the force of the logic in expanding the market to blacks.[5] In addition, the real increase of political risk in South Africa with regard to foreign investors between 1976 and 1978 caused him to recognize the early signs of a restoration of America's economic flow to black Africa.[6] In short, change in southern Africa was supposed to be just around the corner.

The course of events, however, did not support this. The complex logic of the Afrikaner political system is irreducible to well-understood economic interests. The loss of international confidence confronting the South African economy was rapidly overcome by the spectacular increase in the price of gold after 1979. Toward the end of its term, the very same Carter administration ultimately justified the modesty of its means of action by citing the renewed power of an economically vigorous and virtually invulnerable South Africa.[7] The about-face from a voluntaristic and ambitious position to a cautious, fallback attitude could not have been more noticeable. The oscillation between proactive ambition and laissez-faire resignation nonetheless demonstrates clearly the constant difficulty American diplomacy had in proceeding with diplomatic interaction in the region— between the Republic of South Africa and its neighbors, between Afrikaner power and the black majority, and finally between short- and long-term imperatives for global balance. These negotiations, whose urgency was heightened by the collapse of the Portuguese empire, were approached differently by the successive American leaders. The Ford-Kissinger administration sought to defer them by skillfully making South Africa dissociate its own future from that of Rhodesia and Namibia. This choice, which consciously avoided the question of apartheid, very clearly delimited the area of American diplomatic intervention. The Carter administration, on the other hand, did not believe in dissociating the problems of the area and seemed to want to take on the consequences of a polarized regional situation. It also seemed disposed to proceed with the inevitable involvements that would result from, for example, the selective use of sanctions. But it clearly counted on containment of such actions by a shrinkage in South African political options that it believed would continue because of the inexorable rise of black opposition, the irreversible modification of the regional status quo, and the inevitable decline of international confidence in the solidity of white power.

Since the Reagan administration has come to power, American policy has attempted to dispute the validity of any need for diplomatic involvement or arbitration. The emergence of moderate forces in both camps seems to have mitigated the idea of racial polarization in the Republic of South Africa. The inevitability of a political choice between the Republic of South Africa and its neighbors seemed contrary to a regional reality dominated by the density of a network of interdependence. Finally, it thought the strength of its anticommunist commitment around the world could not possibly interfere with its wish, for example, to come up with a negotiated solution in Namibia[8]—a desire demonstrated in its own eyes by its contribution to the treaty between South Africa and Mozambique. Thus, American diplomacy thought of itself as freed from certain constraints and as having thereby expanded its possible choices. In a single move it reconciled its regional ambition of playing a leading role with its deliberate refusal to exert any penalizing pressure on the Republic of South Africa.

This political design, which underlay American behavior since 1981, is under vehement attack today. The modesty of results achieved by the Reagan administration as much on the diplomatic front (Namibian settlement) as on the political (dismantling apartheid) has prompted, since November 1984, the unprecedented mobilization of American public opinion against the Pretoria regime. This protest movement, whose functional influence on the definition of American policy toward South Africa remains uncertain, has contributed to placing the Reagan administration on the defensive and to broadening the split between American public opinion and the South African regime. Indeed, in less than one year, some $450 million in city, university, and retirement fund monies were withdrawn from American companies with investments in South Africa.[9] Moreover, this wave of opinion prompted Congress to retake the initiative vis-à-vis an executive branch that had deliberately held it at bay where its diplomatic conduct in southern Africa was concerned. Albeit modest, the sequence of measures voted by Congress to impose sanctions on the Republic of South Africa reveals the accelerated erosion of South Africa's image. The debate about economic sanctions that American politicians, as a group, had overwhelmingly refused to engage in for twenty years has been reopened in unheard of terms. Henceforth, the central issue is no longer a question of judging the intrinsic efficacy of sanctions so much as their extent.

The Influence of Public Opinion

In a country where historical relations with Africa have been tenuous and where a strong isolationist current predominates, the influence of public opinion on decision-makers' choices seemed negligible for a long time. Nevertheless, this phenomenon appears to have been changing over the last dozen years, thanks to increased United States participation in the African diplomatic game on one hand and the gradual sensitizing of the black community to African problems on the other. Some opinion surveys, although fragmentary, make it easier today to isolate perceptions of Africa in American public opinion.[10]

In the first place, these studies reveal the coexistence of perfectly contradictory perceptions. A large majority of public opinion abhors the apartheid regime. It also seems ready to support any governmental action likely to reduce racial discrimination. But at the same time the predominant American image of Africans remains one of "primitive natives." This prejudice seems all the more tenacious since it is held even among members of the black community.[11] These opinion surveys also reveal the existence of a gap between moral condemnation of apartheid and a willingness to press for direct action to put an end to it. The more cogently the possibility is raised of coercive action by the United States against the South African regime, the more public opinion manifests reluctance. Opposition to military support for antiapartheid forces is virtually absolute, even among blacks. The absence of any significant opinion group willing to support drastic measures against the South African regime is thus real.[12] Consequently, that lack of support imposes a significant constraint on decision-makers. The weight of public opinion, however, is not necessarily an insurmountable obstacle for the government. The dominant fear of seeing Africa move into the realm run by communist powers is barely reflected in public opinion.

Whatever the case, the major conclusion to be drawn from these surveys is without doubt the existence of a real American consensus on the South African question. Neither partisan division between Democrats and Republicans nor racial division is as pronounced as one might think. Certainly, solidarity with the South African black majority is more evident among blacks than among whites. But as soon as there is the prospect of coercive American action against apartheid, black community opinion no longer differs from majority opinion. Finally, the traditional dichotomy between elite views and public opinion is not always noticeable, either. Such a broad consensus has contradictory implications for American behavior. The poor understanding public opinion has of tangible American interests in this area of the world noticeably impedes any mobilization of increased resources (economic aid or military assistance).

The limitation of public interest in African issues enhances the autonomy of political actors under the circumstances, as much within the executive branch as in Congress. The increase in the influence of the House Subcommittee on African Affairs under the Carter administration did not arise out of any political considerations but above all from personal involvement by a select few. In 1979 when the Senate tried to use all its means to lift sanctions against Muzorewa's and Smith's Rhodesia, the subcommittee, chaired by Solarz, engaged in exceptional activism to convince the Representatives, for the most part undecided, to block the Senate's resolution in the House. Had the move succeeded, the course of decolonization in Zimbabwe would have been different. The lifting of sanctions by the United States could have prompted Margaret Thatcher to act similarly and grant the Muzorewa government unhoped-for recognition.[13]

The autonomy of decision-makers with respect to public opinion gave their action an obvious fragility. Lacking an organized network of influence in the American bureaucratic system, United States African policy would always be subject to any considerations assumed to be more important. A change in the political or legislative personnel would set off variations in this policy perhaps more perceptibly than on American conduct in the Middle East.

Economic Dependence and Strategic Vulnerability

The importance of American dependence on certain raw materials produced in southern Africa, and especially in the Republic of South Africa, hardly seems debatable. Most observers recognize the importance of four raw materials (chromium, manganese, vanadium, and the group of platinum metals) whose strategic value arises out of a whole set of factors: namely, their importance for civil and military industry, the low level of domestic production, the excessive geographical concentration of producers in a potentially unstable region, the availability of little or no substitute products, and, finally, the scarcity of alternative suppliers located outside the communist bloc.

America's heavy dependence on the Republic of South Africa can be seen easily in the accompanying table. It is even more visible if one includes certain raw materials imported via a third country. With regard to manganese, for example, taking into account indirect imports through France and Great Britain, actual dependence on South Africa would be at sixty percent. This fact inevitably places America's economy in a situation of dependence that South African policy-makers could not ignore. The geographic concentration of producers and the fact that some of them, like Zambia and Zimbabwe, are landlocked countries, added to the inconvenience of exporting chromium, for example. In a hypothetical situation in which Zimbabwe's production would have to compensate for a South African defection (following an embargo, for example), transporting it would absolutely require access to South African ports. One might well say that without Pretoria's political consent, maintaining or extending Zimbabwean exports (including those via Mozambique) is unimaginable. The crucial importance of the railway system in the transport of raw materials in southern Africa is confirmed daily by UNITA sabotage against the Benguela railway system linking the Shaba region to the Angolan port of Lobito. This access route's vulnerability has forced Zambia to use South African ports more frequently. It has also made Zaire resort to air freight to ensure the smooth transport of its cobalt.[14]

The 1978 Shaba crisis did in fact reveal the real vulnerability of the West in an African crisis situation. The month-long suspension of cobalt imports caused a rapid depletion of the West's reserve stock as well as a tripling of prices by the end of the year.[15] The following year the embargo on chromium from Rhodesia, combined with simultaneous difficulties in

Table 3 United States Dependence on Southern Africa (1984)

	External Depen-dence Rate*	African Dependence Rate**			Extra-African Sources of Substitutes	World Reserves***	
Chromium	92	Ore	RSA⁺	48	USSR, Turkey,	Zimbabwe	28
		Ferrochromium			Philippines	RSA	70
			RSA	44			
			Zimbabwe	9			
		Ore	RSA	33	Brazil,	RSA	69
			Gabon	26	Australia,	Gabon	5
Manganese	98	Ferromanganese			Mexico	USSR	21
			RSA	43			
			Gabon	26			
Group of Platinum Metals	88	RSA		56	USSR	RSA	80
Vanadium	17	RSA		62	Finland Canada	RSA	42

*as a percentage of consumption
**as a percentage of imports
***as a percentage of world reserves
⁺RSA = Republic of South Africa
Source: US Bureau of Mines, *Commodity Data Summaries*, 1984.

Table 4 EEC Dependence on South Africa

	% of imports
Chromium	
ferrochromium	49
Manganese	
ore	41
ferromanganese	8
Platinum metal group	18

Source: Imports of Minerals from South Africa by the United States and the OECD Countries, CRS, Library of Congress, 1980.

obtaining supplies from Canada, forced the United States to dip into its strategic reserves to satisfy domestic demand.[16] American vulnerability appears to have been even more serious if one puts it in the larger context in which all European countries acquire mineral supplies. Indeed, how could the United States not be concerned about the situation of the EEC or of Japan whose dependence on South Africa is more obvious and broader?

Total loss of access to South African raw materials would therefore force the United States to dip into its own strategic reserves to supply its allies and to deal with inevitable inflationary tendencies. Nevertheless, such an outlook, imaginable in a context of total war between the West and the Republic of South Africa, has seemed economically surmountable and politically improbable.

If, indeed, American dependence on mineral raw materials has been significant in all respects, it has not yet reached a critical stage today. A report to the Senate by the committee on American policy in southern Africa makes it clear that for each strategic raw material imported from the Republic of South Africa, there are means available to withstand a break in supplies without turning to the Soviet Union or to any other supplier.[17]

At the cost of invention and substitution efforts, American dependence on chromium and cobalt could have been lessened. The interruption of cobalt imports from the Shaba region in 1978 did enable American industrialists, moreover, to note the fact that a two-thirds reduction of cobalt consumption did not affect the quality of the steel to which it was generally mixed.[18] One should, moreover, take into account the possibilities of recycling, reducing the demand in all sectors where the use of these raw materials is not essential as well as the size of the reserve stock and the existence of sources of substitution. Finally, one has to anticipate repercussions from the inflationary trends inevitable with sharp reductions in United States exploitation of mines that have hitherto yielded rather little, for such trends are engendered by a heavy reduction in supply. The consequences of an economic break are therefore worth specifying further, as are the scenarios in which such a break could actually take place.

An international embargo on South African imports. It is not conceivable that the United States would submit to such a decision without having preventively reduced its own vulnerability. But, by all evidence, American determination would not be enough; it would be absolutely necessary that other Western countries join the boycott. But one could not imagine that Japan, for example, would consent to such a heavy economic sacrifice (depriving itself of South African raw materials) for so paltry a political gain in its eyes (that is, the moral condemnation of apartheid). Even for a country so heavily involved in Africa as France, the need to choose between its interests in black Africa and in the Republic of South Africa has never seriously been imposed by its French-speaking clients. Only Nigeria, in 1979, dared to corner Great Britain to force a choice between maintaining its interests in Nigeria or those in the Republic of South Africa. But this operation, which was indeed more spectacular than it was effective, fell short of its aims. In fact, an embargo on South African imports presupposes the combination of two conditions: the existence of real, international consensus against the Republic of South Africa, and an effective quarantine of South Africa. The former condition would imply that the United States question the priority of its confrontation with the Soviet Union compared to the importance of the consensus. The second condition would require establishment of a system of draconian controls whose efficacy seems doomed from the start because of South Africa's thorough integration in the world economic system.

South African embargo on its exports. This possibility, which South Africa occasionally whispers to the West to remind it of its vulnerability, seems imaginable only at the end of a power struggle initiated by Western countries. An effective embargo on the four strategic raw materials mentioned above would not in the short term cause any noticeable harm to South Africa's economy. On the other hand, the indirect and long-term costs of such a measure would be immeasurable. They would inevitably increase the political risk of the Republic of South Africa vis-à-vis foreign investors and would expose South Africa to Western retaliatory measures. One of the least expensive measures for the international economy would be for South Africa to suspend its gold sales, which guarantee it forty percent of its export receipts. Pretoria would thus find itself enmeshed in a system of sanctions that it has always rejected as much for economic as for diplomatic reasons.

The interference of the Soviet Union? The possible intervention of the Soviet Union in southern Africa to increase the West's strategic vulnerability there might arise out of three generally accepted objectives: to cut off the raw materials route (strategy of denial); to compete economically with Western states in meeting its own foreign demand for raw materials; and to accomplish political and economic manipulations intended to restrain Western access to South African raw materials.[19] These hypotheses, which all implicitly presuppose that the Soviet Union exert some political influence on the Republic of South Africa, are, in many respects, purely speculative.

The "strategy of denial" hypothesis tends to overestimate the strategic factor in the complex equation of southern Africa, while overvaluing the strategic importance of the infamous Cape route.[20] To be sure, the importance of this artery of energy and mineral supply to Western states is hardly contestable. Ninety-two percent of the traffic goes to the West. In addition, this route's vulnerability is accentuated by two little-known geographical constraints. The Cape of Good Hope is in fact an "obligatory passage," comparable to a strait, since beyond forty miles from the South African coastal zone, sharp changes in the weather and the power of currents make any navigation dangerous. Beyond that, the existence of four great marine currents in the region hampers sonar detection of submarines.[21] Nonetheless, one is left to think that the Cape route argument is overestimated. Given the cost to Western economies of cutting off this route, doing so is a possibility the Soviet Union could only entertain in a situation of general confrontation. It would, moreover, presume that the Soviet Union exercise effective political control over the Republic of South Africa. Except by thinking that a non-white South African government might be irremediably condemned to Soviet subjugation, it is difficult to envisage a context in which such a government would serve such objectives (and in exchange for what?).

As it is, the proponents of the Cape route theory overestimate the geographical position of the Republic of South Africa on a route as long as several thousand kilometers. Furthermore, from a strictly strategic point of view, the Soviet Union is not particularly interested in the specific site of the Cape. It could just as well, and maybe even better, intervene at other obligatory passages such as the Strait of Hormuz, the Mozambique Channel, the Cape Verde passage, or Cape Bojador. The "sentry of the West" role played by South Africa, moreover, ought to have been reduced to the extent that the specter of a resource war (born of the oil crisis of 1973–74) has gradually been removed. With the economic recession and the diversification of supply sources taken together, the Persian Gulf no longer retains the strategic value it had not even a dozen years ago. The remarkable restraint of the United States in the face of the regional gyrations in the Iran-Iraqi conflict demonstrates well the relativity of the "peril" in this area of the world. This danger is all the more attenuated with the gradual installation of the Rapid Deployment Joint Task Force (RDJTF), which has given the United States a marked edge in its strategic relations with the Soviet Union in the Indian Ocean.

Hypothetical economic interference by the Soviet Union appears to be even more problematic than the basic hypothesis of "strategic denial." The appearance of the Soviet Union in the African market as an economic competitor of Western powers has seemed improbable, insofar as the end of its self-sufficiency in minerals is scarcely established, and because such an operation would require an additional and substantial mobilization of convertible currency. As for the possibility of a political-economic manipulation to heighten the difficulties of Western access to South African raw materials, it would presuppose either a Soviet political lock on the Republic of South Africa and its neighbors or the ability to offer them an economic option more attractive than the one offered by the Western market. But the international economic strategy of the Soviet Union's African allies, or Soviet efforts to present itself as a possible alternative economic partner in Africa, must negate these hypotheses.

American economic influence. In the American debate about the Republic of South Africa, United States economic influence has been thought of in two complementary ways: what constraints does it mean for United States behavior? And what means does it provide to the United States to curb the rigors of apartheid?

On the level of its global interests, American economic presence in the Republic of South Africa has been unquestionably limited and surprisingly stable. It represents $2.3 billion in investments, that is, one percent of total American foreign investment.[22] The proportion of commercial exchange within America's foreign trade is approximately the same.

Compared to that of Great Britain, ten percent of whose foreign investments have been concentrated in South Africa, America's presence has seemed quite modest after all. To be sure, suspending all economic relations with Pretoria would have been followed in the United States by a loss of 55,000 jobs and would have saddled the balance of payments deficit with another billion dollars. But this measure would not have caused any serious harm to American firms that had a foot in South Africa.[23] For a long time, the profitability of American investments in South Africa was above the international average. In the middle of the seventies, this profitability fell for a time before reestablishing itself at the international average.[24] Thus, while investing in South Africa still remains an interesting proposition, and a better one in any case than that offered by black African states, this country's economic attraction is no longer so exceptional. Chrysler's February 1983 sale of its South African operations to Sygma Motors demonstrated noticeably that monies invested could prove more profitably invested in the United States than in the Republic of South Africa.[25] In addition, any increase in foreign investment would seem ultimately contradicted by the existence of a meager domestic market, which demonstrates clearly the increasing internationalization of South African capital.

All the same, if America's investment in South Africa has represented no more than fifteen percent of foreign investment and if foreign investment in turn only contributes to twenty percent of the country's investments, America's investment has been nonetheless far more significant than the figures suggest. American presence has been, in fact, concentrated in key sectors of the economy such as data processing (controlled by seven multinational companies of which five are American) or the oil market (eighty-five percent of which is held by five firms, four of which are American). The contribution of American computer companies to the economic and military development of the Republic of South Africa has been such that it has quite naturally fed a fair number of controversies. In 1978, moreover, the Carter administration declared an embargo on the sales of computers intended for the South African army or police. But this belated measure, taken unilaterally by Washington, only left the field open to other potential Western suppliers.

Even more essential than that investment was perhaps the introduction of American financial capital into the South African economy. Having been reduced by the end of the sixties, investments began to increase during the early seventies, when the Republic of South Africa launched a broad industrial development program placed under the aegis of its national firms. Its importance was revealed clearly for the first time when the South African debt tripled between 1974 and 1976 to make up for a very high balance of payments deficit. Private American banks ensured a third of the credits that South Africa needed, while the government in Washington supported a $464 million IMF grant. During this same period, grants of export guarantees by Eximbank facilitated the development of strategic sectors in South Africa's economy (the iron and steel industry, energy, aviation).[26] The key role played by the American financial market, South Africa's primary creditor, was revealed a second time in 1981–82, when a conjunction of unfavorable factors again burdened public expenditures. Pretoria then not only came up with the backing of private banks but also with the backing of the Reagan administration, which pleaded successfully with the IMF in 1982 for a grant of two loans totaling $1.07 billion. Even if the strategy of American creditors was geared more toward granting short- rather than long-term loans, there was no sign before the political explosion of the summer of 1985 that South Africa's financial solidity was crumbling.[27]

Nevertheless, the real strengths of the South African economy could not mask its vulnerability. Its pressing need to appeal for foreign capital to reduce certain economic risks over which it had scant control (erratic developments in the rate of gold, drought) gave its creditors, and very particularly the United States, the undeniable means of applying pressure. The decisive influence that Washington enjoyed with regard to the IMF was only one among many. In addition, America's position as primary commercial partner gave the United States government uncontestable trump cards to play.

The simple prohibition of the export of gold coins (*krüggerand*) to the United States would deprive the Republic of South Africa of nearly a billion dollars in revenues. Not only would such a measure cause no direct economic harm to the United States, but it would also alleviate by one-third the trade deficit with Pretoria. On the other hand, it would cut the *krüggerand* market by a half and would provoke a drop in the price of gold that the trading of them is supposed to prevent.[28]

The Search for Diplomatic Arrangements

Zimbabwe: From the Lusaka Speech to the Conference at Lancaster House

Credit for the Lancaster House conference that put an end to the troubled decolonization of Zimbabwe in December 1979 might be chalked up exclusively to British diplomacy. Nonetheless, to say this undeniable success was simply a matter of the ingenuity of the Foreign Office would amount to overestimating the ability of a foreign actor to impose a solution while underrating the complexity of the diplomatic process in which the solution was reached. In fact, the Lancaster House conference was more the result of complex negotiation than of a *sui generis* initiative. The felicitous outcome at Lancaster House stemmed in large part from the fact that at the end of 1979 alternative options to negotiation appeared singularly limited for the opposing parties.

Thus, analysis of America's role in the search for a diplomatic settlement in Zimbabwe between 1976 and 1979 cannot valuably be conducted except by taking into account the gradual diminution of the number of options open to the opposing parties, as well as what was added to this shrinkage by foreign actors. From the end of the Angolan crisis, the United States had to deal with a conflict that can be compared to the crisis in Angola on several points: the failure of diplomatic solutions and the intensification of hostilities, the division in the nationalist movement, the possibility of Soviet-Cuban involvement in the event the situation worsened, the absence of a strong colonial power itself willing to ensure the transition to independence, and the apparent difficulty of African states in finding an endogenous solution.[29]

At the beginning of 1976, the failure of negotiations conducted the preceding summer at Victoria Falls between Ian Smith and nationalist representatives, at the behest of Zambia and the Republic of South Africa, left the nationalist movement no other alternative than to reignite hostilities. As early as January 1976, it moved on the Tete, Manca, and Gaza fronts. Encouraged by Mozambique's independence, the two main nationalist movements—Joshua Nkomo's Zimbabwe African People's Union (ZAPU) and Robert Mugabe's Zimbabwe African National Union (ZANU)—coordinated their military action within the Zimbabwe Independent People's Revolutionary Army (ZIPRA). But this precarious unity of action, imposed by the Front-Line States (Angola, Botswana, Mozambique, Tanzania, and Zambia), was little more than a replay of the Angolan nationalist movement's fruitless attempts at unification.

To prevent internationalization of the conflict, which could turn, as in Angola, to its disadvantage, American diplomacy saw conditions in Zimbabwe as offering the opportunity to regain the initiative and restore its tarnished political credibility—credibility with other African states for whom the Angolan affair had revealed the identification of American interests with those of the Republic of South Africa; and credibility, too, with respect to the Soviet Union, whose influence in southern Africa needed to be blocked, even if it meant shaking up an ever faint-hearted Great Britain a bit. At any rate, such was the significance of Henry Kissinger's first African tour in April 1976 and of his speech in Lusaka in which he announced the recentering of American diplomacy in southern Africa while expressing his desire to maintain a presence in the region.

All the same, if Kissinger expressed the United States commitment to majority rule and committed himself symbolically to favoring repeal of the Byrd amendment, he was also deliberately evasive on the means he intended to use to reach a negotiated solution.

The ambiguities of the Kissinger plan. On the basis of the March 1976 Callaghan plan, Henry Kissinger in fact hoped to extract recognition of the principle of majority rule from Ian Smith, even at the risk of offering him in exchange the broadest guarantees of respect for the rights of the white minority. At the same time, he expected to establish a political *entente* between Ian Smith and the moderate wing of the nationalist movement, which would *ipso facto* marginalize Robert Mugabe's radical wing.[30] To achieve this goal, Kissinger put his faith in South Africa's willingness and ability to impose respect for majority rule on Ian Smith. At the end of 1976, when South Africa's vulnerability seemed to have reached a water mark, Kissinger met with John Vorster, the South African Prime Minister, in Bavaria.

Weakened by the abrupt collapse of Portugal's hold in southern Africa, the failure of its intervention in Angola, and the violent Soweto riots, the South African regime deemed it opportune to join the American initiative in order to reassert itself in the region. It was all the more inclined to do so because it absolutely required American support to put the brakes on the drop in the price of gold and to gain easier access to the international financial market.[31] Besides, it was to Pretoria's advantage in the short run to seek a solution guaranteed by the United States rather than risk, by its unequivocal support of Ian Smith's regime, opening the Pandora's box of internationalization of conflict in southern Africa. Finally, given the considerable means at its disposal to apply pressure on the white Rhodesian regime, Pretoria could scarcely escape American pressure.[32] At the end of September, after a series of meetings between Kissinger and Vorster, between Vorster and Smith, and between Kissinger and Smith, Ian Smith committed himself to negotiating the implementation of majority rule over a period of two years. Ambiguous as it may have been, this commitment would nonetheless bestow an irreversible character on the development of a solution.[33]

Henry Kissinger arrived at these results at the price of major ambiguity. The basis for negotiation proposed to Ian Smith by the United States was a five-point plan that foresaw, in addition to the implementation of majority rule, the creation of a joint state council that would represent blacks and whites equally; the constitution of a black majority government; the establishment of a development fund intended to indemnify departing white colonialists; and finally the lifting of international sanctions against Rhodesia. In fact, Ian Smith only agreed to the demands of this plan in exchange for the presidency of the state council and for giving defense and domestic portfolios to the representatives of the white community. Henry Kissinger, who first withheld his response in order to consult with the Front-Line States, later let Ian Smith think that his conditions had been agreed to by his African interlocutors.[34] Now, neither the Front-Line States nor the liberation movements of Zimbabwe had agreed to these terms. This major equivocation was deliberately maintained by American diplomacy. Indeed, Henry Kissinger's imperative was to make the possibility of a negotiated solution attractive to the parties present, by conceding to nationalists that they would obtain formal access to power within two years while guaranteeing the white minority limited erosion of its own actual power. On the basis of this agreement, he hoped to have anticipated the proper dynamics of the conference and thus to bring together the positions of the opposing parties. Shrewd as it may have been, this plan did not pay off. The Geneva conference, called in the middle of the 1976 American presidential election, robbed the outgoing United States administration of any credible influence. Moreover, far from reducing differences, the conference crystallized antagonisms. Consequently, the basis of the agreement suggested by Washington was tenuous and equivocal. Even on the cardinal principle of respect for majority rule, to which he had previously agreed, Ian Smith committed himself to a restricted interpretation that was closer to suffrage based on property holdings than to universal suffrage. This attitude aggravated the nationalist movements' fears of seeing transition institutions favor the white minority excessively.

Although it did not result in a solution to the conflict, then, the American initiative begun in Lusaka was not totally negative for the United States. It would trigger anew the process of diplomatic negotiation that would continue uninterrupted to the end of 1979. It would legitimate the idea of an American commitment to seeking a solution. Finally, it would popularize the idea in Congress of a financing fund for Zimbabwe, even if in Henry Kissinger's mind such a fund should make a priority of financing the departure of white colonialists.[35]

Ambitions of the Anglo-American Plan

When the Carter administration inherited the situation in January 1977, it seemed to have two strengths: the administration included those in positions of power whose competence and political authority bestowed a choice position on Zimbabwe among initial objectives of American diplomacy: Andrew Young, United States Ambassador to the United Nations; A. Lake, Director of State Department policy planning; and R. Moose, head of the Bureau of African Affairs at the Department of State and linchpin of American strategy in Zimbabwe. In addition, the United States was confronted with a conflict whose equation did not exactly follow the contours of the East-West rivalry. To be sure, the fear of witnessing the Soviet Union's or Cuba's insertion into the diplomatic game had permanently determined American priorities. But insofar as the most radical wing of the nationalist movement mobilized support from Peking rather than Moscow, the search for a so-called moderate solution that included Nkomo and excluded Mugabe could easily gain Soviet approval.

At first, the Carter administration hesitated to understand the problem exclusively from this angle. Rather than playing on the division of the nationalist movement, it relied on its integration into the negotiation, guessing that the exclusion of the Zimbabwe African National Union (ZANU) from a political agreement would be harmful in the long run to stability in Zimbabwe. This analysis was directly based on an assessment of ZANU's military potential, which was in all respects superior to that of the Zimbabwe African People's Union (ZAPU). It stemmed, too, from an estimation of the politico-ethnic basis that the ZANU could mobilize domestically. But, by betting on the integration of the nationalist movement rather than on its exclusion, on its unity rather than on its division, American diplomacy assigned itself a precise goal: to prevent a military victory by the revolutionary forces that would destroy the administrative, economic, and political order that was left by the white minority government.[36]

In defining its line of action in Zimbabwe, the Carter administration tried hard to move away from the Kissinger initiative in order simultaneously to draw lessons from its failure and to improve American diplomatic credibility in Africa. In concert with London, the Carter administration favored including in the Anglo-American plan of September 1977 arrangements that were likely to engage the nationalist forces' interest in negotiating. Where the Kissinger plan allowed for a transition period whose excessive duration (two years) could only give the white minority an advantage, the Anglo-American plan would reduce it to two months. It planned to control the transition by putting a British national in charge who would be assisted by a representative of the United Nations, instead of a white-minority-run state council. In addition, the development fund for Zimbabwe was no longer presented as a subsidy for the indemnities to white colonialists but as a contribution to the development of Zimbabwe.[37] Furthermore, Washington convinced the Front Line that cooperation with Pretoria was hardly something that could be sold for cash and that, failing significant pressures applied to Ian Smith, South Africa exposed itself to inevitable Western sanctions.[38]

Seemingly innovative, the steps of the Carter administration's plan appear the direct descendants of preceding initiatives. Under the Kissinger plan, for example, the Anglo-American plan was to be the basis for a bargaining process in which none of the arrangements was intangible. Further, the negotiators had let the involved parties understand that the process of negotiation was reconcilable with the pursuit of hostilities.

The apparent flexibility of the Anglo-American plan followed from tactical considerations as well as political objectives. In the mind of the Americans, the plan proposed a settlement to the opposing parties that was judged *a priori* preferable to maintaining the precarious and devastating status quo. It validated among all parties the idea that power is conferred after the ballots have been tallied. It also offered nationalist forces the opportunity to deal with their profound differences through universal suffrage.[39] As long as none of the parties rejected the plan wholesale, the United States could keep up its efforts. This was even more the case because the Anglo-American plan defined for the first time the actual stakes of the negotiations by identifying and then separating the central questions of power and constitutional guarantees. This allowed the Anglo-American plan to introduce the draft of a constitution defining Zimbabwe's institutional future ahead of time (and not during the transition period, as in the Kissinger plan). Nevertheless, if this question was of essential interest to the white minority, it was less decisive for the Patriotic Front. For them, the heart of negotiations should focus on the organization of the transition before the elections, namely, on the mode and structure of deliberations on transition procedures, on the role of the British representative, and on the control of Rhodesian security forces.

The success of these negotiations, therefore, required that English and American negotiators establish a balance of the constitutional guarantees sought by some with the conditions of the transition period expected by others.[40] The tactical advantage of this approach, however, failed to become obvious to the English and Americans until late in the game. Initially, their major concern was to extract a basis for agreement at the level of the smallest common denominator (the Constitution) before getting on with the more delicate problem of transition. Dealings carried out between September 1977 and March 1978 under the aegis of the Anglo-American Graham-Low mission were vain attempts to come up with an agreement on this point. The major concessions that the white minority thought it was making on the drafting of the Constitution were disregarded by the Patriotic Front, for whom the Constitution only represented a straitjacket that independence would be able to unfasten.

February 1978 would have to come around—with the conferences in Malta first and then in Dar es Salaam between the Patriotic Front and the Anglo-American negotiators—before the negotiations could be exclusively focused on the question of transition.[41] But, meanwhile, on March

3, 1978, Ian Smith signed a domestic accord with Muzorewa, Sithole, and Chirau, organizing a transition toward majority rule excessively favorable to the white minority.

To assure the survival of their plan, which had been terribly undermined by the Salisbury accord, the Anglo-Americans amended it by granting the Patriotic Front majority representation in the governing council, in exchange for which the governing council would commit itself to participating in a conference of all parties to which the signatories of the Salisbury accord would be invited. But this relaunching of negotiations had no follow-up. Prior to the general elections meant to confer popular legitimacy on them, the representatives in the domestic arrangement had only limited interest in joining negotiations with the Patriotic Front. For that reason at the end of 1978 the Graham-Low mission, which had been responsible for ensuring the artificial survival of the Anglo-American plan, drew up notification of definitive failure of the September 1977 initiative.

The Limits of Boldness

The progressive withering and subsequent abandoning of the Anglo-American plan resulted from the obvious conjunction of numerous factors. But fundamentally they resulted from the general economy of a plan that did not specify the means of reducing the political options of the opposing parties. Afraid of instigating a military power struggle with the white minority, the Anglo-American plan did not foresee securing Ian Smith's departure except with his approval. It underestimated his ability to step down, whereas no one on the American end of things was unaware of the opening of secret negotiations between Smith and Muzorewa in March 1977.[42] This weakness of the Anglo-American plan was to emerge clearly when, immediately after the signing of the Salisbury accords, Washington and London invited Smith and Muzorewa to the negotiating table with the Popular Front, without demanding that they first renounce the domestic settlement.

Though poorly equipped to deal with Ian Smith's intransigence, the Anglo-American plan was even less well equipped to deal with the Republic of South Africa. The primary equation of relations with Pretoria had in fact been laid out by Washington in simplistic terms. But the firmness of his words and the apparent coherence of the initial steps only imperfectly concealed the inconsistency of a policy that was, after all is said and done, erratic.

Throughout the negotiations, South Africa dodged the support-sanction dilemma by carefully refraining from rejecting the Anglo-American plan. It limited itself to letting it be known that it would be difficult to impose upon Ian Smith a solution he deemed unacceptable. Afraid of getting involved with sanctions, Washington ultimately resigned itself to hoping that, with a delay in applying sanctions, Pretoria would bring Ian Smith to a compromise. Initially unintimidated by the Republic of South Africa, the Carter administration evolved a pragmatism that progressively took on the characteristics of a kind of denial. Perhaps nothing illustrates better the diplomatic amateurism of the United States toward South Africa than the Vienna meeting of May 1977 between Vice President Mondale and Prime Minister Vorster. From the beginning, the vice president indicated to Vorster that the Republic of South Africa could no longer expect anything from the United States if South Africa did not commit itself to an evolution toward respecting the rights of the black majority in southern Africa as well as in South Africa. This step toward clarification, from which the Carter administration fully intended to reap political dividends, very quickly backfired. Deftly, the South African Prime Minister purposely exaggerated "the American outrage" in order first to exacerbate the *laager* mentality within the Afrikaner minority and then to enhance his electoral positions with the idea of the "foreign peril." Thus, far from putting Pretoria on the road to reform and concessions, the Vienna meeting reinforced intransigence, Ian Smith's in particular. In fact, one of the unexpected consequences of the American–South African summit was to be the increase in promises to the white minority in the drafting of Zimbabwe's constitution planned by the Anglo-Americans.[43]

If the perverse effects of America's policy came in large part from the lack of specificity of its objectives and the awkwardness of its conduct, they were more fundamentally a result of its refusal to engage in a power struggle with the white regimes. This reluctance seems greater for the fact that the Anglo-American plan would retrospectively seem an initiative with poorly resolved ambiguities. From the first consultations between the two promoters of the plan in March 1977, the British party reiterated its concern with promoting a Smith-Nkomo accord that would marginalize Mugabe.[44] This strategy, which ran counter to the premises of the plan as seen by the American party, would nevertheless continue to be specified further as the prospect of an internal agreement between Smith and Muzorewa mapped itself out. And while Young and Vance countered the Salisbury accord with finely made points in March 1978, Owen did not fail to see in it a "step in the right direction," a necessary step toward a Smith-Nkomo agreement.[45]

Not being able to act toward a solution of the conflict, the United States immediately began to extricate itself, even if it meant supporting initiatives that seriously undermined the initial credibility of the Anglo-American plan. This trend would increase as poorly resolved conflicts and pressing constraints in American policy became more obvious.

Confronted with a conservative Senate on the offensive, President Carter was constantly guarding against neglect of the Muzorewa option, contrary to the advice of the State Department, which believed only in the viability of a solution that would include the Patriotic Front.[46] Given the blocking effect of these negotiations, the Senate's pressure to appeal for the recognition of the Smith-Muzorewa government and repeal of sanctions, and the increasing fear of Soviet involvement after the Ogaden and Shaba crises, Washington's initial interest in a permanent solution rapidly declined. Dreading a rekindling of the conflict or a complete diplomatic failure, the United States was driven to rethink two premises of its approach: imposing free elections to separate competing factions peacefully, and abstaining from exploiting the divisions within the Patriotic Front. By guaranteeing the secret August 1978 Lusaka meeting between Smith and Nkomo, the United States backed an initiative presumably intended to proceed to transfer of power without recourse to preliminary negotiations on universal suffrage. It also favored a solution whose objective was indeed to divide Nkomo and Mugabe. The drift of American diplomacy would turn out to be dangerous in the total failure of the Smith-Nkomo meeting. It would deepen Mugabe's mistrust of the Anglo-Americans, whom he would accuse of wanting to oust him before the verdict of the ballot box. It would incite Nkomo to become henceforth intractable once he realized the trap Ian Smith had set for him. And, finally, it would permit the Salisbury regime to play on hitches in English and American policies by exacerbating their differences or hastening their reversal.

In early 1979, although having lost hope of imposing the broad, or even amended, lines of the Anglo-American plan on the opposing parties, American diplomacy continued to play an essential role during the period preceding the arrival of British Conservatives to power in May. Facing a Senate that was still very much on the offensive and had never stopped calling for the recognition of the Smith-Muzorewa government following the April 1979 legislative elections, the Carter administration agreed to a compromise with Congress that would give it some time—a crucial decision for later negotiations. By proceeding to lift sanctions against the Smith-Muzorewa regime, the United States would be bestowing on it an international legitimacy that the Conservative government would hasten to confirm. Such a decision would definitively undermine Anglo-American authority in the search for a solution, would dissuade the Patriotic Front from joining an international negotiation, and would plunge Zimbabwe into an endless conflict.

The renewal of negotiations at the decisive Commonwealth summit in Lusaka in August 1979 and the happy ending at the Lancaster House conference in December 1979 resulted fundamentally from the opportune reduction of options available to the different actors around the middle of 1979. The Smith-Muzorewa regime, installed by the Salisbury accord, expected that the April 1979 legislative elections would consecrate it at home and legitimate it abroad. On both these levels, its hopes were dashed. Tossed about in unrestrainable conflict, the black coalition of Reverend Muzorewa indeed proved to be a hostage of the white minority. Paradoxically, while holding the essential powers, the black coalition was unable to stem the resurgence of the white exodus. By holding on to its power, all the black coalition had managed to do was to galvanize the Patriotic Front's forces. On an international level, the recognition fully expected from the United States never materialized. Senate pressure as well as Smith's and Muzorewa's trips to Washington did not change anything. In fact, the recognition of the Muzorewa regime would be very costly for Washington and for London. It would ruin American credibility in Africa, a credibility that Young had tried patiently and adroitly to restore; and it would trigger an unprecedented crisis between Great Britain and its Commonwealth allies. If, on its own side, the Patriotic Front did in fact manage by determination to block the success of the domestic solution, it could nevertheless not ignore the risks of an endless conflict—especially as its principal sources of support, most particularly Mozambique, encouraged it to negotiate watching for the highest bid.

To this first series of factors one can add the British determination to exercise its powers of tutelary responsibility fully and directly, hiding behind neither Washington nor the United Nations. This commitment appealed to both parties. It offered the Patriotic Front the guarantee of a British presence during the transition period—an arrangement that limited the margins of action of the white minority. For the member parties of the Salisbury accords, the Carrington plan indicated that the transition period would not be accompanied by any changes in the power structure already in place.

The more important aspects of the Carrington plan were inspired by the Anglo-American plan. It modified the content of the points responsible for its failure: the crucial period of transition was reduced to two months, and the responsibility of controlling this transition was entrusted to British and Commonwealth troops rather than to United Nations troops. Moreover, to avoid getting bogged down in dealing and more bargaining, Lord Carrington rejected the idea of a global bargaining process at Lancaster House. He imposed on his interlocutors a point-by-point negotiation: constitution first, then transition. Nor did he hesitate to float the idea of a "second class solution" resting on a Muzorewa-Nkomo agreement. This prospect therefore prompted Muzorewa to adhere to the British plan in the hope of creating a break between Nkomo and Mugabe. It also led to a compromise with the Patriotic Front, which could not ignore the pressure of the Front-Line States.

Opened in September 1979, the Lancaster House conference led to an agreement on December 21 of the same year. In conformity with the British plan, this agreement included a cease-fire and was followed by elections that installed Mugabe as the head of independent Zimbabwe in April 1980.

Namibia: The Painful Road to Independence

In many respects, the search for a solution in Namibia might have seemed easier than in Zimbabwe. Its stakes could be summarized as the means of access to the sovereignty of a territory whose right to self-determination the war-weary Republic of South Africa had recognized. Even the problem of a white minority was less severe there, since seventy percent of the ninety thousand or so whites who lived there were South African nationals. Real division, which had hindered the unification of the Zimbabwean nationalist movement and weakened it, did not occur in the case of Namibia. In spite of the multiple and tireless South African efforts to divide it, Namibian nationalism was largely identified with the South West African People's Organization (SWAPO). Finally, while the implementation of any solution in Rhodesia remained dependent *in fine* on the British desire to assume its responsibility as tutelary power, in Namibia the United Nations was disposed, in beautiful unanimity, to ensure a transition to independence. One might therefore have thought that the concordance of all of these elements might have made it easier to clarify the stakes and thereby hasten the end of the conflict. Thus, it was generally thought in African diplomatic circles that a solution in Namibia would precede a solution in Zimbabwe.[47] It was even hoped that potential concessions by Pretoria in Namibia would inevitably reduce Ian Smith's options in Rhodesia. This initial schema suffered, over the test of time, a cruel demise. Five years after Zimbabwe's independence, the Namibian situation is still at an impasse.

If it is true that the Republic of South Africa never seriously linked its presence in Namibia to satisfaction of possessive objectives (a formal exercise of its sovereignty over the territory), it did always justify its presence with milieu-related objectives (maintaining an edge in black Africa) whose pursuit was inextricably tied up with the complex stakes of domestic South African politics. Therefore the lack of territorial claims on Namibia did not make it any easier to seek a solution. Quite the contrary, the Republic of South Africa's recognition of Namibia's right to independence helped Pretoria build a skillful diplomatic line of defense around the conditions of access to that independence. Conducted by negotiators whose knowledge of the dossier went back twenty years, South African diplomacy was able to bring to bear priceless, tactical advantages in the international negotiations as they faced American negotiators who were being replaced every four years.[48]

It was the collapse of the Portuguese colonial empire that moved the actors and observers of southern African conflict to think that the death knell of South Africa's presence in Namibia had been sounded. In a temporarily unfavorable international context, Pretoria deferred the project of "bantustanization" of Namibia in November 1974. But while slowly moving toward recognizing the right of this territory's people to self-determination, it did not give up at all on the principle of "ethnic representation" of all parties. The object of the maneuver was simple: to divide the black population and to discredit SWAPO's national representivity. On this basis in September 1975 Pretoria set up a constitutional conference meeting (the Turnhalle conference) that adopted a gradual transition plan for Namibia's independence in April 1976. By leaving things officially to the representatives of the conference, Pretoria gave the impression of acceding to the Namibian population's desire to forge its own destiny. But, in fact, the distance established artificially between its own positions and those of the "domestic parties" would turn out to be a "master trump card" in its negotiation with Westerners.

Whatever the case may be, diplomatic negotiations seemed to be well under way again when in January 1976 the Security Council, in a fit of unanimity, adopted Resolution 385 on the "retreat of the illegal administration" (South Africa) and "the transfer of power to the people of Namibia with the assistance of the United Nations." By voting for this resolution, which was to serve as the basis for all subsequent diplomatic dealings, the United States affirmed continuation of a policy that had since 1966 favored (unlike France and Great Britain) the end of the South African mandate. Simultaneously, it hoped, no doubt, to destroy the negative image in the eyes of African countries that its involvement in Angola had just produced. The diplomatic range of this gesture, however, was limited. In his Lusaka speech several months later, Henry Kissinger relegated the resolution of the Namibian crisis to secondary status in his priorities for southern Africa, even if this implicit hierarchization was officially denied.[49]

In fact, Henry Kissinger, who sensed quite well the importance of the Namibian stakes to the Republic of South Africa, deemed it unrealistic to exert pressure that was too strong at a time when its support was immediately required in Rhodesia.[50] It was also without excessive conviction that he proposed holding direct or indirect discussions at the United Nations (but not under its aegis) between the Republic of South Africa and SWAPO. Anxious above all to promote the representivity of "domestic parties" that came out of the Turnhalle conference and anxious, also, to attack SWAPO's representivity, Pretoria declined the offer of direct negotiations. Instead it suggested opening discussions between the "domestic parties" and SWAPO, but SWAPO objected to the proposition.[51]

Negotiation Progresses

On inheriting the Namibian situation, the Carter administration found that Resolution 385 could serve as a basis for negotiation between the opposing parties but not as the groundwork for any agreement whatsoever. In contrast to what had happened in Zimbabwe, American diplomacy could hardly hide behind a third party's diplomacy to cover up its own involvement or, should the need arise, avoid its responsibilities. American diplomacy offered the United States as the only Western power capable of influencing South Africa, which established it as South Africa's privileged Western interlocutor.

By locating its initiative from the start within the framework of a contact group of Western powers of the Security Council (the United States, France, the Federal Republic of Germany, Great Britain, and Canada), American diplomacy took on several tasks. The fact of choosing the United Nations expressed the importance it intended to grant this organization in the implementation of Resolution 385. But, above all, this choice reflected the desire to gather the most diplomatic support, to channel increasingly lively international pressure, and to counter a potential Soviet diplomatic backfire. As for setting up the contact group, there were two considerations: attenuating African suspicion of the superpowers' actions by putting America's involvement in the context of a collective Western initiative, and inducing Western partners of the United States, most particularly Great Britain, to adopt common measures in the event of a power struggle with the Republic of South Africa.[52]

With negotiations barely reopened, four obstacles to a solution immediately arose along the way: South Africa's refusal to enter into direct negotiation with SWAPO; the issue of the role of the United Nations, which Pretoria held in deep suspicion; the effect of the internal political dynamics of South Africa on the course of the negotiations; and the political developments in neighboring Rhodesia.

As with all the other southern African situations, the Carter administration applied itself initially to proving its determination to throw its weight into the picture. The barely established contact group persuaded Pretoria not to implement the domestic solution and threatened it with resorting to international sanctions.[53] At first, the maneuver seemed to pay off: Vorster agreed not to resort to the "domestic solution" that had been fine-tuned for the Turnhalle conference. He even considered the idea of holding elections for a constituent assembly, in which all Namibians (and therefore SWAPO) would be invited to participate.

Washington then thought it could press its advantage by increasing pressure on Pretoria. In Vienna Mondale tried to make Vorster accept the substitution of the United Nations for the South African administration during the period of transition toward independence. But here American effort met its limits. As in the case of Zimbabwe, the Vienna meetings usefully helped South Africa gauge the measure of American determination to adjust its own behavior accordingly.

Refraining from initiating a harmful break, South Africa developed a two-pronged diplomatic strategy: on one side, it explored with Western countries the possibilities of finding an international solution by skillfully mixing new concessions and demands. On the other, it laid the groundwork for a domestic solution that would offer triple advantage: it would block SWAPO, increase its own bargaining ability in international negotiations, and, if needed, place before Western powers a *fait accompli*. By systematically accompanying its concessions with new demands, South African diplomacy was playing on an advantageous court. It prompted Washington to persevere in its diplomatic efforts while gradually abandoning its potential threats. As long as Pretoria showed an interest in negotiating, recourse to sanctions seemed inopportune: that was, in substance, the basis of American diplomatic reasoning.

By the end of 1977 the South African machine seemed to be launched. Pretoria conceded a place for the United Nations next to its representative during the period of transition, but it insisted that the participation of the United Nations forces be as restrained as possible. Moreover, it was intransigent on the nonnegotiability of its sovereignty over the Walvis Bay enclave. Three months later, it consented to confining its army during the transition period to bases controlled by the United Nations. But on the other hand it expected the West to guarantee nonintervention by Cuban troops in Namibia.[54] Dropping this last condition did not solve the delicate problems of transition. Pretoria, which wanted to control SWAPO quickly and reduce its representation, demanded that elections for the constituent assembly be held a year later, in March 1978. The degree of differences between the parties, each concerned with reducing the presence of the other during the transition period in order to have greater impact on the choice at election time, did not discourage the contact group. At the end of 1977 the contact group proposed holding "proximity talks" in New York between the Republic of South Africa and SWAPO to preserve the essential process of negotiating, and to avoid its getting sidetracked on issues that were supposedly less important.

Begun in February 1978, these discussions ended up satisfying certain South African demands. Pretoria was entitled to maintain two military bases in northern Namibia during the transition phase so as to preempt SWAPO military pressure from out of Angola. At the same time, South Africa's administrator was given police powers. As for the questions left unanswered (such as the size of the United Nations forces, the presence of South African troops after the elections, and sovereignty over Walvis Bay), finding solutions to them was postponed so as not to hinder the implementation of Resolution 385. The first issue was left to the consideration of the United Nations; the second was subordinated to an agreement between the Constituent Assembly and the Republic of South Africa; and the third was relegated to later negotiations between the independent Namibian state and South Africa.

Negotiations seemed to be sufficiently well under way by then that in April 1978 the contact group addressed the President of the Security Council with a resolution proposal inspired by the basic principles of Resolution 435. A calendar was appended to this plan that anticipated the proclamation of Namibian independence for December 31, 1978.[55] At a time when the Anglo-American plan in neighboring Rhodesia had received a fatal blow by the Salisbury accord, Washington's diplomacy hoped to remove the temptation to Pretoria of proceeding similarly in Namibia. It therefore welcomed its conditional agreement to the Western resolution plan as an important step on the road to a solution. And with the decisive help of Nigeria, it then turned to convincing SWAPO, brought up short by South Africa's acceptance, not to hinder the implementation of the settlement plan. But that hope would fade quickly.

Fewer than ten days after approving the Western diplomatic initiative, the Republic of South Africa launched an extensive military raid on the SWAPO camps in Cassinga (Angola). Given the logistical imperatives, the decision to trigger such an operation could only have *preceded* the acceptance of the resolution plan. South Africa's reversal seemed all the more disturbing since Vorster had announced the upcoming Namibian elections in December 1978, at which time Namibia would select its representatives to the Constituent Assembly established in the domestic agreement. This behavior, which had the appearance of a certain duplicity, was nonetheless inspired by the deliberate care of the Republic of South Africa to see its two options (internal and diplomatic) progress at a similar pace, to preserve its maneuvering space and thus to be able to move from one to the other without real harm. The Cassinga raid, an expression of South African constancy in Namibia, nonetheless ushered in a new set of difficulties for the negotiated settlement.

The Cassinga Turning Point

The coinciding of a return to an offensive military strategy with the formal acceptance of the Western settlement plan revealed the intensity of the argument within the Afrikaner regime over the best South African line of defense: the Cunene or the Orange River? But the asperity of this debate was exacerbated following the discovery of the "Muldergate" scandal[56] by the growing rivalry between a weakened J. Vorster and his Minister of Defense, P. W. Botha. The hypothesis that the Cassinga raid corresponded to the army's deliberate wish to discredit J. Vorster's diplomatic initiative is therefore perfectly plausible. Forced to resign finally in September 1978, Vorster tried nonetheless to preserve his political position within the National Party by leaving at the time of the rejection of the Waldheim plan intended to clarify the arrangements of the resolution.

An expression of real tensions that shook the Afrikaner regime, the Cassinga raid also reflected the impact of the general situation in southern Africa on South Africa's strategy. Pretoria analyzed the fearful reaction of Western parties to the Salisbury accord of March 1978 and renewed its interest in activating a domestic agreement in Namibia. It announced that domestic elections would be held in December 1978 and reconfirmed its support of the Democratic Turnhalle Alliance (DTA) to that end. This renewal of South African confidence was not unrelated to the mobilization of certain fringes of Western public opinion favoring white regimes. The interest that one part of the Senate had in a Muzorewa solution in Zimbabwe, together with the clear visibility of divisions within the Carter administration on African policy after the Shaba II crisis, led the Republic of South Africa to be more audacious.

Having thus far believed, or feigned belief, that its original strategy of threatening pressure had not failed to encourage South Africa's interest in a negotiated settlement, the Carter administration seemed particularly disconcerted by South Africa's attitude at the end of 1978. It not only had to exhort Pretoria to honor the international settlement over the domestic one but also to solicit its help in getting Smith and Muzorewa to adopt a similar position in Zimbabwe. The expected extension of the Namibian settlement to the conflict in Zimbabwe never having occurred, it was the fear of seeing a replay at Windhoek of what happened in Salisbury that henceforth preoccupied American negotiators.

Taking note of the new situation, the Carter administration embarked on an in-depth examination of its southern African policy in October 1978 and concluded that it would be necessary to resort to sanctions should South Africa's obstruction of a settlement in Namibia persist. To increase economic efficiency and the political credibility of sanctions, the American administration discussed with its Western partners a sanction plan that would require commitment from all of them. This plan proposed restrictions on the landing rights of South African planes and the blocking of access to Western financial sources.[57]

Armed with this plan, the Carter administration then tried to talk with Pretoria once again, sending Cyrus Vance. The head of American diplomacy, while refraining from invoking the threat of sanctions, set forth a certain number of conciliatory proposals that singularly contrasted with the previous policy of applying pressure. In exchange for a reopening of Namibian negotiations, South Africa's prime minister was invited by President Carter to visit Washington. This offer of international rehabilitation was accompanied by two concessions: Western acceptance of the delay in international elections until the spring of 1979 to increase the Democratic Turnhalle Alliance's (DTA) electoral chances, and a reduction of the presence of United Nations forces to thirty-five hundred men. The Republic of South Africa answered these diplomatic overtures ambiguously: it did not accept delaying the organization of domestic elections but did agree to persuade the delegates of the new assembly to participate in elections supervised by the United Nations. The Republic of South Africa, which had once more managed to avoid the trap of rejecting Western proposals wholesale, had been sufficiently conciliatory to fend off the specter of sanctions. As for Western powers, and especially the United States, they deemed this tentative renewal of negotiations preferable to handling sanctions. But however much the contact group might have considered the establishment of a domestic settlement compatible with the search for an international settlement, as in Rhodesia, the chances of seeing that international settlement succeed were dwindling. Although continuing to participate in the negotiations, Pretoria did not hesitate to make its support of Resolution 435 once again conditional. In particular, it raised the question of control of SWAPO bases in Angola and Zambia during the period of transition. It was also opposed to the regrouping of the SWAPO forces present in Namibia at the time of the cease-fire into camps controlled by the United Nations forces, even though this sort of arrangement offered the advantage of helping to localize these forces better in case the cease-fire ended and hostilities were renewed.

In fact, throughout 1979, the Republic of South Africa played a waiting game—a posture that remained unchanged even after McHenry was replaced by British Ambassador Murray as head of the contact group.[58] At first it appeared just as anxious to know how the domestic settlement had fared in Zimbabwe as it was to learn the results of the British election.[59] Later, it would be reassured by the conservative victories in the British and West German elections, as well as by the increasing diplomatic discredit of the Carter administration (Iran and Afghanistan crises). Finally, and especially, Pretoria extended the lessons of Lancaster House to Namibia. It had reached the conclusion that no international settlement, even one guaranteed by a conservative Western power, could immunize it against a SWAPO victory. But at the same time, the failure of the Muzorewa operation led it to think over the difficulty of conferring legitimacy on a domestic settlement. It is from this angle that one must interpret South Africa's acceptance of participation in the Geneva conference, held under the aegis of the United Nations. For American diplomacy, this conference repre-sented the final bid to save an imperiled diplomatic negotiation. Returning to a tactic that Henry Kissinger had adopted during the Rhodesian situation in 1976, Washington expected a breakthrough in the settlement to come from direct confrontation of South Africa's and SWAPO's positions. This tenuous hope proved to be illusory. The conference having opened barely a few days before the Reagan administration took office in January 1981, it would have been completely unrealistic to hope to see Pretoria give up such a trump card for such fundamental concessions.

Intended to parry the accusation of intransigence, South Africa's par-ticipation in the Geneva conference had one main purpose: to give the DTA the diplomatic credibility that its weak political establishment in Namibia had not permitted it to have.[60]

The Regionalization of the Conflict

Succeeding the Carter administration in January 1981, the Reagan ad-ministration faced a major issue that its own diplomatic interests would broaden: the perceptible shift in the Namibian conflict's center of gravity. Disconcerted by Mugabe's accession to power, encouraged by the out-going Democratic administration's pusillanimity, and stimulated by Ronald Reagan's predicted victory, South Africa opted for a regional strategy after 1980 that was resolutely on the offensive. While its raids in southern An-gola had thus far been meant to destroy SWAPO's striking forces as they infiltrated Namibia, the strategy was broadened thanks to the now perma-nent occupation of a part of Angolan territory. The Republic of South Africa sought to disorganize Angola and ensure revitalization of UNITA's forces. During 1980 and 1981 South Africa triggered two wide-ranging military operations whose extent reflected the breadth of its objectives in the region. By taking the war to Angola, Pretoria increased its pressure on SWAPO and took on two further commitments (territorial occupation of the Angolan south and increased support of UNITA), whose dissociation from the Namibian settlement would become more and more uneasy. Thus, not only did the Republic of South Africa expand its diplomatic maneuver-ing space, but it also altered the problem's basic assumptions. The problem was no longer just a matter of decolonization; it became part of a bilateral Angolan–South African conflict in which the Republic of South Africa had everything to gain. By regionalizing this conflict, Pretoria contributed to taking it out of the framework of the United Nations. By bilateralizing it, Pretoria would eventually force Luanda to choose between its political support of SWAPO and the strict preservation of its national interests. The strength of this policy was all the greater for having been introduced in a domestic political context that was once again strained. Because P. W.

Botha tended to identify, on domestic affairs, with the positions of the *Verligte* (moderates), he thought that an intransigent regional strategy would offer the means of withstanding repeated assaults from the *Verkrampte* (conservatives). The intensity of political debates among white power factions was indeed reflected in the results of the January 1981 legislative elections. The National Party, which was increasingly divided, fell behind while the extreme right wing moved ahead. A year later, nineteen of the thirty-three representatives who had left the National Party founded a new extreme right wing party, the Conservative Party, under the direction of A. Treurnicht. Given the new dynamics, which it would not try to counteract, the Reagan administration would promptly define a line of action whose clarity and voluntarism distinctly contrasted with the ambiguity and erraticism of the previous administration.

The Reagan administration recognized South Africa's central role in the search for a settlement, advocated beginning the effort within the context of the East-West confrontation, demanded a privileged place for the United States in the region, and finally rejected all notions of the inevitability of change in Namibia.

By insisting from the start on the fact that no solution in Namibia could see the light of day without South Africa's consent, the Reagan administration moved beyond simply stating the facts. It made South Africa's new arrangement of priorities its own: a bilateral resolution of the Angolan–South African conflict would have to precede any definitive settlement in Namibia. "Our diplomacy recognizes openly the intimate relationship between the conflicts in Namibia and Angola,"[61] C. Crocker declared in August 1981. In taking note of the shift in the center of gravity of the Namibian conflict, the Reagan administration established the preferred axis of its actions in southern Africa, that of the East-West confrontation. Unlike the Carter administration, the Republican regime asserted the primacy of the fight against Moscow. But, while resolving the traditional dilemma between global and regional approaches to the distinct advantage of the former, the Reagan administration also distanced itself from Kissinger's approach, which understood "globalization" of African problems as necessarily meaning their relegation to the lowest rung in the hierarchy of American preoccupations. Thus, the Reagan administration deployed a *regionalized globalism* in southern Africa—that is to say, a regional activism linked to the imperatives of its global rivalry with the Soviet Union.[62] Perhaps nothing illustrates better that double objective than the establishment of the well-known linkage between Namibian independence and the retreat of Cuban forces stationed in Angola, even if this idea was imposed on Crocker by the White House rather than originally proposed by him. In the mind of its architect, Crocker, the linkage schema offered multiple advantages. Above all, it meant being able to convince the entire Republican administration definitively of the value of a policy of active presence in southern Africa—a policy whose diplomatic dividends on a global scale would for once be significant.

For a profoundly anti-Soviet Republican administration, the advantage of anchoring the main part of its African involvement in the search for a Namibian settlement, leading to a victory only for SWAPO, was quite limited. Even if one supposed that it would improve American credibility in the eyes of black African states, such an objective would in fact only result in ensuring the victory of a cause defended by the Soviet Union. On the other hand, if, along with an outcome that was considered inevitable anyway, Cuban troops could be forced out of Angola, then American involvement in Africa would be singularly enhanced and could be perfectly integrated into the global strategy. Were this plan to work, the United States would demonstrate not only that extension of Soviet-Cuban influence was not unavoidable but also that it was completely reversible.

To get on with its task, American diplomacy proceeded with a perceptible recentering, intended to loosen the diplomatic straitjacket in which the Carter administration had bound itself. Because it took full responsibility for its desire to play a central role in the Namibian settlement, the Reagan administration no longer had any interest in hiding its involvement behind the contact group. Although maintained formally, the group's role would slowly dwindle; its essential function would be reduced to approving the proposals that the American administration wanted to put before it, especially since most of the diplomatic dealings on problems of regional security would escape its attention. But America's wish to marginalize the contact group went beyond a desire to assert itself in southern Africa; it also expressed the desire to discontinue treating Resolution 435 as the be-all and end-all of the Namibian settlement: "We cannot be constrained by a rigid adherence to the letter of UNSC 435 if, by doing so, an internationally acceptable settlement in Namibia is impeded rather than aided."[63] Thus, by carefully avoiding questioning a resolution supported by the international community, the United States also avoided finding itself in a totally unstable position vis-à-vis that same community; but, by prudently keeping its distance, it did manage in the short term to satisfy the Republic of South Africa while simultaneously releasing itself from a commitment that no longer took all of its regional objectives into account.

From June 1981 on, the steps of a settlement process were jointly established by Washington and Pretoria. In exchange for a commitment from South Africa to pronounce itself favorable to independence in Namibia, the United States "offered" South Africa the seductive prospect of a withdrawal of Cuban forces from Angola.[64] This arrangement, later confirmed in writing, seems to have significantly reinforced South Africa's interest in a negotiated settlement. America and South Africa agreed to hasten the process of finding solutions to problems that had arisen thus far from implementation of Resolution 435 before tackling the crucial problem of the Cuban forces.

In the summer of 1982, barely one year after the actual reopening of negotiations, most South African objections to the settlement seemed to have been overcome. Under Washington's influence, Pretoria agreed to be content with a declaration of principles guaranteeing the rights of the white minority, before the elections, instead of insisting on an immediate draft of a proper constitution.

Thinking it had convinced South Africa about the settlement plan, the United States took the risk of setting some dates: the implementation of Resolution 435 was set for September 1982 and the organization of elections for March 1983. The anticipation turns out to have been unwarranted.

While leaving it to Washington to remove the Cuban obstacle, the Republic of South Africa consolidated its strategy of bilateralizing the Namibian conflict. During the summer of 1982, it did not hesitate to invade the Angolan south once again, a few hours after American negotiators had assured Luanda of South Africa's wish to reduce regional tension. In December 1982 South Africa began discussions from which the United States was ostensibly kept at bay. By proposing a month-long cease-fire, followed if successful by a gradual retreat of South African forces from the Angolan south and the installation of a buffer zone blocking SWAPO's infiltration, the Republic of South Africa forced Angola to choose between preserving its national interest and its support of SWAPO. At a time when the Soviet Union was charging Angola a price for its diplomatic autonomy by putting the brakes on its military aid, Angolan authorities saw a chance for relief from the South African proposition. For the United States, direct Angolan–South African negotiations had an ambivalent significance. While reducing regional tension and prefiguring a general settlement, such negotiations still presented the danger of excluding Pretoria from the global framework of the negotiations America had defined. Diplomatic dealings throughout 1983 did not escape that ambiguity. Since that date, the ambiguity has been lifted but not as Washington expected it to be. The bilateralization of the Namibian conflict froze the game in Pretoria's favor.

The Limits of American Diplomatic Bargaining

In southern Africa, constructive American involvement was supposedly based on an approach of instigation and constraint. It presented Angola with the prospect of reducing South African pressure, thanks to Namibia's accession to sovereignty, in exchange for loosening ties with the socialist camp. It offered the Republic of South Africa the turning back of communist influence in the region in exchange for renouncing occupation of Namibia. That plan, based on the traditional rules of diplomatic bargaining, was endowed in addition with two master trump cards. None of the parties involved had the means to make unilateral gains. No other actor could be substituted for the United States in seeking a solution that was at once stable and global. In retrospect, it seems that this diplomatic construct ran up against three major obstacles.

By ostensibly favoring the regionalization of the conflict in order to extricate it from the purview of the United Nations, American diplomacy placed an accent on bilateralization as Pretoria conceived of it. The United States refusal to condemn South Africa's military intervention in the Angolan south confirmed this, even if that was not what Washington had in mind. But in doing so, its diplomacy misassessed the advantages to South Africa and Angola in seeking directly, without United States mediation, a temporary *modus vivendi,* which frustrated the United States as it sought a global success to exhibit to the Soviet Union.

In the second place, the effectiveness of linkage dwindled to a weak power of American constraint on regional actors. For the most part, that is to say, as far as the arbitration of South Africa's or Angola's domestic political situation was concerned, the United States had very little influence. Thus, as soon as Washington seemed to be disarmed vis-à-vis Pretoria, Angola immediately bypassed American mediation to deal directly with its adversary. As for the Republic of South Africa, it went so far as to reverse the meaning of linkage. It turned a child's rattle given by Washington into a straitjacket that confined American diplomacy. As long as the United States could not get Cuban troops out of Angola, nothing forced South Africa to leave Namibia. By transforming the Namibian settlement into an Angolan–South African conflict, South Africa's image in America remained unscathed. South Africa simply applied itself to making the effective implementation of linkage difficult.

In fact the Cuban prerequisite, which might have seemed essential to the settlement, had largely lost its compelling nature. Being less and less convinced of South Africa's desire to reach a settlement in Namibia, or of the ability of the United States to foster one, Angola was forced to choose short-term solutions, even if they constrained its SWAPO allies. Its defiance of linkage turned out to be all the greater for SWAPO's having carefully put aside the question of UNITA. In addition, the failure of the Nkomati accords did not affect Angolan plans about the possibility of an eventual South African commitment to cease supporting UNITA.

Given the insurmountable obstacle that SWAPO representation in Namibia constituted, any immediate interest the Republic of South Africa might have had in American linkage declined. It realized that Cuba's departure from Angola would not protect it anyway from a SWAPO victory at Windhoek.

In southern Africa, the all-powerfulness of the Republic of South Africa and its rejection of traditional rules of diplomatic bargaining harmed the effectiveness of a rather unconstraining American diplomatic involvement.

American Globalism and South African Regionalism

For at least ten years, the United States has been groping to develop a southern African policy that would enable it to benefit from long-term changes—orderly and gradual changes—while preserving its interests as established in the current status quo. Beyond the intentions proclaimed by its successive managers, this policy has had remarkable continuity, even if the version defended by the Reagan administration since 1981 seems relatively more coherent. What can account for the persistent refusal of the United States to commit itself to a decisive power struggle with the apartheid regime? It is insufficient to offer an economic-strategic argument as an answer to this central question. To be sure, United States dependence on the Republic of South Africa is not insignificant. But for a decade now, no determined effort has been made to ease that dependency. In fact the economic vulnerability of the United States, and of the West in general, is such that it reinforces America's immobilism on Pretoria rather than explaining it. As we have tried to show, South Africa's economic, financial, and diplomatic vulnerability under pressures applied by Western forces is much more significant. The crisis of the summer of 1985 sharply revealed the extreme fragility of the South African economy with respect to its creditors. Ten years after Soweto, South Africa found it more difficult than ever to come up with resources for long-term financing. It is rather improbable that this already highly visible difficulty could be redressed. South Africa's dependence on the West seems to have had to increase, especially since the current structure of its *laager* economy is necessarily on a self-destructive course. Except for the possibility of backtracking and accepting the risks of significant deflation, the South African economy is now forced to adapt to the constraints of the world market.

An inflationary policy intended to camouflage the modest competitiveness of the South African economy can hardly be pursued. This sort of manipulation is laden with consequences. On a domestic level, it raises questions about what role the state will henceforth play and therefore about the role of the Afrikaner regime in the economic and social sphere of southern Africa. The ever-increasing pressures on the National Party to relinquish certain traditional functions (denationalization, reduction of farm subsidies) would necessarily affect a party that draws most of its support from state functionaries, tutelary agents, and the overprotected farmers. On the foreign level, the consequences of such action would be even more striking for being more immediate. By dealing with the world market, the South African economy would escape from its state of impending asphyxia. At the same time, the world market would impose some very strict constraints on South Africa, especially where public expenditures are concerned. It would also make the South African economy more sensitive to the irregular rhythms of the international economy and the American economy in particular.

This reality, whose nature the current crisis reveals, would necessarily alter perceptions of the Afrikaner regime. In fact, the supposed indifference that the latter might manifest toward the tightening of an international vise does not stand up to the material facts. From the Muldergate scandal to P. W. Botha's European trip, indications of South Africa's deliberate desire to promote its own image abound (press campaigns, recourse to public relations agencies, opening of honorary consulates, and the like). But America's immobilist policy toward the Republic of South Africa stems less from the prohibitive cost that a break with it would generate than it does from the uncertainty of what gains might be derived from such a decision. This calculation owes as much to rigid American perceptions of the international system as it does to the particularity of its relations with black Africa.

Indeed, even if the international system demonstrated undeniable heterogeneity, it would still remain a prisoner of its original bipolar yoke. In three cases at least (South Africa, Israel, and Taiwan), the identification of these states as United States allies in the Cold War context led to an anticommunist diplomatic conduct that had triumphed over the (real or assumed) determinism arising from America's free market orientation. The prospect of opening the vast mainland Chinese market to American goods probably weighed only slightly in the recognition of the People's Republic of China in 1971. It was prompted rather by the Sino-Soviet schism and by the gains that Washington could generate out of the discord between these two poles of the communist world. The huge development of distributive resources in numerous Arab states has not to this day shaken America's unconditional support of Israel. American perceptions in the Republic of South Africa come *mutatis mutandis* from identical considerations. The South African leadership's doctrinal anticommunism combined with the economic and political power it can mobilize in the event of generalized East-West conflict overrides all else. For Washington, South Africa remains a more reliable anticommunist ally than any other African nation.

The constraints of a bipolar order are, of course, reinforced by the uncertainties of a break with Pretoria. To be sure, such a decision would certainly raise the status of the United States in black Africa. It would also deprive the Soviet Union of several acquired tactical advantages. But on the scale of American global interests, the net gain would seem rather modest. On a diplomatic level, even a spectacular break of American–South African ties still would not convert Tanzania, Zambia, or Ethiopia into champions of anticommunism. On an economic level, a similar sort of reasoning comes to mind. The structure of American investments in black Africa is too dissimilar to allow one to think about a redeployment of American investments to the north of Limpopo in the event of a loss of access to the South African market. To this day, moreover, no African country has managed to impose upon a Western operator a decision between its interests in southern Africa and in the rest of Africa.

Under such conditions, and as long as the costs of supporting Pretoria remain less than the potential benefits of a break with Pretoria, the southern African strategy of the United States has little chance of changing drastically.

It remains nevertheless true that, between complete immobilist policy and a total break, there is room for an infinite spectrum of possibilities determined by the complex structure of the American regime, the multiplicity of factors beyond state control, and the unpredictability of the southern African conjuncture.

In the United States the policy of constructive engagement was hit hard until 1987 by two forces against which it had let down its guard: public opinion and Congress. By inspiring a durable and wholly unprecedented mobilization of public opinion, the antiapartheid movement managed to relay its demands through a Congress divided up to then on the question of sanctions against South Africa. Even if it is entirely possible to imagine the ebb of the opinion movement, its action will have nonetheless contributed decisively to the erosion of South Africa's image in the West. Henceforth, debates about sanctions will be more about their magnitude than about the convenience of using them.

Domestic constraints on American diplomatic behavior are even more real because a legislator's complex political and ideological ideas do not always match a diplomat's interests. In calling for limited economic sanctions against South Africa as well as for the repeal of the Clark amendment, Congress remained faithful to a line of action solidly binding liberalism with anticommunism.

In the final analysis, and beyond the uncertainties that reign in South Africa's domestic evolution, the dynamics of American–South African relations lay bare a number of asymmetrical propositions that nearly all work in favor of the Republic of South Africa.

The first deals with the nature of constraints affecting a global power such as the United States and an actor with strictly regional ambitions such as South Africa. Indeed, even if the search for a *pax americana* in southern Africa necessarily rests on South African hegemony, the underlying logic of accommodation forces Pretoria into certain negotiations, or into inevitable concessions, even if they seem minor in comparison with those imposed on other states in the region. Unlike South Africa, the United States sees no advantage in maintaining the status quo in Namibia, even if the search for a diplomatic solution is not urgent where worldwide interests are concerned.

Conscious of this problem, the Reagan administration tried to avoid it by resorting to linkage in Nämibia. And, indeed, by offering South Africa a political reward (the retreat of Cuban forces in Angola), Washington had hoped to arrive at a strictly even distribution of gains between Pretoria and itself. As the years passed, America's calculations seemed less well founded. The Cuban issue unquestionably heightened South African interest in a Namibian settlement, but it completely failed to call the order of its priorities into question. The retreat of Cuban forces from Angola preoccupied South Africa less than the annihilation of SWAPO. As long as the realization of these two objectives could occur simultaneously, Pretoria was not interested in spurning international negotiations. But as soon as it felt it necessary to choose between accepting a SWAPO victory and getting Cuban forces to withdraw, its interest in a diplomatic solution declined. The Cuban prerequisite, used as a trump card by American diplomacy, was always more important for Washington than for Pretoria. However, this approach changed in 1987 when South Africa recognized that its military supremacy had been eroded by increasing Cuban involvement in southern Angola and by the real improvement in Angolan military capabilities.

The second observation involves the remarkable South African diplomatic know-how concerning the United States. Having assimilated the rules of bipolarity, South Africa was able to assess just how deeply the United States could involve itself against South Africa and just how far South Africa could go. It knew how to use East-West tensions skillfully to extricate itself from limitations, to maximize its regional goals, or to demonstrate implacability. To be convinced, all one need do is recall how Pretoria capitalized on both diplomatic weakening of the United States in 1979–80 and the advent of the Reagan administration to increase its intransigence in the region. Able to manipulate with equal dexterity the symbols of "Western solidarity" and those of the *laager,* the South African regime sometimes presented itself as a durable ally of the West so as to remain in its good graces and sometimes as a country under siege to fend off pressure. In that game, South Africa exploited two essential advantages: its diplomatic experience with regional issues and the structure of

American power. Being especially well versed in regional problems for at least twenty years, South African negotiators had unlimited resources at their disposal compared to their American counterparts, who are replaced every four or eight years.

Furthermore, the multiplicity of decision points, the influence of public opinion, and bureaucratic conflicts in the United States are all elements that South Africa could play on to counteract any potentially hostile action. The American context is not currently favorable to South Africa, but reversal of that situation is not inconceivable. In this regard, the prospect of seeing the United States Congress come out in favor of financial support of UNITA is very encouraging for Pretoria.

Finally, the fluidity of American policy seems even greater contrasted with the extraordinary opacity of the South African regime. In spite of increasing experience dealing with South Africa, the United States has still not managed to decipher the Afrikaner regime's "rules of the game." The Reagan administration, which did tackle the question, constructed its entire southern African policy around the belief that the Pretoria regime was reformist, pragmatic, rational, "detribalized," and little "ideologized." With that hypothesis in mind, the Reagan administration inferred that P. W. Botha's domestic reformism would necessarily continue through regional moderation. Since the South African regime seemed more "reasonable," it was becoming possible to propose, in Namibia for instance, a compelling political settlement.

This optimistic vision was partially refuted by the facts. The precariousness of the internal balance of the Afrikaner regime was greater than ever. Despite the broadening of the National Party's political base to include a "moderate" electorate of Anglo-Saxon origin, the center of gravity of South African politics remains fundamentally Afrikaner. If the creation of the Conservative Party in 1982 seems to have been less traumatic for the National Party than was the creation of the HNP (Herstigte Nasionale Party), its very presence to the right of the National Party will always be more important to the Pretoria regime than the electoral reinforcements from the English-speaking community. The extraordinary emphasis given the smallest partial election tends to prove that great political "clarifications" (the 1983 referendum, for instance, on the extension of the South African political system to include half-castes and Indians) only have a partial and temporary impact on the balance of Afrikaner power.

This is all the more true since the ballot box is not the only way of dealing with conflicts. Despite the considerable influence that current South African head of state, P. W. Botha, once wielded over the South African army and its integration into the highest level of policy decision-making, its autonomy was far from being bridled by political power. The determination with which certain fringe elements could undermine respect for the Nkomati accords between South Africa and Mozambique arose not only out of the problem of the South African regime's internal coherence but also out of the problem of the rationality of its behavior.

Could South Africa hope for any more than to see Mozambique officially accept its outrageous domination in the region?

By limiting its political contacts in South Africa to those politicians congenial to its positions, the United States never did seem to come to an understanding of the profound rationality of South African behavior. The recurrent optimism that America could demonstrate at each diplomatic "breakthrough" highlights this rather clearly. Unable to arrive at some sufficient comprehension of the Afrikaner regime's rules of the game, American policy, for all that, did not give itself the means to engage the expectations of black civil society. A dozen years after Soweto, the number and the quality of its black interlocutors remain laughable. However, things have begun to change.

Alliance Strategies

The Horn of Africa

The Ethiopian revolution, which would be the catalyst of a change in alliances in the Horn, did not *a priori* carry the germ of an inevitable diplomatic reordering. Born nearly by accident in January 1974 of a local mutiny, this revolution took the shape of a "creeping coup d'état" in which corporatist demands by the army accompanied a surge of student demonstrations. Throughout the first half of 1974, the army seemed not so much an adversary power as the guarantor of an orderly evolution toward constitutional monarchy. But, afraid of being marginalized by the Endalkachew cabinet, the army quickly set itself up as a coordinating committee. While affirming its faithfulness to the monarchy and the civil regime, it also showed a firm desire to have a political role. Furthermore, in July 1974 it publicly announced a vague but very nationalist-sounding political program, *Ethiopia Tikdem!* ("Ethiopia first!").

In the fall of 1974, the pace of events quickened. The deposition of the emperor brought about the official establishment of the Dirgue, presided over by General Aman Andom. But lacking a clearly defined program, the military junta governed by guesswork. Furthermore, the Eritrean problem was the source of profound division. Convinced of the need for a quick political settlement of the conflict, Aman Andom talked about linking the future of the Eritrean question to the reestablishment of democratic rights throughout Ethiopia. In November 1974 his assassination annihilated the

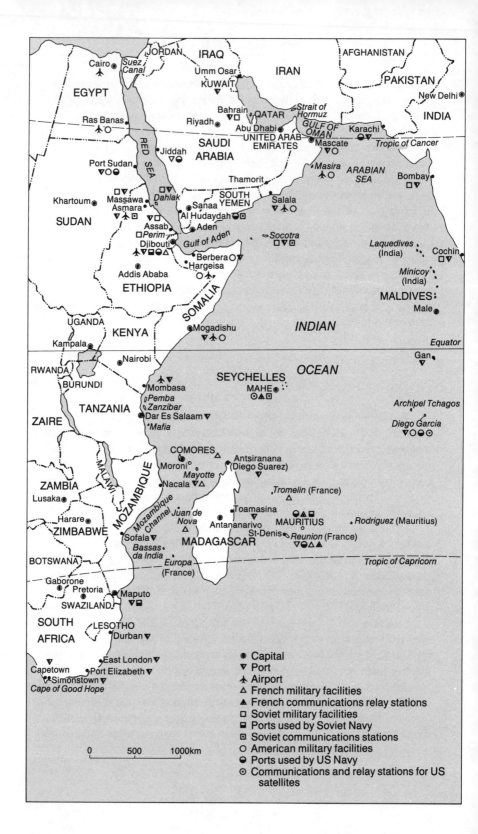

JORDAN
IRAQ
IRAN
AFGHANISTAN
PAKISTAN
Cairo ⊙
Suez Canal ✈
EGYPT
Umm Osar
KUWAIT ▼
New Delhi ⊙
INDIA
Bahrain ▼▼ QATAR
Riyadh ⊙
Strait of Hormuz
Ras Banas ✈○
Abu Dhabi
UNITED ARAB EMIRATES
GULF OF OMAN
Karachi ○▼
Tropic of Cancer
SAUDI ARABIA
Mascate ▼○
Jiddah ▼○
Masira ✈○
ARABIAN SEA
Bombay ○▼
Port Sudan ▼○●
RED SEA
Thamorit
Khartoum ⊙
Massawa □▼
Dahlak □▼
Asmara ●
SOUTH YEMEN
SUDAN
▼▼✈□
Assab ● ▼□
Sanaa ●
Al Hudaydah ▣○▣
Salala ▼✈○
Laquedives (India)
Cochin ○▼
Aden ●
Perim □
Djibouti ●
Gulf of Aden
Socotra ⌁
□▼▣
Minicoy (India)
MALDIVES
Addis Ababa ⊙
ETHIOPIA
Berbera ○▼
Hargeisa ●
○✈
SOMALIA
Male ⊙
UGANDA
KENYA
Kampala ⊙
Mogadishu ⊙
▼✈○
INDIAN
Equator
Gan ●
▼
Nairobi ●
RWANDA
BURUNDI
Mombasa ✈▼
SEYCHELLES
MAHE ●
○▲□
OCEAN
Archipel Tchagos
TANZANIA
Pemba ○
Zanzibar ○
Dar Es Salaam ●▼
Mafia
Diego Garcia
▼○●⊙
ZAIRE
COMORES
Moroni ○
Antsiranana (Diego Suarez) ▼
ZAMBIA
MALAWI
MOZAMBIQUE
Mayotte △
Nacala ●▼△
Tromelin (France) △
Lusaka ⊙
Toamasina ●▲□
MAURITIUS ▼
Rodriguez (Mauritius) ●
Harare ⊙
ZIMBABWE
Juan de Nova △
Antananarivo ●
St-Denis ○
Reunion (France) ▼○●△△
Sofala ▼
MADAGASCAR
BOTSWANA
Bassas da India
Europa (France)
Tropic of Capricorn
Gaborone ⊙
Pretoria ⊙
Maputo ●
▼▣
SWAZILAND
SOUTH AFRICA
LESOTHO
Durban ▼
East London ▼
Capetown ▼
Port Elizabeth ▼
Simonstown ▼
Cape of Good Hope

⊙ Capital
▼ Port
✈ Airport
△ French military facilities
▲ French communications relay stations
□ Soviet military facilities
▣ Ports used by Soviet Navy
▣ Soviet communications stations
○ American military facilities
● Ports used by US Navy
⊙ Communications and relay stations for US satellites

0   500   1000km

remaining influence of those in favor of a political solution and heralded a fresh outbreak of the central regime's military operations. At a time when eighty percent of the Eritrean territory was in the hands of nationalist movements, the centralist regime in Addis Ababa was counting on its survival.

With this broadly sketched background of domestic events in Ethiopia, American conduct followed three principles. The first, heir of the traditional "credibility doctrine," linked the maintenance of an American presence not so much to tangible interests as to the symbolic significance of a possible rollback (especially in the mind of the Soviet Union). The second, stemming from a client-oriented interpretation of American-Ethiopian relations, involved the United States' overestimate of the importance of its network of influence in the Ethiopian army. And, finally, the third, caught up in mechanistic strategic reasoning, considered historical and current Soviet investment in Somalia too significant to imply a change of alliances in the region. These considerations led Washington, then, to stall and not to abandon Ethiopia to its own destiny. Moreover, the regional environment from the Horn to the Red Sea was shaken by deep tectonic movements in early 1975. The first among them had its epicenter in Riyadh: in concert with an Egypt just recently "Sadatized," Saudi Arabia strongly advocated the idea of an "Arab lake" in the Red Sea. Nonetheless, the implementation of this regional design very quickly fell more into line with anti-Soviet action than a true anti-Israeli plan. The banner of the crusade against Israel would serve as a convenient pretext for Riyadh and Cairo to spoil Soviet influence in the Aden and Mogadishu regimes and to prevent its potential establishment in Djibouti.

Now, at a time when the Ethiopian empire was crumbling, the other bank of the Bab el Mandeb could not escape the turbulence of the region. In 1974 el-Hamidi's access to power in San'a helped renew the process of uniting the two Yemens. One year later, King Faisal's death facilitated détente between Riyadh and Aden. Saudi Arabia, which then tried to secure South Yemen for the moderate Arab camp, simultaneously tried to stretch the Arab world to include Somalia. An essential step was made in this direction with the admission of Somalia to the Arab League in 1974.

In the face of the Saudi offensive, which did after all conform to Saudi Arabia's own interests, the United States showed reserve. If anti-Soviet ardor in Riyadh was immensely comforting, the "Arab lake" argument was far less convincing: because it was committed to Israel, the United States could not subscribe to an extension of Arab influence in the region. Furthermore, anchoring Somalia in the moderate Arab camp seemed to the United States to contradict the Soviet-Somali friendship treaty signed at the end of 1974. For reasons of symmetry, Washington did not think the timing was right to cut itself off from Ethiopia. That is why military assistance to the Dirgue, which had been suspended in November 1974, would be mostly restored three months later, even if it was no longer largely gratis.

Addis Ababa, which still had a substantial reserve of strong currency, saw an advantage in trivializing its relations with the United States. America ceased to be an ally; it became a mere supplier of arms. In March 1975 the United States authorized a sale of $7 million in arms to Ethiopia. Compared to the $125 million in arms ordered by Addis Ababa, the American response seemed limited. But by stingily doling out its aid to Ethiopia, the United States was obviously trying to signify that shipments would not take place without political compensation. In April 1975 the United States consented to an economic aid package for Ethiopia amounting to $15 million in exchange for a commitment from the Dirgue to participate in the Sudanese mediation efforts on the Eritrean question. The delivery of eight F-5s (versus the sixteen ordered) would also be subject to the cancellation of the march on Eritrea. Later, when the Angolan crisis in southern Africa turned to his disadvantage, Henry Kissinger would insist on the need to continue supporting the Dirgue. By some curious detour, the most dogged proponents of "globalism" suddenly became choristers of the Ethiopian junta. They praised its moderation and its reformist ambitions. Accompanying its support of the Dirgue with a sizable military effort with respect to Kenya, itself threatened by Somali irredentism, Washington in the summer of 1976 did not seem to foresee the formation of a possible reversal of alliances. In its eyes, the withdrawal of American aid from the Dirgue could only lead to its fall.[65]

The Constraints of a Reordering

Because it had overestimated Soviet interests in Somalia and had few means of influencing an imminent Ethiopian revolution, American diplomacy misassessed the fluidity of the region's alliances. It overlooked the Soviet-Ethiopian rapprochement taking shape bit by bit. Two issues continued to claim Soviet attention: the political options of the military regime and the burning question of Eritrea. On the first point, the Soviet Union subscribed to the nationalization measures taken by the Dirgue in February 1975.[66] On the second point, it advocated negotiation, but it also tentatively allowed its preferences to emerge.[67] Sensing Ethiopia's intransigence on Eritrea, Moscow was to give this question an increasingly restricted interpretation. As a "national question" before the emperor's fall and a "social question" after the accession of the Dirgue, the Eritrean problem was finally defined simply as a question of the protection of the rights of a Muslim minority—a problem exacerbated by hostility toward Ethiopia on the part of certain Arab countries.[68] At a time when the Soviet Union was trying to open the Ethiopian vise on the area, it made sure of contributing to the Dirgue's rekindling of the old anti-Arab sentiment for mobilization against separatist Eritreans.

With increasing exacerbation of Somali-Ethiopian antagonism, Moscow was forced to reveal itself even further. Independently of the OAU's work in January 1976, the Ethiopian delegation produced a document (*War Clouds on the Horn*) citing "irrefutable proof" of an imminent Somali attack against Ethiopia. According to this document, Somalia would object to the results of the referendum on independence in Djibouti planned for the end of 1976, in order to force Addis Ababa to direct its forces toward the Djibouti border. Scattered in this manner, the Ogaden front would have trouble resisting the assaults of the Somali army. That this plan may have been wrong or abandoned on being exposed did not detract from Somali determination to fight with its age-old enemy.

But instead of independence in Djibouti, it was events in Sudan that would precipitate the change of alliances in the region. In July 1976 the Mahdist putsch attempted against the el-Nimeiry regime failed. This operation, undertaken from Ethiopian territory, may have benefited from some powerful support from Libya, Ethiopia's new ally. It therefore poisoned relations between Khartoum and Addis Ababa before being quickly reflected in Soviet-Sudanese relations. Sudan, which had previously been anxious to blaze a new trail of mediation between the Eritreans and Ethiopia, resolutely rejoined the moderate Arab camp headed by Riyadh. But this change took place at a price, that of the expulsion of Soviet military advisers still on its territory. The Soviet Union, which had been watching the gradual tightening of the Saudi vise on its regional positions, saw that it was to its advantage to intensify its support of Ethiopia. This decision met the Dirgue's needs, being short of arms to deal with the increasing danger in the Ogaden, Eritrea, and Tigre. In December 1976 an essential step toward the reversal of alliances in the region was taken with the signing of an accord that anticipated the delivery of $385 million in Soviet military matériel to Ethiopia.[69]

The Reversal of Alliances

February 3, 1977, on the Horn of Africa marked a moment in the evolution of this region whose decisive nature one can measure more easily today. General Teferi Benti was overthrown in Ethiopia and Lieutenant-Colonel Mengistu came into power as the head of the Dirgue. Barely settled in, the new leader of Ethiopia received congratulations from Fidel Castro and began talking with the Soviet ambassador in Addis Ababa. The unusual promptness of Soviet support and the enthusiastic tone of the Cuban press suggest that both the Soviets and the Cubans were, at the very least, informed of the political direction promised by Mengistu's accession to power.

By betting on a military alliance with the Soviet Union, the Dirgue reduced its own maneuvering margin between the two superpowers and favored *ipso facto* an American-Somali rapprochement. By resorting to the Soviet arsenal, Addis Ababa ran an extra risk, since changing from fully American matériel to Soviet equipment required a six-month overlap to bridge the gap, during which Somalia, of course, could try to outwit Ethiopian troops in the Ogaden.[70] In this context of veritable political "implosion," the Addis Ababa regime could hardly count on Washington's parsimonious military support to avert the rise of regionalisms and Somali pressures. In addition, the radical wing of the Dirgue under Mengistu, favoring revolution from above, quickly saw that reference to the Soviet Union could provide additional legitimation to discredit adversaries in the Dirgue not yet won over to the idea of a total break with the United States. The Soviet Union's initial function as a diplomatic and military ally brought with it the image as ideological paragon. At its convenience, the Dirgue would find in the Soviet Union the resources needed to validate the designation of domestic ideological enemies. In this context, the symbolic decision of the Carter administration to suspend free military aid to the Dirgue did not change anything about a break that had been handwriting of the wall ever since the signing of the military accord between the Soviet Union and Ethiopia. The decision essentially enabled the United States to remove itself from a situation on which it no longer had a handle, while it also gave Addis Ababa the opportunity to hasten suppression of the last symbols of American presence: a military mission, the Naval Medical Research Unit (NAMRU) medical mission, the communications center at Kagnew, the cultural center, libraries, and a consulate in Asmara.

If this new situation gave the Soviet Union something to rejoice about, it nevertheless did not guarantee the stability of its influence in the region. On the Arab bank of the Bab el Mandeb, the two Yemens tried to take advantage of all the great maneuvering to hasten the process of unification and to lighten the tutelage of Moscow and Riyadh, respectively.[71] In March 1977 the Soviet Union, through Cuba, proposed a plan for confederation of the Horn of Africa. The plan, which was not very elaborate technically, was intended to regroup Somalia, Ethiopia, South Yemen, and Djibouti. It would attempt to block the process of unification of the two Yemens (by excluding San'a from the plan), to avoid a situation where the Saudis would have a hold on Djibouti (by including it in the federation), and above all to prevent a Somali-Saudi rapprochement in the event of an armed conflict between Mogadishu and Addis Ababa. For the Soviet Union, the political benefit of such an arrangement would be considerable. It would help to counteract plans made by external powers (Saudi Arabia, United States) and to consolidate new position (Ethiopia) without canceling its previous successes (South Yemen, Somalia). But Somalia, which refused to freeze its claims on the Ogaden under the pretext of ideological solidarity with the Soviet Union, rejected the plan. It reiterated its firm opposition to the Soviet regional plan at the time of President Podgorny's stopover in Mogadishu. From then on, Moscow felt free to welcome Lieutenant Colonel Mengistu officially and to sign a joint declaration with him that prefigured a friendship and cooperation treaty.

While Moscow gradually tipped toward the Ethiopian camp, Washington stayed in a holding pattern. The prospect of a Somali-Ethiopian conflict unsettled the new Carter administration. The priority it intended to assign to southern Africa hardly included exceptional concern over Somali-Ethiopian antagonism. At a time when it was seeking to extricate itself from excessive globalism, it accurately saw that East-West machinations in the Horn would ruin that ambition. In addition, it quickly figured out that declared support of Somali irredentism would place it in an unstable situation with respect to the majority of African states. Yet, the definition of a clear course of action to deal with the looming conflict was to be thwarted by the persistence of deep dissension within the American executive branch. The "regionalists," for whom the essence of the conflict on the Horn lay in Somali irredentism, were set against the "globalists," who were preoccupied by the Soviet presence in the region and the necessity of counteracting it. This antagonism was very quickly felt in American diplomatic choices.

When, in the summer of 1977, Somalia became convinced that Moscow had definitely sided with Ethiopia, it sounded Washington out on its willingness to furnish arms. From the outset, the National Security Council responded receptively to Somali demands; but the Department of State was firmly opposed to it and even expressed hostility toward delivering American military matériel through third parties.[72] Initially, President Carter rallied behind Brzezinski: the United States declared that it was indeed willing to meet Somali requests for "defensive arms." Moreover, it immediately let this be known publicly, perhaps to accelerate the break between Moscow and Somalia. But, for fear of exposing itself directly, the United States fostered the idea of delivering military matériel via France and Great Britain. Encouraged by these promises, Siad Barre intimated to the Soviets that they should reduce their presence on his territory in July 1977. As Somalia reinforced its own presence in the Ogaden district, it hoped that the decision to do so would remove the last obstacles to Western military support. This calculation, judicious on the face of it, nonetheless sold American doubts short. Using the presence of Somali forces in the Ogaden as their argument, the regionalists charged back. Their arguments on the dangers of supporting an irredentist state were even more convincing while the Department of Defense disagreed with the National Security Council.

In August 1977 Washington made it clear to Somalia that the benefit of Western aid remained tied to withdrawal of forces from the Ogaden. The United States became all the more firm as Addis Ababa allowed a certain resentment toward the Soviets to show.[73] This attitude, too quickly interpreted by the Western press and the Department of State as an expression of Ethiopian exasperation with a Soviet "double standard," nonetheless cloaked something more complex. It could first of all have been in part suggested by Moscow with the intention of continuing to "mislead" Somalia, on the verge of defecting. But, more fundamentally, this manifestation of Ethiopian moodiness toward the Soviet Union, along with a profession of the "non-aligned" faith, followed from two objectives: to secure from the United States a release of its $100 million in arms ordered but suspended since early 1977; and to prompt the United States to delay arms deliveries to Somalia.

Taking advantage of American hesitation, as well as of Kenyan support for Ethiopian arguments, and the failure of Siad Barre's last-chance trip to Moscow at the end of August, the Soviet Union intensified its military and political support of Ethiopia at the beginning of fall 1977. All that remained for Somalia to do was to expel Soviet military advisers in Somalia, to renounce the friendship and cooperation treaty signed three years earlier, and to close Soviet military facilities in Berbera, Uanle Uen, and Kisimayu. At the end of November, barely two weeks after this decision, the first airlift of Cuban forces to Ethiopia was secured from Havana and Angola. In record time—a month and a half—fourteen thousand Cuban soldiers were channeled to the Ethiopian front to repel the Somali invasion.

In the face of an Ethiopian replay of the "Angolan scenario," the United States was worried about the symbolic dimension of the Soviet-Cuban commitment. Thus, while maintaining opposition in principle to direct military support of Somalia, it reactivated its initial option, that of military support via a third party. At the beginning of 1978 it favored the establishment within NATO of a coordinating group on the Horn that would include the United States, France, Great Britain, Italy, and the Federal Republic of Germany, and acquiesced to the French proposal to hold a regional conference that would tie together the withdrawal of Cuban troops and the departure of Somali troops from the Ogaden. Still, American diplomatic activity in the region was largely hampered by the persistence of rifts between globalists and regionalists inside the American executive branch. Not only did the globalists suggest adopting dissuasive measures to avoid leaving the field open to the Soviet Union, but they even went as far as attempting to relate Soviet presence on the Horn to the signing of SALT accords. On both of these points, however, the battle turned in favor of the regionalists. Through diplomatic channels, both the Soviets and the Ethiopians assured

Washington that Ethiopian-Cuban troops would not push their military advantage at all beyond the recognized international borders of Somalia. In April 1978 the last Somali forces were expelled from the Ogaden; this indeed put an end to the Somali-Ethiopian war.

Rationale for Public Aid

If, in the space of a decade, American aid policy had witnessed noticeable changes both in its geographic distribution and in its structure, it was still rooted in a constant preoccupation on the part of the decision-makers: to make it an instrument of intervention adjusted according to the short-term imperatives of American diplomacy. Even if an effort at rationalization had to include certain inconsistencies and inevitable contradictions, it made a priority of other considerations of an economic and humanitarian order.

Until 1975 the judicious choice of beneficiaries was made in a consistent manner. Within the concepts of American diplomacy, the AID (Agency for International Development) confined its activities to two categories of countries: those where the United States directly assured defense of its interests in the absence of European influence (Ethiopia, Liberia), and those where its credibility as a great anticommunist power had been specifically and durably assured (Ghana, Zaire).[74]

Beginning in 1976 aid policy changed. The concern was to combine preservation of American strategic interests with diplomatic overtures intended to let Henry Kissinger's Angolan clumsiness be forgotten. In addition to restoring American aid to its 1963 level in current dollars, the Carter administration also proceeded to increase the number of aid beneficiaries from 1978 on. In three years this number had increased from ten to thirty-two. Countries that had been thus far neglected in these aid programs, like Tanzania and Zambia, became the objects of attention that increased as their support became needed for American initiatives in southern Africa. This geographic decompartmentalization of aid efforts took place to the detriment of traditional beneficiaries such as Liberia and Zaire. But the geographic redistribution of American assistance reflected above all the precariousness of the game of alliances that the Horn situation well illustrates. Until 1976 the United States only had eyes for Ethiopia in that region. Being on poor terms with Somalia and with Idi Amin's Uganda, the United States scarcely managed to profit from the deterioration in Soviet-Sudanese relations.

With the reversal of alliances on the Horn, and then in November 1977 with Sadat's trip to Jerusalem, the order of American regional priorities underwent modification. In order to counterbalance Soviet influence in Ethiopia, the United States made an effort to support Kenya and Somalia. Washington discovered that Sudan offered not only a useful fall-back position after its mishaps with Ethiopia but also an anchoring point, as the only Arab state that had not rejected the Egyptian president's initiative. The importance—a relative importance—of aid granted by the United States to Khartoum and the ease with which Congress's approval was obtained expressed essentially a consensus in the American political strata on the importance of support granted to favorable states at the Camp David accords. In this respect, there is no doubt that Sudan was above all perceived as a Middle Eastern state. Today, if the separate Israeli-Egyptian peace is no longer at the heart of Middle Eastern stakes, America's interest in Sudan is no less important. The United States continues to view Sudan as an anticommunist ally, a moderating influence within the Arab League, and a major obstacle to the constitution of a geopolitical axis going from Libya to Ethiopia. Marshal Nimeiry's ouster by a military junta anxious to find a new balance for Sudan's foreign policy has not, for the time being, resulted in any interruption of the important American bilateral aid program.

Since the Reagan administration's arrival to power, the geographic distribution of beneficiaries has again been restricted. This trend, begun already in the last year of the Carter mandate, corresponded to a clear objective: to arrest, after the invasion of Afghanistan, the Soviet threat exerted both directly and through Cuban or Libyan intermediaries.

Tanzania, which had been courted by the preceding administration, barely benefited any longer from AID's favors. Economic efforts on behalf of Zambia also slackened. The Reagan administration, believing that the Front Line States had neither the ability nor the opportunity to influence the diplomatic settlements in southern Africa, had less interest in favoring them. Furthermore, Tanzania's economic difficulties, in addition to its refusal to obey the edicts of the IMF, hardly moved Washington to support it. On the contrary, five states (Sudan, Kenya, Zimbabwe, Liberia, and Somalia) received more than fifty percent of American aid. Aid to Kenya and Somalia was inspired by considerations similar to those that motivated aid to Sudan. The case of Zimbabwe and Liberia involved two other, more specific preoccupations. In the first case, American aid reflected a commitment of $220 million that was agreed to at a conference of donors of aid to Zimbabwe (Zimcord) in 1980. In the second, the American commitment, which had been reinforced in the immediate aftermath of the fall of the Tolbert regime, was specifically intended to avoid the "political slippage" of an unexperienced military regime. Overtures to the East and to Libya were interrupted while relations with Israel were established.

The Reagan administration was very preoccupied with Libyan policy in

Table 5 Geographic Distribution of American Economic Assistance
(% of total bilateral economic aid to black Africa)

1962–1975		1976–1981 (Carter Admin.)		1982–1985 (Reagan Admin.)	
Nigeria	18.7	Sudan	7.5	Sudan	19.0
Zaire	16.2	Kenya	5.6	Kenya	9.3
Ethiopia	12.2	Zambia	5.0	Zimbabwe	7.3
Ghana	12.0	Somalia	4.8	Liberia	7.0
Liberia	8.7	Tanzania	4.8	Somalia	5.3
		Ghana	3.5	Senegal	3.5
		Senegal	3.5	Cameroon	2.7
		Upper Volta	3.3		
		Botswana	2.7		
		Mali	2.5		
Cumulative total of the top five beneficiaries: 67.8		Cumulative total of the ten top beneficiaries: 52.5		Cumulative total of the seven top beneficiaries: 57.6	

Table 6 Geopolitical Distribution of American Assistance (1982–1985)
(% of the total)

Horn and eastern Africa (Sudan, Kenya, Somalia):	33.6
Southern Africa (Zimbabwe, BLS**, Zambia, Malawi):	18.6*
Francophone sahelian Africa (Niger, Senegal, Chad, Mali) and Cameroon:	14.2***

*   includes the regional program for southern Africa.
**   Botswana-Lesotho-Swaziland.
***includes the regional program for the Sahel.
Source: AID, *Congressional Presentation, FY 1985, Annex I,* Africa.

the Sahel region; and it naturally became interested in the countries of this region hitherto subject to the more or less exclusive influence of France. This interest was particularly evident concerning Senegal, Niger, and Chad. For these three countries, economic assistance rose from $32 million in 1982 to $72 million in 1985.

One must add to the francophone countries of the Sahel the particular case of Cameroon, where American economic investment was not a consequence of immediate diplomatic preoccupation. The investment was more a result of the determination to make this relatively stable country a place where American economic penetration in francophone Africa could be tested. Although currently only ranking seventh among beneficiaries of American aid to black Africa, Cameroon remains one of the most privileged AID countries in the financing of "heavy" projects. Outside of Zimbabwe, the program to train the higher echelons of agricultural cadres constituted the most sizable financing operation undertaken in black Africa under the aegis of AID in 1985.[75]

While being adapted to alliances and interests, the policy of bilateral aid underwent a very noticeable change in structure, even if this trend was not officially recognized. The "aid for development" component, which included agricultural and rural development, family planning, and training programs, was generally reduced as a proportion of the overall aid programs, in favor of the Economic Support Fund (ESF). That program, whose portion rose from sixteen percent in 1979 to nearly forty-eight percent in 1985, was explicitly intended to lend immediate and localized support to United States allies dealing with serious economic and political difficulties. The ESF has been involved with three types of programs: the financing of imports from America hampered by the absence of convertible currency; direct financial contributions intended to lighten a deficit in the balance of payments; and financing of operations aimed at compensating for the deflationary shock caused by implementation of strict IMF measures.

There were multiple advantages to increasing reliance on the ESF in preference to other programs. Thanks to its flexibility, its specificity, and its immediacy, the ESF could have the most impact in the short run on an economic project whose profitability may be as distant as it is uncertain. Furthermore, from one year to the next, the ESF could be increased, eliminated, or redirected to financing other operations. By reducing the role of development aid projects, American practice ran counter to the dispositions of the Foreign Assistance Act of 1973, which expressly recommended its augmentation.

To conclude that economic aid was subject to essentially diplomatic constraints still hardly explains concretely what sort of benefits the United States might glean. The question does need to be asked, especially if one has the sense that in numerous cases the volume of economic aid was far from attracting a proportional political allegiance on the part of the beneficiary.

The symbolic function. The number and choice of beneficiaries in the first place express the balancing of interests and domestic compromises that the United States was forced to submit to, to impose its order of preference: they involve interactions within the different regional AID offices, between AID and the State Department, between the different regional offices of that Department, and finally between the State Department and the National Security Council.[76] Aid programs are the fruit of laborious negotiations between different elements of the American executive branch and the result also of compromises made with Congress. The actual practice of the last few years nonetheless indicates that, against all expectations, the recommendations offered by Congress, and especially those made by the House Subcommittee on African Affairs, are not significantly different from the propositions drawn up by the White House. At most, one can note Congress's declared inclination to suggest an increase of the part devoted to assistance projects, in preference to the ESF or military aid. This general rule nevertheless does have a few exceptions. One of the most significant involves Zaire, which was constantly held up by the House Subcommittee on African Affairs as the "negative symbol" of American assistance.[77] The subcommittee's argument combining economic perceptions (aid is ineffective) and moral ones (aid to a corrupt and antidemocratic regime is unacceptable) did not fall on wholly deaf ears in Congress. But this liberal-minded attitude did not exempt this same Congress from simultaneously justifying its declared hostility toward certain African regimes reputed to be "communist" or "pro-Soviet." The example of Mozambique, which the Carter administration felt forced to deprive of all economic aid while actively seeking its cooperation in southern Africa, accurately expresses the complexity, or the ambiguity, of American perceptions of Africa.

The compensatory function. In many cases, economic assistance functioned either as payment to an ally whose political support was actively sought or as a trade-off to induce it to adopt a favorable attitude toward the United States. The example of the Horn of Africa demonstrates this type of function well. Kenya and Somalia had just accorded military facilities to the United States when American economic assistance to these two countries doubled. But it is interesting to notice that Kenya and Somalia would use their privileged relations with the United States in different ways. Somalia, whose principal regional adversary remained Soviet-supported Ethiopia, would allow the importance of its ties with the United States to grow. It would view its granting of military facilities not as an obstacle to its sovereignty but as an expression of American support of its cause. The approach taken by Kenya, traditionally more doctrinally anti-communist than Somalia, was different. Nairobi first applied itself to denying, and then to minimizing and trivializing, the breadth of facilities it offered the United States, before demanding the economic benefits to be gained from this deal (marked increase in food aid). On the other hand, all actions in alignment with the United States (on Afghanistan and the boycott of the 1980 Olympic Games in Moscow) were presented as acts of Kenyan sovereignty, and not related to any sort of alignment. Significantly, Nairobi announced its boycott of the Moscow Games two days before the arrival of an American delegation sent to persuade it not to go to the Soviet Union.[78] The contrast between Mogadishu, which took on the East-West conflict to promote its regional interests, and Nairobi, which tried to use this same conflict without taking it on, can be largely explained by internal and regional considerations. On the domestic level, Kenya's economic prosperity, reliant on close economic and cultural ties with the West and especially with the United States,[79] very naturally drew its leaders to come up with a balance or a cover for some of this reality through acts of national affirmation. This prudent attitude was undeniably reinforced by the objective complicity that linked Nairobi and Addis Ababa concerning Somali irredentism. Kenya was therefore better off tempering its traditional anticommunism so as not to block a regional alliance that was indispensable to Ethiopia. Kenya's leaders had, moreover, just signed their agreement with the United States when they conspicuously welcomed Colonel Mengistu. They then asked Somalia to renounce its territorial claims on Ethiopia, Kenya, and Djibouti, and jointly recommended to its arms suppliers that they suspend their shipments.[80]

The integrating function. Since the beginning of the eighties and the Reagan administration, the United States aid policy appears increasingly subtended by a free market doctrine. There is a systematic effort to channel American aid strategy in three directions: to link the United States' financing activity with the strategies of financial institutions (the World Bank and IMF); to rationalize the commitment of Western aid donors by developing programs for the coordination of bilateral aid in close relation with multilateral financial institutions and private banks; and finally to tighten the link between the size of aid programs and a dismantling of the public sector, to the increasing benefit of the private sector.

The increasingly definite movement of African states toward the tutelage of international financial institutions constitutes a major constraint on their international behavior. Confronted with a dramatic fall in their own finances, as many as twenty-one of them in 1982 found themselves forced to accept the painfully humiliating IMF terms, as opposed to only two in 1978. An even more striking fact is that the World Bank's new strategy, outlined in the Berg report, more and more obviously espouses the IMF model of adjustment. In numerous cases (Kenya, the Ivory Coast, Malawi, and Senegal), this type of intervention by the World Bank is explicitly conditional on the preliminary signing of an agreement with the IMF: "More and more, the conditionality employed by each of the two institutions respectively tends to combine so as to give all its force to a policy of neoliberal rehabilitation."[81] With an underlying logic of integration into the world market, the IMF–World Bank approach has defined its involvement on two levels. The first has been to try to hasten the dismantling of economic systems maintained by overvalued monetary parities. In the end, its purpose has been to rationalize the development of African economies on the basis of comparative advantages (development of export agriculture and abandonment of industrial projects aimed at substitution for imports). Such strategies have been actively advocated by the IMF and the World Bank, even in those countries once held up as paragons of free market liberalism, like the Ivory Coast or Kenya.

One can add to this first objective a second one meant to challenge the well-established premises of development strategy hitherto accepted by nearly all of the African states: halting and then reducing the growing role played by the national government in economic life, either by directing the influx of foreign aid directly to the private sector or by financing operations to transfer activity of the public sector to the private sector. For the most part, American bilateral aid has followed this logic. AID programs have insisted more and more explicitly on a preliminary definition of policy reform with the beneficiary states. The development of the ESF reflected the thrust of the Berg report, for which "nonproject" aid constituted an effective mode of economic intervention. In Kenya the (1985) ESF program was largely intended to finance the privatization of the cereal trade and the liberalization of commercial procedures. In Senegal, where in 1985 seventy percent of American aid was "nonproject," AID intervened to support a stand-by agreement signed with the IMF in July 1983. In Zimbabwe, finally, most of the ESF aid was devoted to financing American imports, of which eighty percent was obligatorily allotted to the private sector.[82]

AID wanted to extend this effort to coherent action by all Western partners, calling for their commitment to the development of coordinated bilateral aid. An approach such as this would allow American assistance both to concentrate its activity in those sectors it is best equipped to deal with (food agriculture, health, etc.), as well as to gain entry into those areas where it has not traditionally been well established. As best as one can tell, the function of coordinating health issues given to the United States within the Development Assistance Committee (DAC) in Africa facilitated AID penetration into francophone Africa. By having a principle of coordination of Western aid in each Sahel country approved in 1984, the United States managed, on AID's own terms, to "exert more influence on the development of the Sahel region than that which its contribution [alone] would allow."[83] In the end, the United States' purpose would be to develop an "integrated approach" for each African country that would take into account debt renegotiation, bilateral assistance programs, and domestic economic recovery plans.[84] This approach, inaugurated in 1983 in Sudan, eventually spread to countries where intervention by AID or international financial institutions, or both, was locally significant (Kenya, Senegal, Liberia). Thus, by favoring more and more overtly the macroeconomic logic of the IMF and the World Bank, founded on coherent models, tools of analysis, and statistical operations, American strategy works to distribute its free market neoliberal ideology at the expense of more or less competing logic.

Already in francophone Africa, where France's preeminence had been largely established, the World Bank has managed to dethrone France in the financing of investment aid and "nonproject" loans.[85] If the United States ever were to achieve such an evolution, it would not fail to convert this precious advantage into a political trump card when the time came.

To this date, American economic penetration of black Africa has not provided any spectacular results. The American-African commercial dynamic rests essentially on oil, upon which the United States is less and less dependent. As for American exports, they remain squarely blocked by the financial crisis in nearly all of these countries, as well as the rise of the dollar, and "countertrade" practices (compensation trade) prohibited by American legislation. As much for trade as for investments, the Republic of South Africa still seems today the only truly booming market for American operators, even if recent developments in South Africa seem to be of the sort to shatter such confidence.[86]

This overall view cannot, however, hide America's patient effort to become entrenched economically. This effort can be seen in the United States government's deliberate involvement as the main coordinator of public and private initiatives on this continent. It is also part of the breakthrough of American nongovernmental organizations (NGOs) into sectors as notable as agricultural training and unions, involvement by American banks, and the intensification of oil exploration, notably in East Africa.

The recent signing of bilateral investment treaties with Senegal, Zaire, Cameroon, and perhaps soon with Burundi, Gabon, and the Ivory Coast, demonstrates a desire to formalize African-American economic relations. This effort is reinforced by the development of a network of commercial attachés, by the progress of Overseas Private Investment Corporation (OPIC) commitments, seventy percent of which are concentrated in Africa, and by increased activity of the Trade and Development Board. Created at the initiative of the American government in 1980, this program was meant to help American investors identify projects and potentially take over certain markets. Today twenty percent of its commitments are located in Africa.

This coordinating activity, propelled by the federal government, was carried out in conjunction with a selection of private African operators as direct partners of the United States. The strong interest that AID has developed in this sector has enabled it to finance certain projects and to provide in the same action a whole panoply of services and advice in matters related to management and export. Even more than financial commitments, progress in the areas of information collection, training, and audit attests to the strengthening of America's economic presence. Thus OPIC recently set up a program to assist African states to simplify their rulings in relation to import matters and reduce restrictions on the establishment of foreign firms.

In this effort to coordinate and rationalize, state actors are sometimes powerfully assisted or relieved by a growing network of foundations and charitable and religious organizations. Among them, the very recent African Development Foundation, created by Congress, has come to play a more important role. Financing a small number of essentially agricultural economic projects, it has set itself the goal of making its financial contribution in Africa reach $100 million by 1989.

As for American nongovernmental organizations, more than one hundred twenty of them are, in one way or another, active in Africa. Recent African famines have indeed clearly illustrated the importance of their role. In Ethiopia, where the country's authorities look askance at all Reagan administration initiatives, the very same authorities are helping channel American food supplies. They are also the same ones who have limited the political profit that the Addis Ababa regime sought to gain from the famine to put down the Tigre and Eritrea "rebellions."

As far as training is concerned, organizations such as the African American Labor Center (affiliated with the AFL-CIO), foundations, and universities are all constantly developing programs, meetings, visits, and scholarships. Most of the overseas activity, for example, of a foundation like the Carnegie Corporation of New York is devoted to financing operations and studies focused on Africa. These various actions increasingly receive AID assistance, since AID does not want to see training become a Soviet monopoly.

The growing involvement of banks is also a dimension of American influence worth noting. Even if its credits of the African banking sector do not exceed thirty percent of all foreign banks' assets in Africa, the influence of American banks is no longer negligible, and it is undoubtedly intensified by the progressive "dollarization" of African states' debt. This evolution, significant even in Franc Zone states, makes African economies more sensitive to the rhythms of the American economy. This vulnerability is even more perceptible in that three of the five tropical product exchanges (coffee, cocoa, cotton) are located in the United States. The oil exploration and production sector constitutes another dominant axis of the American economic presence in Africa, even if, as we have seen, United States oil dependence on the continent keeps on shrinking. In western Africa (except in Gabon and the Congo), American oil companies are the most active ones. They produce approximately half of Cameroon's and Nigeria's oil and two-thirds of Angola's oil. In East Africa the activity of these companies is increasingly based on a high-risk exploration strategy.

The Disappointing Results of American Aid*

Between 1963 and 1984, sixty percent of bilateral American aid was aimed at the agricultural sector and rural development, a considerable amount. It is twice the average involvement of other backers in this sector. Such concentration, however, did not enable AID to achieve better results.

*This section was written in 1989 for the American edition.

According to certain unofficial estimates, a third of financed projects have had nearly no impact. As for the other financed projects, they have never managed to function at more than seventy-five percent of capacity once financial support was withdrawn.[87]

Very often the course AID took proved to be disproportionate and overly optimistic. This tendency is particularly striking in all the involvement based on increased production through development of agricultural or agronomic research. A confidential evaluation of AID in Kenya noted that of thirty-seven hypotheses made about a livestock project, fifteen at the very least were arguable.[88] In Cameroon the North Cameroon Seed Multiplication Project, intended to develop a system of production and distribution of improved seeds, rested on the ability of researchers to offer varieties of breeder seeds for five types of cultivation and to enable peasants to benefit from them, all within a five-year period. In fact, it seemed that the simple fact of creating these seeds took, in the best of cases, at least six years. In Senegal a project to develop irrigated cultivation anticipated reaping seven tons of rice per hectare, even though it had never surpassed four tons per hectare anywhere else in Africa.

Poor knowledge in the cycles of research does not explain everything. It very often works hand in hand with failure to use results already available or with simple lack of knowledge of the area. Thus in Senegal the technological packages proposed by AID under the aegis of the Casamance Regional Project recommended that peasants adopt measures they had, in fact, already been using for many years. An AID report noted ironically that the peasants had been urged "to use organic manure and to keep their animals in corrals inside their fields. There is no problem with this plan because it is a custom anyway."[89] The technological packages designed to increase cultivation productivity through logic were conceived in the abstract, as if such an objective could not help but attract peasant participation. As it happened, things turned out to be more complex, not because the peasants would not accept "modernity," but because a certain number of constraints had been splendidly ignored by the designers of these projects. In western Africa, for example, where manual labor is more scarce than soil, a peasant will naturally hesitate to opt for techniques to increase cultivation. The reluctance of Senegalese peasants to undertake irrigated rice cultivation and abandon millet or sorghum stems from an eminently economic calculation. Rice requires three times the labor force of corn or sorghum. It also requires between three and four more times as much water.

The same lack of knowledge about local constraints is also illustrated in the North Cameroon Livestock and Agricultural Development Project.[90] At the beginning, it entailed combating overgrazing by displacing the areas customarily used by nomads during their seasonal migrations. As it was,

Cameroonian authorities were aware of problems. The fact is they were only interested in the project to the extent that it would promote the sinking of wells and help nomads benefit from veterinary services. Instead of taking into account the numerous objections raised about its "deferred grazing" project, AID became stubborn. As is often the case in such situations, opposition by local authorities was not straightforward in character. It took the form of passive resistance (a considerable delay in training the local cadres needed to manage the project), which inevitably led to the total failure of the operation. Again, the temporal dimensions of economic and social change were tragically underestimated. With the help of a "good" project, it was thought, one could rationalize grazing practices, whereas fifteen to twenty years might be needed to put a new transhumance system to work.

None of these problems is particular to AID. The World Bank, for example, has encountered similar obstacles. Indeed, it would be difficult to find a source of funding that could foster better results. This sad fact should nonetheless not obscure certain successes of AID achieved in the specific area of agricultural training. In Nigeria, Cameroon, and Malawi, this sector represented an average fifty percent of American aid to agriculture. In Nigeria the American model of the land grant university was tested at the Nsukka, Kano, and Ife Universities. At Nsukka the demand had clearly come during the 1950s from Dr. Azikiwe, who had sought to counter the influence of the British; but for the most part, these projects consisted in establishing superior agricultural training units and research through the technical assistance of an American university.

The first American university to engage in this type of operation was the University of Michigan, which has continued since then to develop its research on agriculture in Africa. Thanks specifically to AID support, Ahmadu Bello University today is endowed with a good veterinary medicine and agricultural school linked to three agronomic research institutes and four agricultural schools. Paradoxically, AID's greatest achievement took place in a country no longer benefiting from bilateral American aid. Such achievement is probably a result of AID's know-how in this sector and of the close ties between official aid and American universities. But this explanation is not sufficient. In the case of Ahmadu Bello University, it is the conjunction of multiple factors that explains the operation's success. What is immediately striking is the duration and constancy of American support (fourteen consecutive years between 1964 and 1978), considering that American aid generally suffers many, many discontinuities. In the second place, Ahmadu Bello University did not materialize out of nowhere. There had been an agricultural institute in this region since 1922. The University of Kansas, which managed the project, was therefore naturally able to adapt the land grant model to preexisting conditions, whereas in general the temptation of funders is to impose their own ready-made models when they create institutes *ex nihilo*. In addition, it appears that American veterinary medicine was transferable to Nigeria without any major modifications—certainly not the case with, for example, ranching techniques. If one adds to all of this the high quality of personnel sent by the University of Kansas, the support of the project from Nigerian authorities, and the judicious complementarity between AID and the other sources of funding involved, one must conclude that a project's success will always arise from a series of linked effects that is rarely accidental. There exists a dynamics of success, just as there exists a dynamics of failure.[91]

Agricultural training has been and remains one of the strengths of American aid in Cameroon, and AID has indeed understood that well. In 1984 this sector absorbed more than half of the bilateral American aid to Cameroon, whereas in 1981 it only amounted to two percent. The example of the agricultural University of Dschang, by far the shining gem of American aid to Cameroon, demonstrates today nonetheless that the local context overrides the know-how or experience of the funding source. Indeed, although the project was not yet finished in 1988, it seems difficult to detect in it signs of a new success story comparable to that of Ahmadu Bello University. In fact, support for this project is only planned to last seven years, whereas in the Nigerian case, the University of Kansas's fifteen-year presence was not excessive. One can also wonder if AID did not agree to participate in too broad an operation for the needs of the country. The Dschang project should enable Cameroon to enroll eighty students for every million inhabitants, where twenty-six would be entirely sufficient. There is therefore a risk of training cadres who will have trouble finding employment, or, conversely, the risk of difficulties attracting enough students to a university that has the drawback of not being multidisciplinary. Whatever the hypothesis, the project was ill advised, especially if one takes into account the residual responsibilities it will have to shoulder once foreign aid has been terminated. Whatever the case, the example of Cameroon emphasizes the advantages that American aid seems to have in aiming at agricultural training, even if it entails limiting the number of projects. Its visibility is broad and its political consequences not negligible, as indicated in the accompanying table.

A report ordered by AID proposed in 1985 that American involvement be intensified in the area of agricultural research in Africa, yet limiting that involvement to a small set of universities and international organs such as the International Institute of Tropical Agriculture, thirty percent of whose resources come from AID.[92]

American assistance in Africa is thus headed toward increasingly selective aid activity at a time when bilateral aid to that continent has again begun to diminish, while at the core of this very modest effort, concern with development is declining more and more. The number of projects has

Table 7   Current Employment of Selected Cameroonian AID Trainees

Field of Study	Present location
Biology	Vice-Minister of Education
Animal Science	Director, regional agriculture school
Economics	Minister of Commerce and Industry
Economics	Director General, National Council of Transporters
Agriculture	Provincial Chief of Services for Agricultural Statistics, MIDENO
Poultry husbandry	Director, Institute for Animal Research
Education	Secretary-General of Faculty of Sciences, University of Yaounde
Government	Minister of Transport
Agriculture	Station chief, Institute for Agricultural Research
Business Administration	National Investment Corporation
Agricultural economics	Ministry of Planning and Industry
Agriculture	Manager, Cameroon Development Corporation
Educational administration	Vice-Minister of Agriculture
Business administration	Director of the National Railway Corporation
Mathematics	Data Office, Presidency
Agricultural economics	Director of ENSA (Ecole Nationale Supérieure Agronomique)
Agricultural economics	Professor, University of Yaounde
Agricultural economics	Director of Agricultural Education, Ministry of Agriculture
Biochemistry	DGRST (Délégation Générale à la Recherche Scientifique et Technique
Business administration	Director of Finance, National Investment Corporation

Source: AID/Cameroon's own directory of past and current participants. The difficulties in tracking these people are formidable, therefore, this list is likely to be incomplete or in some cases out of date.

thus dropped from sixty-three in 1985 to thirty-three in 1987. Despite support for a policy of comparative advantage, AID is showing increasing reluctance to finance projects intended to promote African exports for fear of competing with American production.[93] That is, moreover, perhaps the only difference between AID and the World Bank. Otherwise the United States continues to adhere to the joint strategy of the IMF and the World Bank in Africa, even if, for obscure reasons, the Kemp-Kasten amendment recommends that AID not submit explicitly to the IMF's conditions.[94] That said, the coherence of AID's free-market liberal discourse should create no illusions. Like any institution of similar scope, AID cannot avoid traditional, bureaucratic conflicts and internal debates. The free-market liberal message may be accepted by all, but there is no unanimity about the modalities of implementation. An appreciable number of AID authorities continue to believe in the virtues of agricultural modernization through training in large units, whereas the "official line" points to the advantages of small farms.[95]

Things are even more complicated in the field. There, AID's local missions encounter the classic constraints of all funding agencies: political pressures from Washington or from the ambassador, and pressure from local authorities with whom one must deal constantly. Add to that the necessity for each mission to disburse funds committed officially, which means that policy orientations coming from Washington are felt in the field only several years later. Finally, AID is paralyzed by the control of a bureaucratic and totally ineffective Congress. AID is thus subject to thirty-three objectives, seventy-five "priorities, two hundred and eighty-eight notifications from Congress, and seven hundred notifications on project changes."[96]

In reality, as with all sources of bilateral funding whose aid follows diplomatic-strategic motivation, AID is a victim in Africa of the "paradox of conditionality."

The Paradox of Conditionality

To understand the paradox, one must put things into perspective. Until the beginning of the eighties, international aid had a double, auxiliary function. The point was to reassure political allies and beyond that to reinforce the actual hold of the state over economic life and society. The social and political sacrifices required of leadership groups were slim. To be sure, during the seventies we witnessed AID following the World Bank in the development of projects favoring the most needy social groups; but on the whole this course of action failed. Integrated development projects in fact reinforced the rural areas' clientage to the state. As for the reformed networks ("sites and services"), in most cases, they were redirected to the benefit of functionaries.[97]

At the beginning of the eighties, things changed. Aid projects were called into question. Priority was given to macroeconomic reform. This was a fundamental change. Henceforth, diplomatic loyalty no longer constituted the only compensation for bilateral aid. What was demanded of African countries was the right to keep an eye on the management of their public finances and their investment programs, as well as on rule changes concerning political power and economic wealth. In the plea for the rehabilitation of market indices is the demand for extinction of economic clientage as manifest in the overcomplement of public enterprises and subsidies of urban consumption.

These adjustment policies thus had the effect of displacing the aid's axis of conditionality. This axis moved from a formal and symbolic level (diplomatic or ideological allegiance) to an economic and social level. Now, firing functionaries is infinitely more costly than aligning one's United

Nations vote with Washington's or Moscow's. The stakes are all the higher since in Africa they are trans-ideological. Clientage to the state is no less powerful in Senegal than in Tanzania.

The change of aid strategy, to which AID subscribed fully, is funda-mental; but its importance should not be overestimated for all that. Ten years after launching these adjustment policies, the liberal transformation of Africa seems slow. And here is where the paradox of conditionality comes in, described as follows: the more an African state is of significant political interest to the United States, the more the United States is forced to handle it cautiously, in other words, into easing the rigor of condition-ality. Inversely, in small countries where the means of theoretical Ameri-can pressure are greater and the constraints on action looser, political interest in expending a great deal of energy to achieve results will be quite limited. Kenya represents the first case and Liberia the second, with a host of intermediate situations between the two.

In a series of reports devoted to American aid, the General Accounting Office set forth the difficulty involved in making the ESF an effective in-strument of macroeconomic conditionality in allied countries. The United States had, for example, a great deal of trouble insisting that ESF funds be consigned to a special account whose activity AID could monitor.[98] In Africa's francophone countries and especially in Senegal, this problem is made yet more insoluble by the regional regulation of the Franc Zone. Indeed, once the West Africa Monetary Union (WAMU) converts dollars received from the United States into local currency, AID can in no way control Senegal's use of dollars made through WAMU.[99] The case of Li-beria is even more serious. The country the United States would gladly have converted into a "little model" for western Africa illustrates the dif-ficulties the United States has controlling an otherwise extraordinarily de-pendent country. Here, food aid and ESF funds have systematically been diverted by a "patrimonial" government.[100] Dispatch of a mission of sev-enteen American cadres charged with regaining total control of macro-economic management met with complete failure. Even in a country like Kenya, where the economy is more advanced and market indices are more respected, AID pressure is not always very effective, especially if one re-members that this pressure is closely linked to the World Bank's. To be sure, tangible results have been obtained in exchange rates, interest rates, monetary management, and the foreign deficit. But in politically sensitive sectors, such as the liberalization of fertilizer distribution or the commer-cialization of corn, obstruction has been total. Privatizing the corn trade would not have harmed the state as much as it would the large producers who, through the expedient of governmental licenses, commercialized corn without competition.[101] In reality, as was noted in a report evaluating AID's activities in Kenya, Americans utterly lack pedagogical skills. They

145

try to impose their views rather than take the time to persuade. "Moreover, we have to think more about ways to address other obstacles, for example, the Kenyan preoccupation with political risks and ethnic issues." [102]

Political and social resistance cannot alone explain Africa's very slow conversion to the beat of free-market liberalism. The complexity of the process of liberalization in the agriculture of Mali, in which AID has been involved, offers eloquent testimony. The Cereals Market Restructuring Program had a triple objective: to privatize grain commerce; to improve the incentives for producers; and, finally, to reduce subsidies to OPAM, the State Cereals Marketing Agency. Over the years, the task has proved more difficult than expected, for the terms of the liberal equation had perhaps been oversimplified. It was realized, for example, that price incentives were not necessarily adapted to a country where eighty percent of grain production is in fact consumed there and where the critical production variable is rain. A report made for AID summarizes the problems well:

> Most Malian families are small-scale, coarse grain producers. Their food production is limited primarily by the adequacy of rainfall, their allocation of labor, and their ability to use animal traction or other yield-enhancing technologies. Most of the grain they produce is retained for family consumption. Since family food security is a priority, surpluses are often stored. Three consecutive years of drought were particularly disruptive for these farmers; many of their limited savings and assets were lost or sold, reducing their capacity to increase output. Furthermore, opportunities for farmers to capitalize on high grain prices were limited, first by the lack of surpluses during the drought and then by OPAM's inability to sustain price supports. For these reasons, the link between price and marketing policy reforms, and coarse grain output was weak. [103]

In the area of trade privatization, results have been ambiguous. The state gave up its monopoly on grain trade; but this measure was largely symbolic to the extent that effectively ninety percent of operations were underwritten by private merchants. The liberalization of the rice trade, however, was far slower, notably because of the authorities' concern for protecting urban consumption from the rigors of another price increase. In addition, the state remained in charge of granting or refusing commercial licenses on importation. All of these factors combined mean that liberalization has had no impact on the volume of commercial grain. Finally, the public sector's taking over from the private sector, where commercialization is concerned, stems as much from the state's resistance to reducing its control as from the extraordinary weakness of the private sector. It was to take five years before AID would decide to participate in the stimulation of this sector by opening lines of credit that had been cruelly lacking.

It is still too early, and anyway very difficult, to draw the bottom line on economic reform policies in Africa and to measure their implications for American policy. What becomes apparent nevertheless is the absence of a causal relation between the economic performance of an African country and its links to the United States—first of all, because bilateral American aid has an auxiliary function and not a driving role in the economic reform of states, and, second, because there exists no direct, or at any rate immediate, causality between the "liberal reformism" of a country and the state of its political relations with Washington. In states with a patrimonial structure such as Zaire or Liberia, results are small, if not nil. With Washington's new clients of the 1980s, such as Sudan and Somalia, results are just as modest, despite the relatively important role of bilateral American aid. Liberia, Sudan, and Somalia, moreover, are considered "weak performers" where reform is concerned. Of this group, only Kenya seems to have made it. But in no way can the result be attributed to, or claimed by, Washington. For the United States, Kenya's relative economic stability is counterbalanced by the worrisome changes in its political regime. As a matter of fact, the two countries with the most promising economic reforms are Nigeria and Ghana; but AID is no longer involved in Nigeria, and in Ghana it is largely encompassed within the World Bank. In the case of Nigeria, moreover, a renewal of the American bilateral aid program would not make much sense. Washington's political support of Lagos in the context of the Brady Plan or a renewal of private American investment would have an impact superior to an aid program.

In reality, there is no incentive for the United States as a state to direct economic effort toward Africa. The reduction of economic assistance projects underscores AID's concern with sticking to a particular number of operations. The considerable drop in ESF allocations and their reduction to simple financial transfers confirms this shift, as well as the absence of illusions about the chances of influencing the economic policy of an African state in any spectacular way. As measured during the 1985 research in Ethiopia, where American action had important political content, food aid did not turn out to be terribly effective. To cap the disappointment, this aid did not convert African countries into importers of American agricultural products.[104]

Strategic Perceptions and Military Assistance

The persistence of certain truisms cannot hide the major reality: for ten years, American strategic interests in Africa have hardly been shaken. At the very moment the Soviet-Cuban presence was spreading to Ethiopia, the Joint Chiefs of Staff conceded that this presence did not yet represent a direct threat to American interests.[105] With the strengthening of American power in the Indian Ocean and the quite noticeable reduction of the Cuban contingent in Ethiopia, it is not rash to envision a potential diminution in this threat. Africa, moreover, ranks last on America's list of geostrategic preoccupations; Washington still does not have an articulated strategic vision of its interests in this part of the world. At most, one can recognize reaffirmation of broad principles concerning the control of maritime routes for communication, the need to guarantee the internal stability of those states that are purveyors of raw materials, and the exclusion of all Soviet influence supported by a direct or indirect military presence. Such an imprecise definition of military force is justified in two ways. First of all, the United States has no tangible interests to defend outside of southern Africa. And for the most part Africa constitutes an area for contingency planning (the Horn) but above all an area for preventive exclusion. Africa is not regarded as a primary strategic site one would want to occupy but as a regional totality in which one would want to keep Moscow to the sidelines. One understands then that American strategic interests essentially flow from perceptions of Soviet involvement in this part of the world.

Globalism or Regionalism: An Apparent Dilemma

In the form it often takes, the debate opposing globalists and regionalists is perhaps poorly presented. As a comanager of the world order, the United States cannot put aside the global dimension in which all Soviet involvement in Africa is inscribed. By the evidence, the Soviet Union profited from American inconsistency and indecision in Angola as in Ethiopia, the same way the United States is now able to profit from the rigidity of Soviet strategy in Africa. That is why the core of the question resides perhaps less in the globalist or regionalist nature of this or that action, than in how these two inseparable planes are articulated. The globalists, generally well represented in the Department of Defense, the National Security Council, and the non-Africanist divisions of the State Department, raise questions about the means to penalize Soviet involvement and suggest using action in extra-African arenas assumed to be more important to the Soviet Union (for instance, linking the signing of the SALT accords to the withdrawal of Cuban forces from Ethiopia). It is recourse to linkage in this very sense that globalists immediately justify by domestic political constraints prohibiting a United States response to Soviet incursions "in the field."

However, it all leads one to think that this essential debate has never been properly clarified by American decision-makers. While the status of the actors in the American bureaucratic system or the influence of their own ideological convictions may determine their globalist or regionalist orientation, this distinction remains a question of sensitivity and not of doctrine. In addition, professions of globalist or regionalist faith often envelop conduct that is not so different.

The regionalist reputation of the Carter administration does not in and of itself make it easier to understand its hesitancy on Angola. For, while the Democrats in power were careful not to link Namibian independence to the withdrawal of Cuban forces stationed in Angola, they also refused to recognize the Angolan regime officially as long as that regime enjoyed Cuban protection. The Carter administration also succumbed to the temptation of adding an extra condition to the Cuban settlement: negotiation of a political arrangement between Luanda and UNITA.[106] In 1978 the White House even seriously considered repeal of the Clark amendment. It only backed down when the Senate expressed vigorous objection.[107]

In the conflict on the Horn, the Carter administration's regionalist approach was more convincing. But the Republican regime that replaced the Carter administration remained quite prudent. The Reagan administration, playing out its African "anything-goes" policy in southern Africa, never seriously raised the issue of Cuban forces stationed in Ethiopia. The irony of the story is that Cuba has mostly completed its withdrawal from Ethiopia while it continues to hang on in Angola.

In fact, the choice of and the benefits gleaned from either approach result much less from deliberate intention than from the power relationships imposed both by the African and by the global contexts. The relative victories of the Carter administration in Africa were recorded during the most regionalist phase of its mandate. But since 1981 it has been a more globalist approach that has assured Washington of some advantages in Africa.

The Perception of the Soviet "Push"

Since the colonization of lusophone Africa and the Ogaden war, the United States has wondered about the Soviet Union's African motives, about the coherence of its strategic design, and finally about the receptivity of its African allies to the "Soviet model" and their ability to disengage from it. Again, the answers that have been proposed have hardly been clear-cut, especially since the constraints of diplomatic action impose a sort of double-talk on Washington. To convince Congress or to express its determination regarding the Soviet Union, the United States thinks that there is some advantage in exaggerating Soviet penetration to the point of caricature, in denying Cuba's autonomy of action, and in insisting on the dangers of an irreversible Soviet presence. But this discussion often coexists with another one that glorifies the historical superiority of liberalism over socialism. It might thus invoke the Soviet Union's inability to offer its allies anything other than arms and might suggest a pessimistic prognosis for the solidity of any alliance between an African state and the

Soviet Union. But the whole ideological discussion does not sum up all of American policy. The Reagan administration—a prisoner of unshakably anticommunist convictions—has never seriously considered the Angolan regime an African extension of Moscow.[108] And even when its rhetoric enjoyed going as far as denouncing the Soviet "empire" in Africa or the enfeoffment of Cuba to the Soviet Union, its diplomatic practice showed that, for Washington, the key to withdrawal of Cuban troops from Angola was to be found in Luanda rather than in Moscow.[109]

Given that, the traditional split between official declarations and kid-gloved diplomacy cannot be excessively overestimated. The conflicts within the Angolan regime were for a long time viewed in Washington through a prism that reduced the number of participants to only two: partisans and adversaries of the withdrawal of Cuban troops. It was only after long and arduous direct negotiations with Luanda that the United States was forced to modify its initial position without, however, renouncing its primary objective: to obtain the withdrawal of Cuban troops.

Finally, United States appraisal of Soviet influence in Africa may need to define the threshold of incompatibility between Soviet and American interests in black Africa. But, as useless as it may seem to expect the United States to explicitly or publicly specify this threshold, it also seems difficult to believe that it could avoid doing so. American diplomatic discourse and behavior suggest that the broad scope of organic relations between Africa and the West has been considered the major obstacle to the success of Soviet implantation. But, to admit the possibility of coexistence between American and Soviet interests in an implicit division of labor (with soviets to the Soviet Union and electrification to the West) would amount either to entrenching a *de facto* situation or to depriving oneself of being able to object to such "sharing." Should the United States give up on demanding the withdrawal of Cuban troops just because American oil interests in Angola happen paradoxically to be protected by Cuban troops? This solution, implicitly suggested by the Soviet Union throughout Africa, has been rejected by Washington. However, if the United States seemed to be inclined to reject such a compromise in the specific case of Angola, other comparable situations on the African continent did not afford them such a clear-cut choice.

In fact, the difficulty for the United States has been rooted in its inability to circumscribe the extent of Soviet "control" over certain African regimes. Between using the Soviet Union as a symbolic stake or source of legitimation by African powers and the direct involvement of the Soviet Union in these same states' political struggles, there exist an infinity of configurations that the United States perhaps does not always manage to grasp.

This margin of indeterminacy simultaneously reflects the unknown character of Soviet-Cuban influence in Africa, the mediocrity of American thought on African societies and their position in the international system, as well as the relative misunderstanding of the social fabric of Africa. American diplomacy has therefore limited itself in the meantime to the principle of a "zero-sum game," wherein any advantage gained by the Soviet Union is deemed negative for American interests.

Military assistance and global contingency planning. In many regards, the United States has seemed handicapped in crossing swords with the "Red Army" in Africa. The rigidity of the legislative straitjacket and the weight of public opinion have made prolonged involvement rather improbable. On the other hand, mounting a quick and pointed response (Grenada for example) is included in the "horizontal strategy" advocated by the Reagan administration. The French-American crises of the summer of 1983 and winter of 1984 on Chad did indeed clearly reveal how very few African areas escape the strategic vigilance of the United States.

On a strictly military level, however, the United States has still remained a small purveyor of arms to sub-Saharan Africa, as much because of legislative constraints as because of the poor financial means of potential clients. For the most part, arms transfer to black Africa requires use of the channels of bilateral assistance. Between 1976 and 1980 all transfers to southern Africa did not exceed $385 million, while the Soviet Union's transfers are said to have reached $4 billion.[110] But this imbalance, which the United States evokes with the regularity of a metronome to vilify "Soviet militarism," only corresponds to one aspect of reality. As soon as one compares the respective military efforts of each of the superpowers with the military effort of all NATO countries together or all Warsaw Pact countries together, the imbalance decreases. In the period in question (1976–80), NATO transfers are said to have totaled $2.6 billion, as compared to the Warsaw Pact transfers totaling $4.1 billion.

Table 8   Arms Transfers to Black Africa (1976–1980)
(as % of total)

Suppliers		Beneficiaries	
Soviet Union	47.6	Ethiopia	27.3
France	10.4	Angola	11.3
Federal Republic		Somalia	8.9
of Germany	6.5	Sudan	6.8
Italy	6.2	Tanzania	5.5
United States	4.5	Others	40.2
Others	24.8		

Source: World Military Expenditures and Arms Transfers 1971–1980, DAC, 1983.

While still very modest, America's military presence in Africa, how-ever, has not ceased to intensify. The United States, which once refused to take responsibility for the training of African military cadres, is now anx-ious to make up its lag in this area behind the Soviets. In 1983 the number of African trainees reached an unimpressive 852. But compared to the figures of the seventies (239 in 1975), the increase seems remarkable.

Just as significant is the blurring of the traditional separation between military efforts and economic assistance. As of now, the complementarity of these two tools is well demonstrated in the "security assistance" pro-grams designating both ESF and military assistance programs. One would not be surprised therefore to find the list of military aid beneficiaries more and more neatly a carbon copy of a list of recipients of economic assis-tance. Sudan, Kenya, and Somalia alone received three-quarters of the American military loans granted to black Africa between 1981 and 1984.

Nevertheless Washington has accepted this military effort in the context of a perspective that extends considerably beyond African borders. For about ten years now, the United States has addressed itself to the military means of counteracting Soviet political involvement in the Third World and protecting its own access to Persian Gulf oil resources. As early as August 1977, while Soviet-Cuban forces had not yet entered Ethiopia, President Carter ordered study of a development project for a rapid deploy-ment force. But this plan, just barely conceived, ran up against the inertia of both the Department of State and the Department of Defense. The ac-celeration of events in southwest Asia (the Iranian and Afghani revolu-tions) nonetheless forced the executive branch to react vigorously. In the summer of 1979, several months before the hostages were taken in Teheran and the Soviet invasion of Afghanistan, the Rapid Deployment Joint Task Force (RDJTF) was officially established.

In the American mind, the creation of the RDJTF ought to enable the United States to make up for its political handicap with respect to the So-viet Union in the Indian Ocean region. It also fit in with the declared desire to restore the political credibility of the United States in this area after so many misunderstandings. Since 1980, $871 million have been allocated by Congress to develop a network of military facilities (matériel stockpiles, mooring rights, landing and air reconnaissance rights) in Egypt, Kenya, Oman, and Somalia, and to increase the permanent presence of the United States in Diego Garcia. This vast program, which will only be completed in 1989, has already had a considerable impact on American strategy. Shifting the RDJTF to autonomous command constitutes the most impor-tant conventional military effort ever made by the United States since the creation'of NATO. Its aim is to make the RDJTF the fourth pillar of an American global strategy (on a par with the nuclear triad, NATO forces, and the Navy) and to situate the American military set-up within a "two wars" hypothesis and no longer only in a "one-and-a-half wars" hypothesis.[111] This renewal of strategic interest has worked hand in hand with a redefinition of the content of relations between the United States and certain select African partners.

Redefining American-African Relations: The Case of Nigeria

The dynamics of American-Nigerian relations suffice to illustrate the redefinition of American-African relations in the aftermath of the Angolan crisis. On one hand, there is the American desire to ensure a more stable and stronger footing in Africa. On the other hand, there is the Nigerian concern to make the best of the renewal of American interest in Africa in a direction favorable to its own interests. But the singularity of American-Nigerian relations does not stop there. Both sides envisage construction of a network of stable relations, not only out of diplomatic convergence but also taking into account real economic complementarity and numerous ideological affinities.

America's economic gamble in Nigeria can be explained both by the strategic value of oil imports and by the considerable weight acquired for the first time by an African state in America's international economic relations. In 1978 Nigeria was not only America's second largest source for oil imports, it was also the seventh largest foreign supplier in the United States economy.

Until the end of the seventies, Nigerian oil offered the triple advantages of quality, proximity, and security. The fact that Nigeria did not belong to the Arab world and the vital importance of oil for its economy encouraged American operators to consider their Nigerian oil supply serenely stable.[112] In addition, the extent of Nigeria's domestic market was perceived as essential to American economic penetration into black Africa. The Carter administration, as originator of this approach, quickly evaluated the long-term political benefits that it might gain. In its eyes, American economic success in Nigeria would have a stimulating effect on all American investors potentially interested in the African market. It would then prefigure a redeployment of the flow of investments by South Africa in the rest of black Africa. As Soweto events were shaking Pretoria, the gamble did not seem to be all that wild.

Above all economic, the American gamble in Nigeria was also political. It took into account the unprecedented activism of Nigerian diplomacy, its voluntarism, and its influence as the head of the ACP (African, Caribbean, and Pacific Countries) in 1973 and later at the creation of ECOWAS (CEDEAO). But it was especially the Angolan crisis of 1975 that revealed the full measure of Nigeria's ambitions. The initial prudence it demonstrated concerning inter-Angolan rifts arose from its fears of witnessing the birth of a new secession in Africa and also from the differences among its leaders. Despite the pro-FNLA sympathies of the head of Nigerian diplomacy, the Lagos government ended up consenting to aid the MPLA on the order of $20 million in November 1975. Three months later, it used its decisive influence on its OAU peers to admit the Popular Republic of Angola into the pan-African organization. This diplomatic affirmation, conducted on a foundation of anti-Americanism, ruined the credibility of Henry Kissinger's actions in Angola and silenced the echoes of his Lusaka speech. The Lagos government refused—indeed, three times—to welcome Kissinger, even if the facts suggest that its opposition to American policy was more measured.[113]

A Complementarity of Interests

The Carter administration's reevaluation of American-Nigerian relations took two directions. Lagos's diplomatic radicalism was no longer perceived as a hindrance to American policy (with "nuisance value") but as a political resource likely to restore, in the eyes of the Front Line States, a potential American-Nigerian initiative. Washington's optimism was then fed by the indisputable anchoring of Lagos in the Western system and the existence in that country of pro-American cultural potential, whose expression had been thus far restricted by the awkwardness of America's African policy. To a large extent, the terms of this rapprochement, as outlined by Washington, overlapped with Nigerian preoccupations of the moment. As a young economic power, Nigeria had every reason to consolidate its position in the vast, stable, and profitable American market. Even in periods favorable to producing nations (1974–79), Nigeria had always had a difficult time diversifying its sales outside of the United States. Besides oil, Nigeria also relied on increasing interest in natural gas, in which it counted on interesting American operators. Alongside economic concerns were political calculations that bear witness to the vitality of the African strategy of readopting bipolarity. Indeed, of all black African states, it is Nigeria that best understood the heretofore structural nature of the commitment of the superpowers in Africa. It was also one of the first states to measure the benefits to be gleaned from this new arrangement. While showing some hostility toward interference by the superpowers in Africa, it did not hesitate to channel their involvement in ways that remained favorable to its own interests. It refused to condemn Soviet-Cuban intervention in Angola and Ethiopia. In southern Africa, it militated for stronger diplomatic involvement of the United States.

The balance that Nigeria tried to maintain between the two superpowers nevertheless rested on a false symmetry. The militant positions it adopted on the African scene (refusal to condemn Soviet-Cuban intervention, political support of Angola, and adherence to the Front Line) all follow strict consideration of national interest. They usefully enabled Lagos to obscure certain domestic and diplomatic choices of a pro-Western bent. Poorly disposed toward Great Britain and France, whom it saw as wielding only little influence, Nigeria perceived the United States as the sole international actor able to bring about the peaceful break-up of white domination of southern Africa. From the United States it therefore expected a sustained commitment in this region and official recognition of Nigerian preeminence on the whole of the continent. On this last point, Nigeria's comparative perception of its relations with the superpowers is noteworthy: In dealing with the Soviet Union, it gets the impression of dealing with a state that is prepared to consider several options and a state that is cognizant of the status of Nigeria as an influential African state.[114]

Channeling Nigeria's Rise to Power

It was the prospect of settlements in Zimbabwe and Namibia that sealed the American-Nigerian alliance in February 1977. Even if Lagos continued to affirm its support of armed struggle in southern Africa, the differences between the two countries on this issue seemed to be more verbal than real. In fact, if Lagos pressed Washington to act, it was precisely because Nigeria thought that the armed struggle was at an impasse.[115] The obvious interest in the history of American civil rights struggles expressed by top-level Nigerian leaders was quickly interpreted by Washington as indicating Nigerian moderation.[116]

The rules of the new American-Nigerian game were therefore quickly determined. At the United Nations, the United States conspicuously sponsored Nigeria's candidacy to the Security Council, even if it meant treading on the sensibilities of the African group that favored Niger. In the plan for Zimbabwe worked out with London in the spring of 1977, the American government suggested without flinching that Lagos be associated with the constitution of a United Nations Peacekeeping Force. Impatient to create a new image for itself in Africa, the United States saw an advantage in linking Nigeria with the fortunes of its plan. More than that, it expected Nigeria to convert African mistrust of the United States into the political capital of confidence.

In concert with Tanzania, Nigeria put all of its pressure on the Patriotic Front to persuade it to approve the Anglo-American initiative. In April 1978 it favored a decisive meeting between the foreign affairs ministers of the Front Line and the American presidential delegation visiting Lagos at the time. It was during this very visit that General Obasanjo committed himself to organizing an initial meeting between the United States and

SWAPO.[117] Through Lagos's diplomatic commitment, the United States found a privileged axis for diplomatic integration into Africa, the surest means of keeping the Soviet Union at a respectable distance and the most useful intermediary for the moderation of demands by the liberation movements.[118] In this respect, SWAPO's reluctant acceptance of the contact group's plan in May 1978 under decisive Nigerian pressure illustrated the accuracy of American expectations. America's concern that Nigeria lend itself to moderation efforts was compounded by its concern that Nigeria's "rise to power" be oriented toward realization of diplomatic arrangements favorable to American interests. When in April 1977 the Carter administration hesitated to come to the aid of President Mobutu, threatened in Shaba, it expediently protected itself behind Nigerian mediation between Luanda and Kinshasa in order to defer its arms deliveries to Zaire. In Chad also, the United States encouraged Nigeria, even if Nigeria cut into the influence of France. Finally, in southern Africa, it tempered the hostile reactions of J. Nyerere, S. Machel, and R. Mugabe to the secret Nkomo-Smith negotiation of August 1978, by taking refuge behind Lagos's backing of the proceedings. Aware that Nigeria might reach the status of military power able to prevent potential Soviet-Cuban intervention, the United States opened its doors to sizable contingents of Nigerian officers.[119]

Unequal Alliance

On the face of it, the problematics of American-Nigerian relations may appear to conform to a simplified schema of independence. Since the dynamics of the relationship were profitable to both parties, the cost of a unilateral break would become prohibitive. Such an interpretation is no longer possible today. In the space of a few years, American-Nigerian relations have lost their intensity.

The apparent interdependence and reciprocal vulnerability have yielded, since the beginning of the eighties, to a situation of "unequal vulnerability and imperfect reciprocity." [120] Nigerian power has crumbled. Its implosion has set off the asymmetrical nature of the American-Nigerian relationship in even greater relief.

Nigeria's rise to power was supposed to have been based on a creative combination of oil power and political voluntarism. But its economic prosperity, founded solely on the worth of its petroleum, made it vulnerable to a reversal of the oil situation. When this began to happen in 1981, Nigerian revenues plummeted by half under the cumulative effect of a drop in the net price and reduced production. The United States was not entirely uninvolved in this reversal. American imports of Nigerian oil fell from 8.8 million barrels per day in 1977 to 4.2 million barrels per day in 1982.[121] This decline, accentuated by the diversification of American imports, relegated Nigeria to the rank of fifth highest supplier of oil in 1982.

Thus, at the very moment when Nigeria particularly hoped to maintain its privileged access to the American market, the United States saw an advantage in reducing its oil dependence. Nigeria's grave economic difficulties did, of course, have almost automatic repercussions in the course of its international conduct. Even in eastern Africa, a likely area for extending its influence, Nigeria did not manage to impose itself as a regional federator. In Liberia, for example, it was the direct involvement of the United States and not Nigeria that facilitated the reinstatement of Monrovia's military regime in the Western lap. But it was in Chad especially that Nigeria proved its impotence. In April 1979, one month after being approached by Chadian factions to guarantee the implementation of the Kano accords, the Nigerian army was asked to pack up. Admittedly, in that amount of time it had demonstrated a lack of discipline and inefficiency.[122] Nigeria's discredit in Chad is today even greater because Lagos's official policy is largely contradicted by Chadian policies in the various states of northern Nigeria.

In other African areas of supposedly active Nigerian involvement, its performance seems yet more modest. From the failure of the Anglo-American plan in December 1978, Nigeria ceased to play an active role in ending the Rhodesian crisis. In the phase that preceded the signing of the Lancaster House accords, intervention by Tanzania, Zambia, and Mozambique seems to have been more decisive—and that despite the Nigerian government's nationalization of British Petroleum interests. In the Namibian conflict, the effacement of Nigeria is just as perceptible. A participant in the Front Line deliberations during 1977–78, Nigeria was now being distanced from them. Luanda's rejection of President Shagari's proposal in 1984 to replace Cuban troops stationed in Angola by armed forces of the Commonwealth confirms the diplomatic marginalization of Nigeria in southern Africa.

In fact, if American-Nigerian relations have been considerably deemphasized over the last few years, it is because both partners have been interacting in a field of asymmetrical forces too powerful to lend themselves to lasting alliances. In Africa, the progress of United States influence has not been necessarily antithetical to the precariousness of its diplomatic strategy.

5

The Soviet Union: Thwarted Plans

Soviet Perceptions and African Expectations

In its appreciation of African reality during the past ten years, the Soviet Union has taken a combination of multiple factors into account: the collapse of the Portuguese colonial empire and the Ethiopian empire, which have both led to the retreat of Western positions and especially of American positions; the development of a certain economic collective nationalism enabled by the success of OPEC during the period between 1973 and 1979; the disappearance of China from the African scene as competing ideological headquarters; and, finally, the development of socialist African experiments claiming Marxist-Leninist inspiration. Even if, since the beginning of the eighties, the Soviet Union has come to temper its optimism under the double impact of American political pressure and the aggravation of the economic crisis that has increased the vulnerability of the African actors, it has always thought first of the future of socialism in Africa.

The disappearance of China from the African scene and the increasing number of socialist experiments have offered Moscow two complementary advantages. Becoming again the sole standard for socialism, the Soviet Union is finding it easier to legitimate here or qualify there any given socialist-inspired African experiment. But as the facts demonstrate, the manner in which the Soviet Union presents and especially decides on its relations with socialist regimes is inspired by the Khrushchevian pragmatism of the sixties. It always relies on a double process of ideological gratification and control wherein the process of exclusion is applied only very exceptionally.

Through the process of "gratification," whose most concrete embodiment is attribution of the label "socialist-oriented" to a given state, the Soviet Union tries to assert the existence of a link between African claims of socialism and its own idea of socialism. It is indeed for that reason that the near-totality of African states explicitly claiming socialism are classed by Moscow in the category of states "of socialist orientation."[1] This pre-occupation is even more clearly confirmed if one looks at the ideological status accorded by the Soviet Union to states claiming not only socialism but also Marxism-Leninism. Indeed, the simple act of claiming Marxism-Leninism entitled Benin and the Congo to be categorized as being "the left wing of socialist orientation," just like Angola, Ethiopia, and Mozambique, even though, in contrast to these three cases, their diplomatic-strategic ties to Moscow are infinitely less secure.[2] In fact, if the Soviet Union has appropriated *a posteriori* all of the formal declarations of Marxism-Leninism in Africa, it is primarily out of a concern not to lend credence to the notion that experiments of this order do not owe anything to Soviet influence. That is why, as Moscow ably seizes upon all of the socialist experiments in Africa, it does not give up its role as ideological censor. While implicitly contributing to the reinforcement of legitimacy of Marxist-Leninist regimes by conferring upon their ideological orientation a particular ("advanced") character, the Soviet Union does not recognize in any of them the qualities characteristic of a socialist state.

For Moscow, the simultaneous employment of ideological acquisition (or reward) with control (or sanction) has been doubly advantageous. The ideological control game has helped it impose upon states of the "left wing of socialist orientation" the conditions for their potential integration into the socialist community. In the rest of Africa and the world, the acquisition process feeds its arguments concerning the "progression and radicalization" of socialist ideas in Africa and thereby legitimates its diplomatic-strategic incursions.

One can best glean what Soviet perceptions are on this subject through research undertaken by Soviet africanists, even if this body of research fails to mention some essential dimensions of Soviet policy (such as its military policy) or expresses them in some highly coded manner.

To analyze African problems of the past ten years, the Soviet Union takes into account what it calls "the attempt of the third form of the power struggle between the two world systems." In the Soviet Union's eyes, the exceptional scope of the "deepening process of national liberation" during the second half of the seventies has significance comparable to the emergence of the world socialist system and to the Soviet Union's accession to strategic parity.[3] The Soviet Union has perceived the signs of this evolution in Vietnam since 1975, as well as in Laos, Cambodia, Afghanistan, Nicaragua, Ethiopia, Mozambique, and Angola.[4]

For the Soviet Union, the meaning of the new configuration is clear: at the same time it erodes the significance of the Third World as a "historical community," it prefigures an increasingly marked differentiation between countries closer to the world socialist system ("countries of socialist orientation") and countries that are increasingly allied with capitalist developed countries ("countries of capitalist orientation").[5]

In Africa, where, other than the Ivory Coast, Kenya, and Nigeria, there really has been no "country of capitalist orientation," the Soviet Union has been inclined to make a priority of the future of socialist orientation. In analyzing this orientation in differentiated terms, Soviet research distinguishes between "popular revolutionary development" and "democratic revolutionary development" also called "national revolutionary development." Thus, for certain analysts, the situations created, for example, in Angola, Mozambique, Ethiopia, and also in Yemen and Afghanistan, all accurately express "the transformation of socialist orientation into a revolutionary process of the popular democratic type."[6] Others, refusing to commit themselves quite as much, only admit to applying the term "popular revolutionary" to Afghanistan alone and prefer applying to the other countries the more restricted label of "democratic revolutionary."[7]

In many regards, this categorization would appear to be purely formal and without any operational value for Soviet policy. In fact, all it does is transpose into coded terms the uncertainty that the Soviet Union has as to the maturity, and therefore the irreversibility, of certain African political experiments. That is why, while some authors might dare to imagine the possibility, for states with a socialist orientation, of near-direct integration into the socialist world system, others would rather insist on hindrances to this evolution: "It would be a serious error to liken the process taking place in noncapitalist developing countries to the process in socialist countries. We should not underestimate factors as important as the power of the working class, the Marxist-Leninist party's leadership, the cancellation of capitalist relations, and the irreversibility of changes in progress."[8]

Soviet africanist research—an ideological expression of Soviet perceptions and their gains in the Third World since the middle of the sixties—appears to be having a more difficult time understanding the concrete processes actually experienced by those countries of a socialist orientation.

Despite an impressive number of analysts, the Institute for Africa, where Soviet africanist research is carried out, is the smallest of the institutes for international research. It is incomparably less prestigious than the Institute for Study of the USA and Canada and infinitely less far-reaching than the Institute for Oriental Studies. Its director, Anatoli Gromyko, son of the head of state, is a newcomer to africanist studies. Originally a specialist on American issues, his knowledge of the African domain seems limited; one perceives it in the conformation of his writings. His predecessor, V. Solodovnikov, who was more familiar with African realities, acquired international notoriety by becoming the Soviet representative in Lusaka in the mid-sixties. But his conversion to diplomacy does not seem to have had any beneficial influence on Soviet behavior. Solodovnikov is said to have totally neglected the Mugabe option in Zimbabwe in favor of exclusive relations with his unfortunate rival, J. Nkomo. Compared, for example, to Soviet sinologists, in whose number stands the current Deputy Minister of Foreign Affairs, Kapitsa, Soviet africanists seem relatively distant from the centers where Soviet policies are articulated. And, within the international bureau of the Central Committee, the two principal "scientific advisers" (K. Brutens and Oulianovsky) are not africanists by training.

Even within the structures where research on the Third World is conducted, africanists are not the ones leading the way. Most of the time, original analyses of the national liberation movements in liberated countries owe more to the work of orientalists (Kiva, Khoros, Kim) than to that of africanists. For the latter there is a double constraint: they are up against the weakness of their primary documentation (trips into the field are the exception) and up against the insufficient and disparate nature of their secondary documentation as well. Evidently receiving their information from Soviet press agencies and from work published in the West, Soviet researchers do not seem to be in a position to benefit from (or to study) the information in the hands of the military or the diplomatic corps.[9] Furthermore, investigations in africanist research constantly come up against the constraints of Soviet diplomacy. For that reason, the more their thinking bears on concrete and particular situations, the more the content seems imprecise and repetitive.

This very real problem can be felt as soon as one tries to understand what content the Soviet Union ascribed to a state with a socialist orientation during the seventies. Now, one must note that the tasks generally given to such a state do not significantly differ from those once assigned to "national democracy" states in the early sixties: expropriation of foreign capital, nationalization of the economy, economic planning, cooperativization, and nationalization of agriculture.[10] Still, it remains uncertain whether the lack of originality of the Soviet model of economic nationalization, proposed tirelessly for more than twenty years now, derives solely from the difficulties of empirical validation that Soviet analysts encounter. The central explanation lies in the Soviets' primary interest in the structure and organization of political power in Africa, since it is, of course, at this level that they understand the specific nature of regimes inspired by Marxism-Leninism: "It is in the necessity of creating a party endowed with avant-garde ideology and the power to mobilize the workers . . . that one can locate the essential difference between the second and third generations of revolutionary democracy."[11]

It all leads one to think that, in all states where the parties in power (MPLA–Labor Party, PRPB, Frelimo, PCT, WPE) are indiscriminately identified as workers' avant-garde parties acting as functional substitutes of the communist party, the Soviets invariably limit themselves to the Leninist power grid. This conception of state power, once characterized by Rosa Luxemburg as the theory of the "inverted capitalist state," projects the postcolonial state as a simple mechanism whose content will be exclusively determined by those who assume responsibility. Thus, rather than defining the contours of a new state, Soviet analysts prefer to evoke a simple rearrangement of the colonial state—the "re-education" of its cadres and "the utilization of existing structures." [12] Thus, they validate a vertical, centralized, and hierarchized conception of state power and reiterate the critical importance of the selection of those who make it work. [13] An even more remarkable fact is that they do not evade the delicate question of the maintenance of power of regimes with a socialist orientation, including recourse to force. Thus, one can read that "revolutionary power cannot be eternally maintained it there aren't the means to defend itself [and if] . . . the army generally has techniques that have no equivalent in any other branch of the national economy." [14]

This voluntarist and authoritarian conception of state power, which the Soviet Union does not hesitate to endorse in black Africa, appears all the more significant since it must integrate a rather sizable sociopolitical factor: the persistent incongruity of the situation on a continent where the process of class differentiation is the least advanced and "avant-garde" urban minorities exist that are supported neither by the peasant masses (predominant in black Africa) nor by the still embryonic working classes. The Soviets overcome this hiatus—which, by the way, they do not deny—in their analyses by resorting to a Leninist grammar that has been tested elsewhere: the autonomy of the ideological superstructure with respect to the economic infrastructure, the determining role of "subjective factors," and the decisive influence of political voluntarism in the political orientation of the state.

While occupying a central position in Soviet perceptions of Africa, the question of power is nevertheless not the only criterion by which the Soviet Union judges the quality of the various socialisms in Africa. Another decisive factor continually comes into play: the privileged relationship with the Soviet Union. The necessities of ideological coherence do indeed force Moscow to challenge any discrepancies between diplomatic and ideological dimensions ahead of time. This explains why it will always be difficult, if not impossible, for the Soviet Union to accept, for example, that a state of socialist orientation might develop a declared hostility toward it. It therefore makes the quality of the ties with "states of socialist orientation" an obligatory part of the route to socialism and discredits in advance any socialist experiment that does not follow this route: "The alliance with the countries where socialism has triumphed creates the foundations without which the transition of backward countries toward socialism is impossible. For this reason, if such and such a country departs from that alliance, it will be felt in the nature of its choices after development." [15]

Thus, from the deterioration of relations between the Soviet Union and Somalia and the resulting change in alliances on the regional level, Somalia lost its "socialist orientation." But, interestingly, the Somali power itself no longer legitimized itself in socialist terms, as if in this case the ideological label "socialist" were primarily a response to diplomatic imperatives.

The Handicaps of "Tropical Sovietology"

Defining the framework of Soviet perceptions by using Soviet sources usefully delineates the interpretative field of Moscow's policies. It introduces into the debate an element of rigor and thereby lessens the credibility of too often poorly supported assertions. [16] Nevertheless, to take into account only the tenets of Soviet positions is of little help to us to evaluate concrete expressions or to appreciate the receptivity of its African partners. Concerning African Marxist-Leninist states in particular, an analyst cannot help but raise two questions: How does the Soviet Union interfere in the legitimation and consolidation processes of these regimes? And how do these regimes define and interpret their relationship with the Soviet Union?

To answer these two central questions, Western Sovietology—which is to be credited for first considering the Soviet Union's role in the Third World—is poorly equipped. Even when it tries to undo itself from the "Soviet-centric" straitjacket, its problematics always remain unilateral. To a Soviet logic with a reputation for being articulate, it applies partial, uncertain, and changeable logic, sometimes described as "radical" (to explain a pro-Soviet choice), sometimes as "nationalist" (to argue the contrary), without ever explaining the meaning of this inexact labeling. The methodological weaknesses and the ideological biases appear even more pronounced in "tropical Sovietology," which aims not only at understanding Soviet policy but also at analyzing the strategies of Third World actors with respect to the Soviet Union. Thus, in the introduction to an essay on "A New Communist Third World," P. Wiles makes the simple, nominal claim to Marxism-Leninism the criterion for belonging to the socialist community. [17] This interesting but inadequately supported approach neglects two dimensions of the dynamics of Soviet-African relations: (1) the ability of African actors to adopt unto themselves, in a fragmentary or global manner, the components of the Soviet model for purely instrumental ends and not necessarily ends congruent with what the Soviets expect; and (2) the often decisive dissociation of concrete Soviet intervention in the consolidation of an African regime (military aid, technology transfer) from the symbolic presence of the Soviet Union in the domestic political rivalries.

The Soviet Model and the Deficit in Legitimacy

From what one can tell, the conditions under which Marxism-Leninism functions as a *lingua franca* of African regimes differ remarkably from one country to another. In Angola, Ethiopia, and Mozambique, the Marxist-Leninist choice followed a break with preexisting political orders. In Benin and the Congo, it appears above all as a mode of legitimation *ex post* for regimes born of simple military *coups d'état*. In all cases, however, the Marxist-Leninist option emerges in conjunction with the exercise of state power and not after long and profound social maturation.[18] Neither Frelimo nor the MPLA, much less the Dirgue, had initially thought of its project in Marxist terms. The implication of that historical given concerning the conditions for adoption of Marxism and the Soviet model is crucial: in Africa, Marxism is not the expression of a social movement but an operational ideology at the service of political forces facing a "structural deficit in legitimacy" and severe difficulties in asserting their international identity. To be sure, the size and simultaneity of problems confronting these political forces vary noticeably from one country to another. But the more acute they are (the combination in Ethiopia, for example, of the threat of domestic implosion and peril at the borders), the broader the adoption of the Soviet ideological model is, and the more pronounced the direct role of the Soviet Union in its diffusion and consolidation.

Since the beginning of the seventies, the emergence of Marxism-Leninism as a mode of legitimation of state power in Africa has been related to a disapprobation asserted by ideologies vying for access to contemporary state control. Having been too compromised, "African socialism" had become an exhausted political resource for elites "without a fixed place in the division of economic labor and unsatisfied with their place in the division of political labor."[19]

The attractiveness of the Western representative model is even weaker both because it answers poorly the unitary imperatives of national construction but also because it remained identified with colonial domination. In this regard, the political itinerary of the MPLA offers a good demonstration of the conditions needed in the seventies for African socialisms to mature. Influenced from its inception by certain Marxist currents, the MPLA could measure the disillusions born of experiments imprinted with an image of "specific socialism" even before its arrival to power. In addition, since its political hegemony was being challenged by movements claiming "nationalism" only, it naturally found Marxism-Leninism its sole source of legitimation. Its choice proved to be all the more profitable given that its arrival and tenure in power involved in part political-military support of the socialist camp.

The case of the Congo is markedly different. The integration of a Marxist-Leninist referent into the political field goes back to the *"trois glorieuses"* of 1963 during which the pro-Western regime of Fulbert Youlou was overthrown. It was accompanied by the introduction of the Marxist-Leninist genre of discourse by the intellectual elite and the proletariat of Brazzaville.[20] Masters of the street but also of discourse, these organizations for the masses, particularly the *Jeunesse du Mouvement national révolutionnaire* (JMNR), quickly came to defiance of the central power symbolized by the National Council of the Revolution (Conseil national de la révolution). By creating a Marxist-Leninist party in 1969, namely, the Parti Congolais du Travail (PCT), the military regime offered an ideological response to the formidable opposition of popular organizations with a Marxist-Leninist referent. By claiming Marxism-Leninism in its own turn, the Congolese regime thus regained the ideological initiative before making its claim to hegemony concrete through forceful mobilization of the state machine.

Combined with the use of "revolutionary violence," Marxism-Leninism also allowed the Ethiopian regime to better exercise its ideological monopoly over public life in the face of adversaries (PERP and MEISON) also making their own claim to Marxism. The Ethiopian regime, bearer of the aspirations of the urban classes, demonstrated an instinctive hostility as much to the emergence of intellectual avant-gardes in the cities as to peasant power in the country.[21] The Ethiopian regime took from Soviet discourse a whole reservoir of references that allowed it to obscure its actual position on the social gameboard (by declaring itself bearer of the ideals of the emerging working class) while discrediting its rivals. The "spontaneity of the masses" justified the recruitment of the peasantry, while "leftist illusions" announced the repression of intellectual elites. By using a vocabulary new to the Ethiopian political imagination, the military regime thus managed to entertain the illusion of a radical break with the past while the two principal organs of the old regime prospered, the army and the administration.[22] Still today, recourse to the idioms of Soviet discourse makes it remarkably easy for Ethiopia to obscure its realities. In its report to the constituent congress of the Ethiopian Labor Party of September 1984, Colonel Mengistu only mentioned the term "famine" twice. Conversely, explicit reference to Marxism-Leninism, to the Soviet Union, and to the "Great October Revolution" occurred thirty-nine times.[23]

Such recurrence of legitimizing, obscuring, and discrediting functions, proper to the original Soviet discourse, prove even more "performative" (*"performante"*) in periods of "peril at the borders." The Soviet political discourse, a discourse of war *par excellence*, facilitates the formal actualization of what Pierre Bourdieu calls the *effet de fermeture* ("closure effect") of the political field. Because the whole of social and international reality is slanted toward the main conflict between "imperialism" and "the people," political opponents can only be "infiltrating foreign agents." In a symmetrical effect, international reality is itself presented in Manichaean terms, for admitting that the reality of the world is not reducible to a confrontation between socialism and imperialism would implicitly mean accepting that the internal, domestic enemy is not necessarily a foreign agent. And, on this level, the political texts of the Angolan, Mozambican, and Ethiopian regimes indisputably lend themselves to this sort of interpretation.

Thus, in African societies, where more than anywhere else in the Third World the challenge of nation-building is difficult to deal with (what with the preponderance of segmented allegiances, the fragility of the national will, the weak internalization of ideologies offering access to contemporary statehood, and war conditions), recourse to Marxism-Leninism and to the Soviet model should be interpreted neither as a choice imposed by the Soviet Union nor as an erroneous solution. For those who lay claim to it, the Soviet referent functions primarily as a tracking system, a "legitimate problematic" (*problématique légitime*, Bourdieu), which preliminarily specifies the locus of the setting (the people versus imperialism), the hierarchy of the roles (the working class, the peasantry), the plot (class struggle), and the denouement (the victory of socialism).

For societies in quest of totalizing political structures, the ideological justification and practice of the "intangibility of the social system" proposed by the Soviet Union have an undeniable emotional and concrete impact as well. To this day, the historic efficacy of Marxist-Leninist regimes has held up. In spite of strong domestic and foreign pressures, the Luanda, Maputo, and Addis Ababa regimes endure. In Congo, factional struggles for power still continue within the group of leaders that emerged in the 1968 *coup d'état*. And finally in Benin, President Kerekou's regime has been in power since 1972. In a country whose public life had to that date been punctuated by numerous coups, *"performance"* is not insignificant.

Marxist-Leninist Discourse and Political Irreversibility

As one can see, the spread of the Marxist-Leninist idiom in Africa expresses the political aspirations of its users to a totalizing mode of expression. The rare studies undertaken so far on Marxist-Leninist discourse in Africa permit validation of the general properties of Soviet language.[24]

Must one, however, argue from the internationalization of the Soviet discursive genre to support the thesis of the spread of the communist system?

In truth, the debate about irreversibility, so precious to the West, lacks rigor. Whether fortuitously or deliberately, the irreversibility of Marxist regimes finds itself largely confounded with or assimilated into the irreversibility of Soviet presence. Thus the political autonomy of African actors with respect to the Soviet Union is minimized or ignored, as if the occurrence of Marxism-Leninism in these states were inextricably dependent on allegiance to the Soviet Union.

In many respects, such reasoning is specious. To speak of Marxism-Leninism in Africa first of all requires that one define its contours and content. Should one characterize as Marxist all African parties claiming that ideology? Or is it appropriate to judge its applicability by using a grid of predetermined Marxist-Leninist indicators? The first approach has the advantage of a nominalism that excuses the analyst from any empirical validation. The second raises the problem of the choice of indicators.

The conformity of African Marxism-Leninisms to the Soviet paradigm might be assessed on the basis of their alignment with Soviet foreign policy, the degree of state control over public life, and the avant-garde structure of their party. Such a grid, offering the advantage of tying domestic dynamics to international diplomatic maneuvering, is nonetheless hardly convincing.

African diplomatic alignments with the Soviet Union have not always made a lot of sense. Of all the regional groups represented in the United Nations, it is precisely the African group that displays the greatest homogeneity in voting and, when all is said and done, the group in which echoes of the East-West conflict are the most muffled. In addition, the considerable coincidence of interests between the Soviets and the Africans at the United Nations expresses much less a deliberate alignment of the group with the Soviet Union than it does a more or less tactical convergence with it. In fact, only the questions of Afghanistan and Kampuchea (to be examined below) present a real problem. But there, too, nothing indicates that the Marxist-Leninist option in and of itself leads to an alignment with the Soviet Union. On the question of Afghanistan, certain Marxist states take refuge in abstaining (Benin, Congo), while other non-Marxist states choose to align themselves with the Soviet Union (Madagascar). Thus the coincidence of interests with the Soviet Union cannot be set forth as a distinguishing characteristic of the foreign policy of Marxist-Leninist states. Neither does the degree of state control of economic life seem to be a criterion permitting a full understanding of the specific nature of African Marxist-Leninist regimes. The grip of the state on economic life is no less noticeable in a non-Marxist country like Cameroon than in a Marxist state

like the Congo. Neither do the nature and the influence of the ties woven
with foreign capitalism help in making sense of the particular traits of
Marxist-Leninist policy. The fiscal regime of the oil companies seems, for
example, more constraining for foreign operators in Cameroon than in
Angola.

Of these three criteria, reference to a party structure of the avant-gardist
type is perhaps the most relevant. But there again, an avant-gardist quality
is not solely characteristic of Marxist-Leninist parties. Nearly all African
parties function on the basis of property-related recruitment. Thus nothing
allows one to assert that the mode of selection of Party members in the
Congo differs from that employed by any other non-Marxist party. The
operation of the Party and its different organs (Congress, Central Committee, Politburo, Control Committee), as well as its articulation in popular
organizations, is also insufficient for a judgment as to the unique character
of Marxist-Leninist parties. The RTP (Rally of the Togolese People) in
Togo, whose formal organization and operation owes a lot to North Korea,
nonetheless did not set itself up as a Marxist-Leninist party. Conversely, it
took a Marxist-Leninist party like Frelimo nearly ten years to create a
worker's union under its leadership.

Since the formal level does not allow one a solid grasp of the particu-
larities of Marxist-Leninist regimes, one can wonder whether sociological
problematics of totalitarianism might offer more satisfying answers. Based
on the interpretative grid presented by J. Leca, the question becomes
whether African Marxist-Leninist parties actually meet the criteria of totalitarian parties insofar as they are *monist, teleocratic,* and *revolutionary.*[25] One can add to their political claims the power of their effectiveness
in eliminating any intermediary between the Party and society, in setting
up the social order around a rigorous relation of inclusion-exclusion, and
finally in exerting an absolute monopoly on economic, social, and cultural
exchange. Relying on social constraint rather than brutal repression, the
totalitarian party limits its relations with civil society to provisional and
fully reversible compromises.[26] At the outset this classification proves to
have little pertinence to Africa. Although numerous parties, though not
exclusively Marxist ones, display totalitarian pretensions, none of them
has enough effective power to match its ambitions. Political control of the
dominated, including in Marxist states, is far from irreversible. Everywhere, the edifice of the dominators is being eroded by the press of
subordinate social actors. In the oldest of the African Marxist-Leninist
regimes, the Congo, political claims of the PCT are continually challenged
by the vitality of ever more numerous social networks. The lethargy of
popular organizations, most notably the women's organization URFC
(Union révolutionnaire des femmes congolaises), contrasts sharply with

the dynamic nature of mutual aid associations for women (the *mozikis*) whose creation was sometimes encouraged by certain cadres of the Party. In fact (and with the possible exception of Ethiopia), most of the research is, for now, in agreement on the idea that Marxist-Leninist states have more in common with other African neo-mercantilisms than with a totalitarian model.[27] The only regimes with a potential for totalitarianism prosper more under the banner of "authenticity" (Togo, Zaire) than under that of Marxism-Leninism.[28]

In truth, if there exists a specific trait of Marxist-Leninist regimes in Africa, it may involve the choice of the mode of political discourse and the constraints that this mode of discourse imposes on the legitimation of regimes laying claim to it.

As a revolutionary ideology, Marxism-Leninism reproduces the fundamental trait conferred by F. Furet on the ideology of the French Revolution: "an ideology where representations are at the center of the action and where the semiotic circuit is the absolute master of policy."[29]

Based on the primacy of the political, Marxism-Leninism also makes discourse in the acquisition of legitimacy the central stake of power.[30] To be sure, the mastery of legitimate discourse does not apply only to Marxist-Leninist political societies. In a Muslim society such as Egypt, it is precisely the Islamic intelligentsia's exclusive access to the translated order (*l'ordre traduit*) that enables it to eclipse the discourse of the mullahs.[31]

But the monopoly on scholarly discourse in Islamic societies is not necessarily expressed through conquest of the power of the state. In addition, its horizons stretch beyond the national framework and extend to the whole of the Muslim community, the *ouma*. In the societies we are dealing with here, the problematics of discourse take on importance precisely because they are intimately linked to the control of the central power of the nation-state.

Thus the specific nature of Marxist-Leninist regimes could provisionally be sketched out based on overrepresentation of the *logocracy,* that is, the position of ideological power in the political arena, on the rigidity of formal political choices, given the "closure effect" marked in Marxist discourse, and on partial dependence with regard to the Soviet semiotic center.

Under all African skies, including in states of "soft ideology," ideocrats manage, by the very mastery of discourse, to rise in the power hierarchy and thus to invest in certain of their positions. In Marxist-Leninist states, this tendency seems more pronounced to the extent that revolutionary ideology is "coextensive" with power, to the point of making "the higher ideological bid the rule of the game in the new system."[32] H. Ossebi has demonstrated quite well apropos the Congo how the simple mastery of the

French language and the management, however rudimentary, of Marxist concepts were sufficient in 1963 to propel candidates politically to the highest positions of responsibility.[33]

A detailed study of Angolan political life since 1975 would perhaps confirm the importance of ideological positioning in struggles for power. In the Congo the "Nzé Affair" underlines the importance of language in domestic debate. In using the Party's weekly newspaper to validate the Ethiopian political experiment, the head of foreign relations for the PCT was perhaps trying to discredit the Congo's current political line. The promptness of the response to his encoded message by Party superiors confirms the "performative" nature of the charge.[34] Here Marxist discourse fits well into the problematics of language that Bakhtin proposed: that of a "password" known to a limited number of actors and belonging to the same social horizon (in this case the Party machine).[35]

The overinvestment of ideologic discourse in the political field necessarily leads to valorizing the places and the actors that are "producers of meaning," such as Party schools, for example. That is why, even when Marxist-Leninist language seems purely formal, its ability to structure the political field is never insignificant. In all of the African states, the Marxist-Leninist choice introduces modes of legitimation and discredit whose presence in each one's political culture deserves in-depth study. All of these regimes have developed the ideological ability to generate and maintain "event-based crystallizations," to the point of making them the constituting act of a new political culture.

One can note, for instance, that formal political independence is rarely treated as a break point by these countries. For Mozambique, the break point came with the eruption of the war of liberation. In Angola, one may refer to the liberation war, too, but also to the civil war that became the "second war of national liberation." To be sure, most African regimes have had a hand in the game of "event-based crystallization" to legitimate their own authority. But in most cases (Togo, Zaire), it remained personalized and devoid of any teleological interpretation. Thus the "myth of Sarakawa" had little chance of surviving in Togo after the death of Eyadema, while the "1963 revolution" underscores the "legitimate problematic" of the different Congo regimes since that date.

Able to structure a modern political culture, Marxist-Leninist ideology contributes therein to the rigidification of the rules of political language. Because Marxist-Leninist discourse in Africa is always accompanied by initial acts supposed to attest to its effectiveness (nationalization, for example), justification of new economic choices seems a betrayal, the abandoning of an initial model of conformity. In the Ivory Coast resistance to potential denationalization will probably be as lively as in the Congo. But it is not certain that the terms of the debate are set the same way in the two

Table 9 The Marxist-Leninist Code

Formal Context—Ethiopia Valorizing Idioms	Real Context—Congo Discrediting Idioms
Correct (Party) line, hardline	Intrigues, tribalism, plots, clans
Unique experiment, avant garde spearhead	Ideologic confusion, *fuite en avant* (escape by attack)
Faithful and tough Party	Infiltration, fissure, *embourgeoisement*
Masses	Middle classes
The continuing struggle	Managing difficulties
Irreversibility	Retreat

Source: P. Nzé, "Le Congrès constitutif du PTE," *Étumba,* October 23, 1984

countries. In the Ivory Coast those terms will probably increase the unpopularity of the regime without, however, diminishing its legitimacy. In the Congo denationalization means incurring the risk of "no longer acting socialist."

The constraints of the Marxist enunciative mode can also be found naturally in the diplomatic arena. There is no doubt that the current political crisis in Mozambique stems from the failure of the Nkomati Accords. But did the very signing of these accords bring with it an "enunciative crisis" in a state where the idea of a South African plot had until then served as a rallying point?

It is nonetheless in its relation to the Soviet Union that the enunciation of Marxist politics derives its distinctiveness.

The dependence that ties these states to the Soviet Union is both symbolic and instrumental. For better or worse, all the Marxist African states entrust the Soviet Union with the role of pilot country in the construction of socialism or view it as the successful example of real socialism, even if they reject the idea of a model. This political choice forces them constantly to seek its sacramental unction. The report of the last PCT congress adequately emphasizes that "certain fraternal and friendly countries are already starting to consider the PCT a proletarian workers' party conducting a real struggle for national liberation. They recognize that our party really practices real democracy in the working of its institutions." [36]

This link necessarily leads to systematic obscuring of all deprecatory references to the Soviet Union or of all conflict or disagreement with it. If there is a difference of opinion with the Soviet Union, it will be carried on through unspoken channels. But rather than practicing the self-censorship of diplomatic restraint or allegiance, the process will in fact obey the rules of a dialogic code in which formal enunciation is more important than the concrete behavior it supposedly prompts. That is why, for the Soviet Union, the Congo's abstention at the United Nations on the question of

Afghanistan will prove less important than its formal support of the "Popular Republic of Afghanistan" at the signing of the Soviet-Congolese friendship treaty in May 1981. Grafted into this tie is instrumental dependence, in which the training of cadres plays an essential role.

Indeed, through sending training personnel or accepting students, socialist countries have become the principal centers for training Congolese, Ethiopian, and Mozambican cadres. Thus, in the space of ten years, the Soviet Union has trained seven thousand Angolans. During the same period it contributed to assuring the training of eighteen thousand Workers' Party of Ethiopia (WPE) cadres, not including the three thousand Ethiopian scholarship students it welcomed to the Soviet Union.

With respect to Mozambique, the Soviet effort has been more modest, probably because of the active role played by the German Democratic Republic. Along with Cuba, East Germany has assumed, after the Soviet Union, the most important role in Africa's socialist arena.

Since 1982, for example, more than six thousand Mozambicans have been trained in the German Democratic Republic. This program is all the more impressive in taking a totally unprecedented form. Indeed, it not only assures the training of technical and professional cadres who are funneled upon their return into projects that the German Democratic Republic is financing (the coal complex at Moatize, for instance), but it also ensures the training of elementary and high school children, and of skilled workers as well. The amplitude of cooperation in this area justified the creation of a "GDR–Mozambique Friendship School" in Stassfurt. The establishment of such a school grew out of the concern of African states for extending, to all sectors and at all levels, the training of technically and politically reliable cadres. At the same time, the leaders of these states are careful to keep their future cadres in close contact with their countries of origin, especially those who, since adolescence, have followed the path of socialist countries—and thus the interest in a school like that at Stassfurt where part of the final training is carried out by Mozambicans trained earlier in the GDR. At Island of Pines in Cuba, where 2,445 Angolans, 2,000 Ethiopians, and 2,500 Mozambicans are enrolled in six-year cycles of primary and secondary schooling, the principle of bi-national functions is approximately the same.

The emphasis henceforth placed by socialist countries on training young people and skilled workers probably expresses a decisive, qualitative evolution in the development of their African policies. Aside from the fact that most of the time they are the responsibility of the beneficiary countries, these programs permit socialist countries to act on two different levels: assuring, from a very early age, basic political training for future national cadres and aiding the establishment of a workers' elite.

Beyond the broadening of training programs in socialist countries, and beyond sending eastern European assistance personnel, the nature of Soviet relations with Angola, Ethiopia, and Mozambique also depends on the proliferation of undertakings designed to make Soviet realities more familiar.

This dimension seems very evident in Ethiopia, where the Soviet Union and other socialist countries have contributed a great deal to the establishment of the Party and popular organizations, launching a ten-year plan, to creation of an institute for nationalities, to the constitution of a militia, and to the founding of a military service, not to mention the logistical support in the questionable transfer of hundreds of thousands of drought victims. The Ethiopian press, which has reported extensively on this cooperation, particularly underscores the benefits of a single party for the purposes of consolidation. The ideological training program of the WPE thus planned to develop the *Yekatit 66* school, to send trainees to socialist countries, to create a Party organ, to launch a theoretical journal, to translate Marxist-Leninist works into Amharic, and to create secondary schools and a social science institute.

The process of "implantation" in Angola and Mozambique has been quantitatively just as significant. Chronological examination of the Soviet Union's relations with these two states reveals the sizable number of delegate exchanges between parties, press organs, cooperatives, unions, youth groups, and churches.

In states claiming Marxism-Leninism, the Soviet Union thus largely bets on the emergence of ideological nuclei steeped in Marxist-Leninist culture. In the Congo, for example, it aided the creation of a new Higher Party School. Having provided a portion of the financing of this institution, it also kept an eye on the final training stages in concert with the GDR. Thus in 1985 nearly one hundred trainees had been trained by fifteen Eastern European professors and four Congolese full-time professors, in addition to more than thirty part-time professors.

Given the facts, the functional mode and the content of the teachings of this school reflect the standardized character of the Soviet ideological model. In many respects, the content of the courses (scientific communism, Marxist ethics, scientific atheism, party edification, typology of African states, international relations, critique of bourgeois philosophy and society) and of the documentary materials made available to the trainees (Lenin's complete works, photocopies of material written at the Soviet Union's Academy of Science, publications of the Social Editions) seems primarily intended to facilitate the learning of the Marxist-Leninist vulgate. It also facilitates reinforcing ideological power positions within the party, as the selection process becomes more and more constricted.

Is this to say that the Higher Party School has reproduced the process of "creeping sovietization," pure and simple, in the Congo? Is this also to say, generally speaking, that Soviet training of African cadres feeds and maintains the "prosovietism" of certain elites?

In fact, since its creation in 1971, the Higher Party School has only slightly contributed to the strengthening of the Party's hold on society. While offering students a diploma valuable in the employment market, it paradoxically contributes to inflating the numbers of state bureaucrats, to the detriment of party structures.

The answer to the second question seems singularly difficult, competent monographic studies being as painfully rare as they are. But it seems already the case that the presence of communist political culture in Africa, to which Moscow contributes, is far from guaranteeing in and of itself the irreversibility of Soviet influence in Africa.

The Levels of Influence in Soviet Policy

"A Power like Others"

On a continent where it had no leverage or influence in 1960, the Soviet Union has tried for the last twenty-five years to establish itself as "a power like others." In conformity with the process of globalizing its power, it fixed itself to this goal, eating away at the strong anticommunist potential left behind by European colonialism and denying the West any exclusivity over this area of the world. Thus, what the West perceives as a Soviet "breakthrough" in Africa since 1975 is interpreted by the Soviet Union as legitimate accession to the status of African power.

This minimum threshold of influence, which Moscow has sought patiently since 1956, has now been reached. Only the Ivory Coast and Malawi still refuse to establish diplomatic relations with the Soviet Union. Without having fully managed to dissipate the mistrust generated by its double status as a communist power and strategic superpower, the Soviet Union has managed to gain admittance into Africa as a full-fledged power. Thus, from the end of the 1975–76 Angolan crisis, the question of the presence of Soviet-Cuban forces is no longer brought up at the OAU. The unanimous rejection by African states of any idea of linkage between the presence of Cuban troops stationed in Angola and Namibia's independence confirms the marginalization of this problem in Africa.

Paradoxically, moreover, the Soviet Union's negative image in Africa seems to have been more marked in the good old days of the "Soviet-American condominium" than it has since the beginning of the "second cold war." The evolution in debates about the Soviet Union within the nonaligned movement and in the Soviet Union's own perception of its image within the movement, between the Algiers summit (1973) and the Havana summit (1979), supports that hypothesis.[37]

The intensification of the diverse ties between the Soviet Union and various African capitals clearly attests to the routinization of the Soviet presence. Thanks to the signing of general economic and scientific cooperation agreements with twenty-nine African countries, the Soviet Union has been able during the last ten years to sign eight fishing agreements, open twelve air stations (particularly useful for relaying trawler equipment, for sending assistance personnel, and for African student travel) and increase its civilian presence to at least ten thousand assistance personnel.[38]

These vectors of potential influence are unquestionably reinforced by an annual grant of three thousand scholarships (North Africa included) to nearly all African states, and not just to the most faithful of its allies.[39] Granted directly by the Soviet Union or through various intermediaries (friendship associations, solidarity committees, mass organizations, unions, universities), these scholarships play a role in the different paths of African social life. Even when partially financed by the beneficiary states, training programs in the Soviet Union offer the advantage of being less onerous than those proposed by Western states. In a fair number of African countries, this aspect of the issue often seems more decisive than the attraction of a "socialist paradise."

The influence of these training programs on their beneficiaries, on their perceptions of the world, as well as on their social position once they have returned from the socialist countries, must be assessed. Given the lack of studies of representative samples of the African student population sent to the Soviet Union, evaluating this situation remains extremely difficult. Nonetheless, a few observations and some correlations of fragmentary information suggest that the "Soviet experience" of African students has not fostered either massive ideological conversion or systematic rejection. Furthermore, the subjective evaluation of Soviet reality cannot be dissociated from another, more basic question: does the possession of a Soviet diploma enhance one's political or social worth? In the case of an affirmative answer, the resentment in response to the "daily racism" that most African students experience in the Soviet Union has a good chance of being blurred. But it is not even sure, furthermore, that in the case of a negative answer, perceptions would be systematically unfavorable to the "fatherland of socialism."

In the Congo, for instance, where Marxist ideology is the official ideology, a Soviet diploma does itself constitute the indispensable asset needed to acquire a position of power and enrichment. Sometimes afflicted by ostracism, those trained in the Soviet Union may militate in favor of a firmer ideological line, of a cleaner subordination of the state to the Party, in order to attain a more favorable position of power. In such cases, their obligatory "prosovietism" could accommodate a negative image of the Soviet socialist system.

In fact, in those countries not entertaining any privileged ties with the Soviet Union and where Western meritocratic norms are largely still vital, the possession of a Soviet diploma involves lowering one's status more often than it does social improvement. In Nigeria, for example, lawyers educated in the Soviet Union are scarcely able to find openings in the job

**Table 10   Scholarships and Training Programs
For African Nationals in Socialist Countries**

Beneficiaries	Scholarships Granted		African Nationals Present in Socialist Countries	
Angola	Cuba	100 (1984)	Cuba	2395 (1983)
Benin			USSR	400 (1983)
Congo			USSR	1500 (1984)
Ethiopia	Cuba	200 (1980)		
		600 (1983)		
	USSR	175 (1980)	Bulgaria	480 (1985)
		30 (1981)	Cuba	2000 (1982)
		600 (1982)		
		500 (1984)		
	GDR	70 (1981)		
		374 (1983)		
	Czechoslovakia	30 (1981)		
	Poland	12 (1981)		
Ghana	USSR	175 (1980)		
		150 (1984)	Hungary	60 (1985)
	Cuba	600 (1983)		
Guinea	USSR	57 (1980)		
	Romania	27 (1980)		
Guinea-Bissau	USSR	96 (1981)	USSR	500 (1984)
		70 (1981)		
		112 (1984)		
Madagascar	USSR	240 (1980)	USSR	1000 (1981)
		310 (1982)		
Nigeria			USSR	1800 (1981)
			Bulgaria	800 (1981)
Mauritius	USSR	60 (1981)		
Mozambique	USSR	150 (1982)	GDR	6000 (1982)
		100 (1983)	Cuba	2500 (1981)
		25 (1985)		
	Cuba	188 (1981)		
Tanzania		100 (1984)	GDR	100 (1985)
Zambia	USSR	75 (1984)		
	GDR	1000 (1981)	GDR	675 (1984)
Zimbabwe	Bulgaria	50 (1982)	Cuba	100 (1985)
			USSR	300 (1985)

Source: This non-exhaustive list was based upon information gathered from the African press of various African states (*No Pintcha, Madàgascar-Morning, Horoya, Jornal de Angola, Étumba, Ethiopian Herald, Daily Graphic, Noticias, Daily News, Times of Zambia, The Herald*).

market. In a fair number of francophone countries, the professional integration of a Soviet graduate only takes place after further training in France.

The situation in Marxist-Leninist countries is more complex, since certain formal structures (the Party, for instance) want to attract cadres who are ideologically trained. But outside the Party or civil service, jobs offered to graduates of Soviet institutes remain extremely limited. In the Congo, as in Angola, key sectors of the economy, dominated in large part by Western interests, attract only very few educated in the Soviet Union. In December 1984 the Central Committee of the MPLA was particularly concerned about the poor rationale behind jobs offered, especially to graduates of the socialist camp.

The extension of training programs for Africans in the Soviet Union has logically been accompanied by an increase in the visibility of Soviet assistance personnel in the field, even if their sociability has remained just as poor. In Nigeria alone, some six thousand assistance personnel have been participating since 1982 in the construction of the Ajeokuta iron and steel works complex.[40] The rest of the Soviet Union's assistance personnel (geologists, medical doctors, engineers, and educators) are for the most part divided among Ethiopia, Angola, Mozambique, Madagascar, and Zambia. Alongside efforts in economic aid, the Soviet Union has facilitated instituting a "sociability network" (comprising friendship societies and associations), meant in principle to enhance reciprocal familiarization with Soviet and African realities. In reality, these efforts have, above all, assured cultural and ideological penetration by the Soviet Union. For, while African programs in the Soviet Union offer primarily "cultural" content, Soviet activities in Africa more clearly work to promulgate the "Soviet model" (construction of socialism, settling the question of nationalities).[41] Seen in this light, the Soviet Union is largely encouraging the dissemination of initiation rites following the Soviet liturgy: the commemoration of anniversaries (the Great Patriotic War, the Great October Revolution, Lenin's Birthday), the sanctification of the Founding Fathers (erecting statues of Lenin), the distribution of breviaries (gifts of Marxist-Leninist works), and the teaching of the language of the "scriptures" (opening the first African Pushkin Institute in Brazzaville).

The Soviet Union's desire to affirm itself thus has been essentially prompted by diplomatic preoccupations, compounded in certain specific and limited cases by economic preoccupations. In West Africa, for example, where the Soviet Union realized eighty-five percent of its 1983 imports from black Africa with only four partners, it had managed in the course of the previous fifteen years to develop a strategy for access to agricultural raw materials (cocoa, coffee) and minerals (bauxite). Now, thanks to the stabilization of its economic presence in precisely that area where its diplomatic positions were always weak or precarious, the Soviet Union has managed to check certain disappointments and avoid being expelled from the area.

Thanks to its contribution to exploitation of the Kindia bauxite mines, the Soviet Union has succeeded in preserving the main thread of its shaky cooperation with Conakry. Significantly, Moscow has always accorded Guinea the label of "socialist-oriented" country, even after its loss of access to Guinean military facilities and the opening to the West by the Sékou Touré regime in 1975. Still today, the stability of Soviet-Guinea relations seems to be confirmed by the Soviets' grant of two loans in the amount of $230 million.[42]

As an element of stabilization, the instrument of economics can be a factor, even a symbolic one, in reintegration with a hostile or mistrustful state. In other circumstances, it can be used to mark the path laid out for the long term. This is how, in Ghana, Lieutenant Rawlings's accession to power permitted the 1982 reactivation of Soviet economic projects abandoned in 1966. In Nigeria the Soviet Union's strictly commercial participation in the Ajeokuta complex reinforces its presence in a difficult country with which it has faltering ties.

Thus, short of having any real influence on its partners, the Soviet Union is giving its presence in Africa an ever-increasing stability. In a limited number of cases, its economic and especially its military assistance policies allow it to influence the renegotiation of its partners' debts. During the last few years, it has thus been able to alleviate or defer debts incurred by Guinea-Bissau (1978), Madagascar (1981), Angola (1983), and Mozambique (1984).

Compared nonetheless with what it represents for Western states, such an economic weapon continues to play an ancillary role in the Soviet Union's African strategy. In 1983 its commerce with black Africa did not exceed eight percent of the total of its trade with the Third World. This level, stunningly stable since 1960, would be even lower if one subtracted the flow of "return aid" that Soviet statistics identifies with purely commercial exchanges.[43] It would, on the other hand, be markedly higher if one added the statistics for "nonapportioned products," usually corresponding to arms shipments.

The Soviet Union, Ally in Protest

The Soviet Union at first made an effort to appear "a power like others"; but having attained that objective, it never once has failed to present itself as a different power, as a concrete alternative to the West. On a continent where local expectations are not all the same, Soviet policy lends itself easily to that ambivalent game.

For the most part, this second level of influence can be summarized as an exercise in the function of an ally "in protest" vis-à-vis partners anxious to maximize their position in the East-West conflict. Having influence "by default," the Soviet Union can easily integrate itself into those areas where Western strategies prove insufficient, heavy-handed, or costly.

Even in the most marginal manner, Soviets and Africans have not hesitated to start from a basis of *comparative disadvantage,* that is to say, to exchange products of relatively poor quality that neither of the two parties could channel to the West. In other cases, it is the nonparticipation of the Soviet Union in certain international agreements, like that on coffee, that enabled countries like the Ivory Coast to sell a large part of their production "outside quotas." Until the middle of the seventies, commerce with the Soviet Union was characterized by another peculiarity: that of prospering outside the monetary circuit—thanks to the practice of clearing. Since then, the merits of this system have been blurred in the face of the shared imperative that the Soviets and the Africans come up with strong currencies—the former, in order to procure Western technology without dipping too far into their gold reserves; the latter, in order to ease oil constraints and to honor their growing debts. Added to the poor economic complementarity of the Soviet Union and Africa, this situation explains the relative stagnation of Soviet-African exchange and the general abandonment of clearing accords.

Nonetheless, in the dynamics of mercantile ties between the Soviet Union and Africa, two salient characteristics deserve to be noted.

First, despite the parsimony of Soviet bilateral aid, loans toward investments in the mining sector reimbursed in the form of deliveries in kind on the completion of a project are multiplying. This approach, tested in Guinea, has long since been extended to Mali, the Congo, and Ethiopia. In northern Africa, this integrated strategy of investment and supply materialized in a spectacular agreement for exploitation of Meskallah phosphates. Even if the quality of the products may have fallen short of the desired level, Soviet projects still remain less costly than those proposed by Western firms. Moreover, payments in kind avoid disbursement of currency. That is why, while clearing has disappeared from Soviet-African trade, this practice of barter has intensified. Finally, Soviet investment projects often anticipate the training of cadres, such that travel to the Soviet Union normally would allow avoiding a "brain drain."

Second, in an increasingly marked way, the equation of commercial ties between the Soviet Union and Africa has included arms shipments by means of downgrading them. Managed in the Soviet Union by a civil agency (the State Committee for Foreign Economic Relations), sales of military matériel generally figure in Soviet commercial statistics under the heading of "nonapportioned products." This growing integration of arms sales into traditional commercial circuits is significant. It expresses the Soviet desire to exercise its function as an effective arms merchant while no longer having to overlook the political orientation of its partners. Armaments are no longer considered a particular commodity reserved for political clients, as was the rule in the sixties, but rather as an operative and competitive commercial article.

Thus, Soviet armaments have remained payable over rather a long period (ten to twelve years) and at moderate rates (two to three percent), even if the traditional discounts of forty percent now seem exceptional. Similarly, the usual practice of compensation with tropical products has been diminishing as well. It was systematically abandoned with all of the oil countries (Angola, Congo, Nigeria) in favor of convertible currency settlements. In other cases, the Soviet Union is inducing its partners to settle their payments in the form of mineral raw materials (gold from Mali or Ethiopia, copper from Zambia). It would nonetheless seem that these general arrangements continue to be modulated largely in terms of the Soviet Union's political interests in the beneficiary country, the financial situation of the partner, the political benefit to the Soviet Union in maintaining its "ally" in a dependency situation, and its receptivity to Soviet demands for military facility loans. Thus, in Madagascar, the delivery of fifteen MiG-21s, eight of which were free of charge, was to have permitted Soviet installation of three land-based centers for long-range marine surveillance.[44] In Mali and Benin it is said to have built two airports in exchange for stopover rights for its military aircraft.

Besides the specific advantages to certain African states (the speed of delivery, the sturdiness of the matériel, the ease of maintenance, the low prices), military cooperation with the Soviet Union escapes the excessive "conditionality" of Western military aid. In delivering arms to Zambia in 1982, the Soviet Union had none of the motives invoked by the United States for declining Zambian demands: the excessive burden arms sales might mean for an anemic economy and the futility of such deliveries in the face of a South African adversary of crushing superiority.[45]

Beyond its immediate political interest in inserting itself into a key country in southern Africa, the promptness of the Soviet response expressed its willingness to reinforce the attributes of African sovereignty. On a continent where the precariousness of sentiment loyal to the nation-state is offset by strong symbolization of the power of the state, the objectification of loci of authority (stadiums, palaces, roads, MiG planes) does not necessarily bend with the imperatives of economic or military rationality.

Acting as an ally "in protest" at the political-military level very naturally has had repercussions in international diplomatic enclaves. For the Soviet Union, Africa does indeed constitute the best (and perhaps the last) echo chamber for its classical antiimperialist strategy. In Asia, where it

Table 11   Soviet Arms Deliveries to Black Africa
(1975–1980)
(in millions of dollars)

Angola	550	Madagascar	60
Benin	20	Mali	110
Burundi	10	Mozambique	180
Cape Verde	50	Nigeria	90
Congo	60	Somalia	150
Ethiopia	1900	Tanzania	320
Guinea-Bissau	30	Uganda	40
Guinea	50	Zambia	220

Source: World military expenditures and arms transfers, 1971–1980, ACDA, 1983.

had based its activities during the fifties and sixties on the anticolonialist potential of states in the area, this approach is now no longer operable. The reality of Sino-Soviet competition, the military disengagement of the United States, the Vietnamese hegemony in Indochina, and the success of the newly industrializing countries of Southeast Asia are all elements that constrain Soviet impetus.[46] To survive, the Soviet Union has adhered to its classical diplomatic alliances, of which the treaty with India represents the best example. In the Middle East where the antiimperialist dimension of Arab claims has fed the potential for Soviet influence, it is the congruence of strategies rather than ideological conniving that would now assure Soviet influence in the area. In Latin America, finally, opportunities open to the Soviet Union in Nicaragua nonetheless cannot obscure the obstacles to its involvement there. There remains Africa, where anticolonial claims remain lively (Namibia, Mayotte Island) and where hostility to apartheid cements the diplomatic cohesion of African states.

At the United Nations, the Soviet Union has thus managed to maximize its functions as a "protest-ally" by supporting without reservation African resolutions against apartheid, South African policy, and survival of any last bits of colonialist confetti. Such convergence of interests has very naturally led the Soviet Union to consider the African group the most coherent geopolitical grouping among the nonaligned states, even as it accurately recognizes the gap between declared radicalism and the pragmatism of conduct.[47] In any case, the Soviet Union has managed, on the basis of fundamental agreements, to make a fair number of its interests coincide with the specific demands of African states (the denuclearization of the African continent, the proclamation of the Indian Ocean area as a peace zone).

The Soviet Union's enviable position as a privileged diplomatic ally of the African group has reemerged in most basic debates pitting Third World states against Western states. Thus, on the central question of human rights, the Soviet view of those rights (the prevalence of collective rights over individual rights) coincides better with the definition advanced by Third World countries (the rights of peoples to peace, to development, to noninterference) than with those rights advocated by Western governments.

The dividends Moscow receives from this rather inexpensive support of the near-totality of African demands are not negligible. Implicitly, the Soviet Union has managed to establish with its African partners a diplomatic code of conduct on both the bilateral level and the multilateral level. It presupposes, in the first place, that the Soviet Union never appear to identify with the United States, for which reason the tone of "anti-Soviet" resolutions on Afghanistan or Kampuchea will always remain softer than the tone of resolutions against the United States (on Grenada, Puerto Rico). Although largely condemned, the invasion of Afghanistan did not mobilize African diplomacy, even the more anticommunist elements.

The Construction of Privileged Alliances

At the core of its ability to create and maintain alliances in the Third World, the Soviet Union is particularly interested in treaties of friendship and cooperation. Inaugurated in the 1971 Soviet-Indian treaty, this Soviet "pactomania" has been continually extended since then to a growing number of partners. Five treaties were signed with Arab countries between 1972 and 1985 (Egypt, Iraq, South Yemen, Syria, North Yemen), while five others were signed with African countries.

While expressing the Soviet Union's stated wish to institutionalize its relations with diplomatic partners of choice, the signing of such treaties nonetheless has occurred in concrete conditions that have been rather dissimilar. The treaties signed with Egypt and Somalia were essentially aimed at pinning down allies with a capricious fidelity to the Soviet Union. The abrogations of their treaties with the Soviet Union first by Egypt and then by Somalia suggest that on this point at least the effectiveness of such pacts is quite limited. In the case of treaties with India, Iraq, and Syria, it was the special influence of these states in their respective regions that

Table 12   Soviet-African Friendship Treaties

Countries	Dates
Somalia	July 11, 1974*
Angola	October 8, 1976
Mozambique	March 31, 1977
Ethiopia	November 20, 1978
Congo	May 31, 1981**

*Treaty abrogated on November 13, 1977 by Somalia.
**Does not include a military assistance clause.

motivated Soviet action. Finally, in the African and South Yemeni situations, the diplomatic-strategic dimension was compounded by a political-ideological dimension equally obvious. Angola, Mozambique, Ethiopia, and the Congo, like South Yemen, officially claimed ties to Marxism-Leninism along with a privileged alliance with the socialist community.

The diversity of these situations is even more pronounced if one considers not only the Soviet interpretation of these treaties but also the respective meaning each partner confers upon them. Through understanding the specific case of the Soviet-Congolese treaty, one can thus see that signing such a treaty was much less a response to pressing diplomatic-strategic preoccupations than a response to a concern for counterbalancing, in political-ideological terms, growing economic extraversion toward the West.

Friendship Treaties on Trial

The central axis of such treaties indisputably rests upon political-military guarantees that the Soviet Union grants to regimes that are potentially threatened and that it wants to maintain in power.

Beyond reaffirmation of the general principles of peaceful coexistence, all of the treaties invoke, significantly, the necessity of ensuring the conditions for the maintenance and development of social and economic victories for their peoples as well as the respect by each one of them of their natural resources. Simply put, Moscow vouches for the "socialist orientation" of its allies. Without, however, considering changes in these countries irreversible, the Soviet Union hopes, through these treaties, to attract the attention of the international community to the fact that it will not remain oblivious to any attempts to overthrow these regimes. Thus, when South African troops in August of 1981 penetrated deep into southern Angola, Moscow opportunely reminded all concerned of the existence of the Soviet-Angolan treaty.[48] That same year, shortly after a South African attack against ANC positions in Mozambique, the Soviet Union dispatched three naval units to be anchored in Mozambican ports. In December 1983, having caught wind of a South African plan to overthrow the Luanda regime with UNITA's backing, the Soviet Union addressed a severe word of caution to Pretoria directly.[49]

It goes without saying that granting such guarantees cannot be divorced from the considerations the Soviet Union expects of its partners. In Africa, for instance, the Soviet Union has always tried to exchange its support for military facilities. However modest, such facilities are operational in Angola (the use of Angolan airports for air surveillance of the seas, mooring rights in Angolan ports for the Soviet West African naval detachment previously anchored in Conakry), in Mozambique (stopover rights for its craft en route to Antarctica, repairs of its trawlers), and in Ethiopia (naval and air facilities on Dahlak Island). At the time of preparatory negotiations for the signing of the Soviet-Congolese friendship treaty, the Soviet Union insisted several times on access to harbor facilities in Pointe-Noire. The Congolese refusal to grant these Soviet demands explains in part the absence of a military clause in the Congolese-Soviet treaty.

An expression of a political-military guarantee, a friendship treaty also functions as an instrument of control or potential pressure for the Soviet Union over its allies. In January 1982 the Soviet Union reminded an Angolan delegation of its willingness to fulfill all of the treaties obligations. It even consented to participation in the large project to cofinance the Capanda Dam with Brazil. But in exchange, Moscow expected Luanda to offer stronger resistance to the regional *pax americana*.[50] At first, Luanda's diplomatic resolution largely matched the Soviet Union's interest in the area—to wit, the support it reiterated for the Angolan-Cuban declaration of February 4, 1982, on the conditions for a withdrawal of Cuban forces. But faced with the intensification of American-Angolan negotiations during the summer of 1982, Soviet concern resurfaced. Lacking the ability to control an ally worried about maintaining its decision-making autonomy whatever the cost, the Soviet Union finally modified its guarantee. Significantly, it reacted to the summer 1982 South African offensive by invoking an American–South African "plot" against Angola rather than by referring to its obligations under the friendship treaty.[51] And, as if in order to express more clearly its reprobation of Angola's diplomatic autonomy, the Soviet Union in 1982 and 1983 slowed the pace of its arms and spare parts deliveries.[52] In the spring of 1983, the head of Angolan diplomacy sounded a note of real alarm before the international conference on Namibia. A month later in May 1983, the Angolan head of state, who had until then never seemed in any hurry to go to the Soviet Union, boarded a plane to Moscow. His thinly veiled criticism of the slowness and the insufficiency of the Soviet Union's cooperation then confirmed clearly the true tensions existing in Soviet-Angolan relations.[53]

Soviet-Mozambican relations have in large measure been subject to tensions of the same order. In 1980, in a tense regional context and with deteriorating relations with Portugal and the United States, Mozambique afforded absolute priority to the intensification of its ties with the socialist camp. Immediately after his return from a visit to Moscow in November 1980, M. Machel designated one of the Frelimo principals, Marcelino Dos Santos, to "supervise and make more dynamic the relations of the Party and the state between the two countries, as well as the relations among mass organizations."[54] Thinking it could benefit from increased military assistance and from a socialist division of labor, Mozambique was counting on integration into the socialist camp. It reasserted membership in the CMEA and perceived assistance from socialist countries not as aid but as an international duty: "Cooperation between new socialist countries and advanced socialist countries should be established . . . on the basis of an unswerving defense of the expansion of socialism, since a socialism that is defended spreads." [55]

Although expressed in actions with greater realism than in the simple adoption of Soviet discourse on "international duties," Mozambican expectations were indeed real. Thus, sending a commercial delegation to the socialist countries in December 1981 was seen as necessarily leading to a "profound transformation of Mozambique's economic relations." [56] Other than the March 1982 signing of an economic protocol with the Soviet Union on cooperative farms and mining and oil explorations, the Soviet Union's economic commitment remained small. [57]

In the realm of the military, Soviet support proved to be as indispensable as it was insufficient. In February 1981, in the aftermath of a South African raid, the Mozambican regime discovered great breaks in an army trained by the Soviet Union and heavily bureaucratized.

Faced with the undeniable pressure of RENAMO (Movimento Nacional de Resistença) encouraged by Pretoria, Maputo's regime tried hard to rehabilitate veterans of the war of liberation, to create a militia, and to promote the formation of antiguerrilla units. To this end, he made certain to turn to Lisbon, which offered a meager supply of armaments and advisers. Fearing an erosion of its position, the Soviet Union unsuccessfully attempted to prevent this agreement from being implemented, through the mediation, it seems, of the Portuguese Communist Party. For Maputo, such actions offered proof that its allies were then "more preoccupied with their political intrigues than with respect for [its] sovereignty." [58] At any rate, when the delivery of seventeen tons of Portuguese armaments was announced, a sizable Soviet military delegation arrived in Maputo to evaluate Mozambique's new armament needs. Directing its military support to the formation of a classical army, Soviet assistance to Mozambique would remain too parsimonious to help confront the Republic of South Africa, and it was largely unadapted to assist in resisting RENAMO. Moreover, the slenderness of Mozambican financial resources does not seem to have been totally unrelated to the slimness of Soviet aid.

In Angola, on the other hand, where the stakes of its presence were significant, and where the reduction of military assistance was essentially dictated by political considerations, the Soviet Union progressively reestablished a balance of forces in the area. Apparently soothed by the Angolan president's explanations in May 1983, Moscow consented to reinforcing the qualitative potential of the Angolan army (with MiG-23s, Sam-9s, and MI-25D attack helicopters) and to renegotiating the Angolan military debt of $600 million and discussing the reorganization of its commercial debt, assessed at $1 billion. [59] The arrival of Soviet matériel in Angola at the end of the summer of 1983 was complemented by a noticeable reorganization of the Angolan defense apparatus. With some new systems, classical anti-air artillery could now be detected by radar, whereas pursuit was now subject to ground control that could detect South African crafts as soon as they took off from Namibia.[60] Several months later in December 1983, when the Republic of South Africa launched the Askari operation in southern Angola, it ran up against unexpected resistance by Angolan forces and registered its largest loss of men since the 1975 war. In spite of the fact that it maintained its superiority, the Republic of South Africa estimated that introduction of the new generation of military matériel into Angola was such that the cost of its military interventions had quickly become prohibitive.[61] And, as if to emphasize more clearly its support of Angola, the Soviet Union officially put Pretoria on notice regarding any attempt to overthrow the Angolan regime. A month later in January 1984, a joint Soviet-Cuban declaration of military support for Angola was also made public.[62]

Seemingly unequivocal, the significance of these "signals" sent out by the Soviet Union was, as it turns out, rather ambiguous. Coming only a short time after the South African cease-fire proposal in December 1983, the Soviet warning to Pretoria was related to the Soviet wish to insert itself into the United States–South Africa–Angola diplomatic game and to dissuade Angola from responding favorably or precipitously to Pretoria's offer. Whereas the MPLA regime took advantage of the strengthening of Soviet aid to increase its room for diplomatic maneuvering, the Soviet Union dispensed its aid only to induce it to oppose a regional settlement sponsored by the United States. This difference of interpretation led Moscow to express, in veiled terms, its opposition to the Lusaka accords and to dissuade SWAPO from facilitating their implementation.[63] Similarly, Moscow expressed skepticism about the chances of seeing the Nkomati Accords put an end to the "aggressive strategy" of the Republic of South Africa.[64]

Alliances without allegiance? If the effort of socialist countries committed to training cadres was indeed sizable, its political profitability still remains uncertain. A decade seems too short to gauge the degree of "sovietization" of certain elites. Moreover, the implementation, even advanced, of the components of the Soviet model is not necessarily incompatible with preservation of political autonomy vis-à-vis the Soviet Union. The examples of China and Vietnam are particularly illuminating on this point.

In fact, the main benefit to the Soviet Union of its alliances in Africa is at the diplomatic level. At the United Nations, for example, on the political issues important to the Soviet Union and diplomatically expensive for its African allies (Afghanistan, Kampuchea), the Soviet Union has succeeded in effectively mobilizing those allies and limiting its own diplomatic isolation.

Table 13 Soviet-African Diplomatic Solidarity

	Afghanistan					Kampuchea				
	1980	1981	1982	1983	1984	1980	1981	1982	1983	1984
Resolutions[1]	35/37	36/34	37/65	38/29	39/13	35/6	36/5	37/6	38/3	39/6
Results	112-22-12	116-23-12	114-21-13	116-20-17	119-20-18	97-23-29	100-25-19	105-25-19	105-23-19	110-22-18
USSR	no	no	no	no	no	no	no	no	no	no
Angola	no	no	no	no	no	no	no	no	no	no
Mozambique	no	no	no	no	no	no	no	no	no	abst.
Ethiopia	no	no	no	no	abst.	no	no	no	no	no
Congo	abst.	abst.	abst.	abst.	no	abst.	abst.	abst.	abst.	abst.
Madagascar	no	no	no	no	no	abst.	abst.	abst.	abst.	abst.
Sao Tome e Principe	no	no	2	abst.	abst.	abst.	abst.	abst.	abst.	abst.
Seychelles	no	no	2	abst.	abst.	no	no	no	2	2

1. The first number indicates "yes" votes, the second, "no," and the third, abstentions.
2. Absent at the time of the vote.
Source: Resolutions and decisions adopted by the General Assembly during the first part of its 35th, 36th, 37th, 38th, and 39th sessions.

With reference to the votes of the General Assembly on these two issues in 1980 and 1984 (see accompanying table), two observations deserve to be made.

In the first place, the bloc of countries siding with the Soviet Union never numbered more than approximately twenty. If one subtracts from this number the states of the CMEA and Laos, what remains is a bit fewer than ten countries, of which three are Arab states (Libya, Syria, South Yemen) and four are African states. This, then, is a first indication of the relative importance now taken on by Africa in the "reservoir" for mobilization of Soviet diplomatic support. Among these states, three demonstrate (almost) unfailing support: Angola, Ethiopia, and Mozambique. These three states voted identically with the Soviet Union nine times out of the ten votes taken on these questions.

Outside this diplomatic "square" is drawn a second circle of African countries that regularly abstain on one question or another in order not to hinder Soviet diplomacy. Thus, the Congo regularly abstains on the Afghan question while voting systematically with the Soviet Union on Kampuchea. Inversely, Madagascar, which has supported the Soviet Union on the Afghan question since 1980, has abstained just as regularly on Kampuchea.

Political interpretation of this voting pattern is often uncomfortable inasmuch as it seems difficult to isolate the comportment of a state at the United Nations from the whole of its foreign policy. This being the case, three keys to interpretation can be offered here.

In the first place, the coincidence of voting patterns reflects the coincidence of perceptions of the international order. For those societies at war, the affirmation of solidarity with the Soviet Union makes it possible to give the appearance of belonging to a single community and stems from concern not to weaken this tie in the face of the prime adversary, the United States. Although expressed with less clarity than by Angola, Ethiopia, and Mozambique, the regular abstention of countries like Burkina, Cape Verde, Guinea-Bissau, or Uganda on the questions of Afghanistan and Kampuchea expresses a real desire not to judge Moscow by the same standard as Washington.

In the second place, diplomatic fidelity often reflects a diplomatic bargain between "patrons" and "clients." In different cases, the meaning of a vote involves complex preoccupations. Because they identify themselves as Marxist-Leninist and confer official privilege on their relations with the Soviet Union, states like the Congo and Benin officially support the Soviet position on Afghanistan. But at the decisive moment of voting, they take refuge in abstention.

In fact, everything suggests that the Soviet Union itself is not wholly sure about future relations with its privileged allies. In this respect, a careful examination of the order of countries cited at each anniversary of the October Revolution almost unerringly points to the uncertain evolution in Soviet diplomatic priorities at any given time. In 1979 and 1980, neither Angola nor Ethiopia nor Mozambique was singled out for mention. In 1981 Angola was cited for the first time, ahead of Ethiopia, and with no mention of Mozambique. In 1982 these three states were jointly cited for the first time but in a significant order: Ethiopia was placed at the head in front of the other two, which were both mentioned at the same level.[65] The disappearance of any mention of these three states after 1983 seems to signal diminishing Soviet attention to Africa. Even if it seems probable that Soviet interest in Ethiopia is continuing to increase, it seems difficult for Moscow to single out Ethiopia without such an action being considered an abandonment of its southern African allies. At the same time, Moscow seems to have been too put off by the Lusaka and Nkomati accords to grant Angola and Mozambique as much importance as before.

In southern Africa the Soviet Union has found itself well placed at a juncture that limits both the progress of its influence and the collapse of its positions. It is perhaps in this particular and paradoxical relationship that one can apprehend the specific nature of its privileged alliances in Africa. In the aftermath of the Lusaka and Nkomati accords, which one might have thought sounded the death knell of Soviet influence in southern Africa, it has become interesting to take stock, at the United Nations, of the ties that have united the Soviet Union and its allies. Such observations seem particularly useful in light of the fact that the price imposed by Washington on Mozambique for certain Western favors (the development of bilateral aid, its speedy admission to the IMF and the World Bank) involved a softening of its anti-Western diplomatic behavior. On the question of Afghanistan, the Mozambican position, like that of Angola, did not budge one iota. In January 1985 Mozambique even went as far as establishing diplomatic relations with the Kabul regime. Addressed primarily to the Soviet Union, this diplomatic signal meant that the privileged nature of the Soviet-Mozambican alliance would not be blemished by the signing of the Nkomati accords. On the question of Kampuchea, on the other hand, the Mozambican position changed slightly after Nkomati. Here, the message was addressed more to the West and most particularly to the United States. It tends to demonstrate that a diplomatic alignment with the Soviet Union is in no way unconditional, even if the distancing must remain cautious and gradual.

Finally, diplomatic solidarity has often resulted from the strong political-military dependence of certain states on the Soviet Union and from the inevitable shrinkage in their margin for diplomatic maneuvering with respect to the Soviet Union. Nevertheless, it is difficult to imagine states like Angola, Ethiopia, and Mozambique going so far as to condemn the Soviet invasion of Afghanistan. Aside from the pressures the Soviet Union could exert on them at the time of a vote, these states would not breach their solidarity with the Soviets unless such a move assured them of a diplomatic gain clearly superior to that offered by their alliance with Moscow. As far as one can tell, it is not opposition to the Soviet Union on the question of Afghanistan that would help put an end to South Africa's support of UNITA.

The End of "Exteriority"?

Soviet policy rests upon a dual basis to which it owes the majority of its positions in the Third World. As a "power like others," the Soviet Union has made an effort to control the international system's rules of function to its own advantage. As an "ally in protest," it has sought to modify the system's constraints by associating itself obviously with the demands of subordinated states. This double position of "interiority" and "exteriority" has helped it combine diplomatic-strategic gains with ideological victories, without getting involved in constraining negotiations. Nevertheless, as it has experienced the need to manage its presence and consolidate its influence in the African arena, its plan of action has become fixed. That plan could only unfold with the construction of a relational framework assuring the benefits of exteriority while simultaneously releasing it of the constraints of interiority. The specific advantages, moreover, that the Soviet Union has conceded to its allies has imposed sometimes considerable responsibilities on them.

It is undeniably in the area of economics that the Soviet Union has the most difficulty in managing the duality of its strategy, for it is precisely in that sector that the advantages to African states prove the most uncertain. Without any ambiguity, indeed, the Soviet Union has conceived of its economic relations with the Third World only insofar as the Soviet economy can profit from them.[66] Its refusal to accept Mozambique's membership and that of other African states in the CMEA clearly expresses its concern for curtailing the number of beneficiaries of its unilateral economic support. Protected by the rule of "mutual advantage," the Soviet Union has imposed on its partners draconian economic and financial conditions containing a weak element of liberality.[67]

In the argument the Soviet Union has developed to justify its economic behavior, it has stressed that, unlike Western aid, its own economic assistance does not present any political constraints. In addition, the priority it accords to the public sector could reinforce the sovereignty of young states, whereas Western aid would tie them down to the capitalist system. Nonetheless, the Soviets have strongly counseled their allies against breaking their ties with the West, feeling that the arms race imposed by the United States deprives them of the financial means to come to their allies' aid.

This essentially political exercise was nevertheless accompanied by considerations of a quantitative nature for the first time in 1982. In a letter to UNCTAD, the Soviet Union announced that its assistance to Third World countries had attained 1.3% of its GNP in 1980. Notwithstanding, in the absence of specific indications of the conditions on that aid, the distribution among different beneficiaries, the distinction between the commercial flow and aid, and the specific geographic delimitation of the Third World, such figures seem devoid of any credibility. In order to find in Soviet statistics the 30 billion rubles it claims to have disbursed to the developing world between 1976 and 1980, one would have to add the total equipment deliveries to developing countries in the context of technical assistance projects to the whole of commerce with non-European communist countries.[68]

In fact, the need for the Soviet Union to become involved in the debate on aid while continuing to be vague on the financial flow to the Third World expresses its growing difficulty in maintaining a position of total exteriority with regard to the New International Economic Order (NIEO). Whereas in 1976 it officially informed the United Nations that the idea of a mandatory transfer of a part of its GNP to developing countries was unacceptable, by 1982 the Soviet Union found itself forced to justify its contribution to development using that criterion. Meanwhile, and under the growing political pressure of the UNCTAD, the Soviet Union eventually had to leave its "splendid isolation." At the 1979 Manila conference, it even expressed its opposition to measures of compensatory inequality promoted by southern countries. Because the NIEO demands seemed to the Soviet Union to arise far less out of the emergence of a radicalized political coalition than from a desire to accommodate the West, it has kept its distance from the UNCTAD. It has sought to make it a locus of commercial discussion between East and West rather than a center of expression for the Third World.[69]

Still today, while approving of the general direction of Third World demands, the Soviet Union demonstrates the most extreme reservations about any demands that might contradict its perceptions of the world (the division of the world between North and South, the refusal to take into account the givens of the East-West conflict) or that might harm its interests (plans for restructuring international economic relations without trying to integrate the demands of the socialist countries, and imposition of constraints on those countries equivalent to those by Western countries).

The sort of difficulty the Soviet Union has in proposing to the Third World an original model of economic relations is also clearly seen in the complicated bilateral relations it has been forging with its African partners. Outside of the training of cadres or the financing of certain projects to be reimbursed in kind, Soviet economic cooperation does not offer African states any clear advantage.[70] Quite the contrary, this economic cooperation has generated constraints that hinder their expansion.

On a commercial level, the structure of Soviet-African trade matches that which rules West-South relations at all levels. The Soviet Union sees itself above all as an exporter of equipment and African states as suppliers of raw materials. Moreover, commercial accords do not escape the fluctuations of world market rates. The Soviet-Tanzanian accord of 1980 on the sale of twenty thousand tons of cotton included a quarterly price revision clause, whence the concern of an increasing number of African states seeking a stabilization of the prices of goods exchanged with socialist countries.

Even when the payments for projects are expected to be made in kind, African economies find themselves in no way immune to certain abusive practices. Reported in the case of the mines of the Congo and Guinea, such abuses are even more frequent in the business of fishing. By not respecting the international rules on netting, Soviet ships directly imperil the reproduction of aquatic fauna. Moreover, Soviet trawlers have fulfilled the fish deliveries expected under Soviet-African fishing agreements only very incompletely.

In the industrial sector, the implementation and proper functioning of projects have been compromised by the exceptionally slow pace of deliveries and the very imperfect quality of materials supplied. Thus, in Kindia (Guinea) the railway system built between Debelé and Conakry with the help of the Soviet Union has proved particularly defective. In five years, 147 cars, 5 locomotives, 500 meters of tracks, as well as 54,300 tons of bauxite were lost.[71] In Ajeokuta the implementation of the iron and steel project was hindered for a long time by the inferior quality of Czech and East German materials.

The rigidity of functional norms for the Soviet economic system is necessarily reflected in the working methods of its assistance personnel. In the Congo, for example, a mission of planners dispatched at the time of the preparation of the 1981–85 five-year plan largely failed. In proposing planning norms mapped out following those of Gosplan, Soviet planners demonstrated a poor ability to adapt to the Congo's peculiarities. Whether ignorant or feigning ignorance of the political criteria governing the selection of investment projects, they found themselves logically remote from the decision-making process. As for their proposals for establishing an integrated system of planning indicators, they were hardly retained.

The Soviet Union is timidly beginning to recognize the difficulties that it has had trouble admitting to itself for a long time. It has admitted its lack of experience in constructing industrial units in tropical environments and recognized that the industrial norms it was proposing were out of scale for the needs of African states. Finally, it has noted that the rigid rules of its planning aggravate delays in deliveries.[72]

Soviet assistance, which persists in concentrating on energy and industrial sectors, can therefore only contribute marginally to the recovery of essentially agricultural African economies. In Mozambique, the dismantling of the Limpopo agro-industrial complex, in which the Soviet Union, the German Democratic Republic, and Bulgaria were involved, confirmed the inadequacy of such projects given African limitations.[73]

Lacking the ability to remedy the slenderness of its financial resources quickly, the rigidity of its planned economic system, and its technological weaknesses, the Soviet Union has gradually had to entertain the possibility of cooperating with third parties (Western countries or new industrial countries). At Capanda (Angola), a dam and an electrical power station will be jointly undertaken by the Soviet Union, Brazil, and Portugal. Thus everything would indicate that a better economic integration of the Soviet Union into Africa should go through a cross-fertilization of its operations with those of Western capitalist powers.

The disadvantages for the Soviet Union of settling on a position of exteriority concerning African problems is accompanied by an erosion of its valorized image as a "power unlike the others." Certainly, there is the example of the Ethiopian famine of the fall of 1984 to demonstrate that the modesty of its economic aid was amply compensated for in the eyes of Ethiopian authorities by its willingness to facilitate massive deportation of "uncontrolled" populations into Tigre. But the attractiveness of such solutions often recommended by "big brother" cannot dissipate the growing propensity of the Soviet Union to cash in on its aid with military advantages that it nonetheless denies seeking. During the course of the last ten years, the Soviet effort has particularly been focused on West African states to enhance its observation of maritime activity traveling via the Cape route. Heavily solicited, Congo and Guinea-Bissau have both refused to give in to Soviet demands.

Without any decisive political anchor points, the Soviet Union therefore finds itself inclined to make its military cooperation its particular lever of influence. In southern Africa, Angolans and Mozambicans have quickly recognized the Soviet capacity to use Soviet arms and spare parts deliveries to interfere with their diplomatic choices. Soviet military assistance programs are, moreover, accompanied by a weighty presence that is more than the beneficiaries really need. That is why certain African states do not hesitate to reduce (Madagascar), indeed expel (Nigeria), Soviet military missions.

Even with allies reputed to be most faithful, the Soviet Union has had a hard time limiting the weakening of its position. In the Congo the laughable amount of its economic commitment, along with its political pressure for access to certain naval facilities, have eaten into its capital in political confidence in that country. This disillusion will nevertheless not dissuade the PCT from seeking its ideological imprimatur at the same time.

At any rate, the suspicion that arises because of "certain practices" of the Soviet Union's leads most of the Marxist-Leninist states to counterbalance the Soviet presence with that of other socialist states. In sensitive areas such as state security, for example, the presence of Cuban or North Korean advisers is generally judged preferable to that of Soviet experts. The historical examples of Yugoslavia and China indicate that maintaining state security apparatus outside of all Soviet control is essential to escape subjugation to it. The expulsion of Soviet diplomats from Ethiopia at the beginning of 1984, when it was alleged that they had tried to influence nominations within the Party, demonstrates clearly that implementation of an external model is not without dangers for those who engage in this activity.

In fact, the privileged nature of alliances forged by the Soviet Union with selected partners cannot totally obscure the partial disagreements between Soviets and Africans. For the Soviet Union, it is primarily a matter of seeing that the partial reproduction and recurrence of communist political culture in Africa occur hand in hand with maintenance of a constraining diplomatic-strategic alliance, whereas for its partners, being anchored in a socialist universal should favor the preservation of their decision-making autonomy. In the middle of the eighties, Soviet-African relations still rest upon a contractual relationship of yet undispelled ambiguity.

6

Conclusion

The thirty years of African independences draw to an end on an ambiguous note for the superpowers. Their influence on the continent is considerably greater now than in 1960. Without having become masters of the game of African crises, they have managed to have a durable influence on the rhythms of exacerbation and resolution in Africa. The exclusive tête-à-tête between the African states and the European powers is finished. The multilateralization of Africa's international relations is probably an irreversible fact. And Africa is presently set to world time. It submits like other regions to the rhythm of relations between the superpowers. From this point of view, the Angolan crisis did indeed play the role for Africa that Dien Bien Phû played in Asia and that the Suez crisis did in the Near East.

That being so, Africa continues to fail to command the stable, primary interest of the superpowers, even taking into account the stakes of South Africa. And that is, moreover, where the greatest ambiguity in their actions lies. Unlike Latin America, the Near East, and Asia, which maintain relations of historic, geopolitical, or economic proximity with at least one of the superpowers, Africa falls short of fitting into this network of determinants, or else it fits episodically, indirectly, or fragmentarily. In this regard, the media attention focused on certain African issues cannot be overestimated. The Antiapartheid Act of 1986 only succeeded because it came out of a coalition of diverse interests, some of which were totally irrelevant to South African problematics (e.g., the decisive role played by protectionist lobbies in blocking certain imports from South Africa).

Indeed, the superpowers' ambition is more to reduce the "nuisance value" of African tensions than to extirpate its causes. Their concern is thus less to promote "socialism" or "liberalism" than to dissuade their respective clients from using internal or regional conflicts to ends that are

This chapter, written in 1989, replaces the Conclusion of the original French edition.

incompatible with their own global priorities. This ambivalence of action deserves emphasis. For it is precisely when the *concertation* [action in concert] between the superpowers shows signs of apparent effectiveness in the Horn and southern Africa that liberalism's and socialism's chances seem weaker than ever. In this regard, any ideological failure of the Soviet Union should not cause us to lose sight of an American failure, even if the latter's is less acute. Political allies such as Sudan, Somalia, and Liberia are in a state of total political entropy. This disjunction between strong diplomatic-strategic control and a devaluation of "rational ideologic expectations" suggests the value of not overestimating the consequences of Soviet-American cooperation for definitive settlements in the Ethiopian, Angolan, Mozambican, Sudanese, or South African conflicts. And this hiatus deserves particular note at a time when Africa is dealing with the logic of loss of status, in other words, of the process of international marginalization.

The Logic of Loss of Status

The loss of status rests on several paradoxes. While Africa may have little influence at the level of production and exchange, it is not for being unintegrated into the world economy. Quite the contrary, African states are among those whose share of the wealth in world trade is the greatest, three times that of southern Asia. This same paradox exists in foreign aid. The most marginalized continent is also the one where foreign aid amounts to the greatest share of internal gross product. It averages ten times more than aid to eastern Asia. One of the sources of Africa's current loss of international status lies, for example, in the excessive assimilation of Western models of consumption by certain African elites. Indeed, those models have had the effect of increasing production costs and thereby reducing the continent's economic competitiveness. Thus Africa suffers from neither an excessive nor an insufficient integration into the world system but from a lopsided integration. It is insufficient where it should be strong and over-extended where it should be more contained.

This being said, if all of these factors are evident in the eighties, they are nevertheless not new. The changes in economic indicators do not in and of themselves help to explain the unfavorable status of Africa on the international scene. The loss of status is a result of the new hierarchy of values in the world system, of conditions unfavorable for African participation, of production and exchange networks, of its poor contribution to international equilibria, whether these are seen as nuisances or contributions.

In the sixties, Africa was able to capitalize on the dynamics of the ideology of decolonization that placed less value on the economic importance of states than on their political or diplomatic activity. To simplify things, let us say that the collective importance of Africa, in such situations as at the United Nations, compensated for its economic handicaps. Multilateralism was thus relatively effective in the double context of East-West conflict and Sino-Soviet rivalry.

In this context, the diplomatic-strategic level was in fact the only one on which the superpowers acted; their action was not correlated to any economic or cultural sort of strategy. This last point has probably been neglected by the United States, although there was substantial pressure from the Nigerians, for example.

In the seventies, the problematics of the relationship with the international environment modified. What is especially striking immediately is Africa's change in level, i.e., its apparent integration into an originally economic dynamic at a time when the problematics of independence were unclear. In examining the changes in net entry of foreign capital, for example, into Africa in the seventies, one is struck not so much by its absolute value as by its increase in frequency. The evolution is particularly spectacular in countries as different as Malawi, Tanzania, Niger, Sudan, Madagascar, Kenya, Cameroon, the Congo, the Ivory Coast, and, of course, Nigeria. Between 1972 and 1980, guaranteed public debt increased from $7 to $40 billion. Two financial sources, up to then only marginally used, enter the scene: private bank financing and private investment in the oil sector. In the space of a few years, and without any change in the conditions of the global system of production, Africa witnessed a singularly improved position on the ladder of world trade dynamics.

Four elements of an economic, strategic, and ideological nature converged in an unprecedented manner to allow strategic valorization of Africa. On the economic level the quadrupling of oil rates had an explosive effect on Africa in two ways: directly, on the new generation of African oil countries (Angola, Cameroon, Gabon, Nigeria), and indirectly, on all of the other producers of raw materials, who in turn found themselves drawn upward by the new oil dynamics. Africa thus ended up endowed with a new level of resources wholly unequaled. Between 1970 and 1977 Nigerian oil receipts increased twenty-five times. Such solvency then eased the entry of Africa into the private financing network and freed it to a certain extent from the political constraints of public aid. In this context, the World Bank made a strong showing by granting non-concessionary loans. Africa's indebtedness to this institution increased from $600 million in 1972 to $1.2 billion in 1977. Export credits were not far behind; they increased to thirty-five percent per year between 1975 and 1980.

This new economic situation naturally had considerable political consequences. On a psychological level, the logic of OPEC gave credence to the idea that the nature of world power relations was in the process of fundamental change.

Like other countries, certain African states began to feel that the possession of new resources enabled them to "buy" development without inference in their political choices. The fact that between 1977 and 1983 countries such as Angola and the Congo were the principal beneficiaries, along with Nigeria, of the increase in net income to Africa is in this regard very significant. The fact that this income was apparently not subject to obstacles of a political sort probably fed the sense of being able to mix and choose external referents. This sense of increased autonomy was then reinforced by an unprecedented factor: Africa's perception of being endowed with unused "nuisance value" power. Nigeria, for example, became the first African state having significant interest for the American economy. The conjunction in time of the oil crisis and the crumbling of Portuguese colonialism gave rise to the West's hitherto unknown sense of precariousness of access to natural resources, which enhanced Africa's position in several ways:

1. as a stable source of oil supply to mitigate the effect of the Arab embargo (western Africa);
2. as a support to strategic control of Persian Gulf supplies (the Horn);
3. and, finally, as a source of raw mineral materials whose supply was no longer guaranteed (southern Africa).

Thus, almost concomitantly, three African subregions were endowed with significant strategic significance for the West. Each of these regions was suddenly involved in at least two or three major tensions of the moment (the East-West conflict, the Israeli-Arab conflict, the North-South conflict). Strategic valorization would nonetheless have been less pronounced had it not been symmetrically reinforced by the strategic availability of the Soviet Union to the urban political elites modeled in statism and mistrust of the peasants and merchants, and bent on making up for their weak representivity by taking obvious recourse to military and ideological resources generated by a communist system reinvigorated by Cuba. The political genius of African leaders will then have been not only to have taken advantage of all opportunities offered by this new global situation working to the West's disadvantage (in the East-West conflict, the Israeli-Arab conflict, and the North-South conflict) but also to have known how to amplify the meaning and scope of the superpowers' commitment to Africa, beyond what this continent might have represented for them. That was what the Ethiopians, Angolans, and Mozambicans were doing for a time in the Soviet camp in making their diplomatic alignment and their recourse to the Marxist-Leninist vulgate the signs of a "serious" ideological radicalism needing proportional Soviet support. That was what Nigeria successfully accomplished in "dramatizing" the problems of southern Africa for the United States while playing the economically stable and politically indispensable partner. This was also what Somalia managed to do in turning its newfound Arabism and its situational pro-Westernism into the sources of an undreamed-of valorization. Between 1978 and 1982, an important time in Africa's strategic valorization, the net disbursements of public aid for development increased from $4.7 to $7.3 billion. Thus, except in some very specific situations, most African countries managed to profit from the classic benefits of diplomatic bargaining, from the valorization of sources of economic exchange, and also from access to resources external to the diplomatic-strategic system. In addition, they were able to use external referents to obscure less admissible strategies. Marxist radicalism, for example, was the chosen weapon in strategies of exclusion. In the Horn, Marxism was for Ethiopia an instrument of ultranationalist strategy.

At the end of the seventies, the African states gave the impression of being able to play successfully in several registers. This dynamics was totally reversed in the eighties, to Africa's disadvantage. What one thought of as a modification of Africa's relationship to its environment has turned out to be but an exceptional "political moment," largely reversible.

The sources of Western economic vulnerability were quickly reduced by the lessening of constraints on oil supply. In 1979 oil represented twenty-two percent of OECD countries' exports. In 1987 the figure dropped to seven percent. Nigeria was one of the first victims of the double process of diversification of American sources of oil imports and the sharp reversal of the oil situation. The dynamics of this decline has had a negative effect on other raw materials. Africa has thus discovered the volatility of its "nuisance value" power. It has suffered in this crisis three ways: through the reduction in exchange rates, which cost it $3 billion between 1981 and 1987; through the changes in consumer habits and technological advances that reduce interest in raw materials; and, finally, through market losses to Asia. The debt crisis, a particularly sensitive issue for the oil countries of Africa, intensifies the darkness of the general picture.

Africa has thus ended up being dependent again on bilateral flow, in other words, on resources dictated to by diplomatic-strategic imperatives. The superpowers' direct responses to its requests have been a mockery. American bilateral aid to Africa is regressing; the Soviet Union's, negligible on the economic level, has weakened on the military level.

Economic considerations do not by themselves explain the strategic decline of Africa. The decline is also a result of modification in the superpowers' priorities. For a long time, the superpowers have tried above all to purchase the silence of clients to whom economic and military aid had been granted. From this perspective, being numbered among supporters was a sign of international respectability or, conversely, of reprobation. The Soviet Union played extensively in this register, taking note of the numerical importance of the African states. Today, in a context of relative ideological appeasement and exacerbation of economic tensions, alignment with the superpowers is changing its meaning. On the Soviet side, for example, gaining diplomatic support or ideological conformity is much less attractive for the Soviet Union as soon as it has to guarantee a large financial cost in return. It is ready to accept ideological distancing of its clients to the extent that doing so reduces the Soviet Union's load. For the United States, the process is even clearer. In a context of weakening global American power, the quality of a client really only has any value if it agrees to participate in reduction of costs to the United States or in lessening its decline in power. On the Soviet side as on the American side, we are witnessing, then, a process of selecting allies according to their political faithfulness. To be sure, this process is neither irreversible nor linear. But it nonetheless indicates a trend that is not in Africa's favor.

The relative decline of the superpowers' commitment has thus logically cast new light on the importance of third party actors. On the economic level, bilateral European actors have increased the grant portion of their aid over the course of the last few years and maintained their commitments in Africa at approximately thirty percent of their public aid for development. As for the World Bank, under the joint pressure of the United States and France, it has committed itself to reserving fifty percent of International Development Association (IDA) resources for Africa. But these apparently reassuring figures unfortunately must not be interpreted as mitigation of the loss of status. Between the era of 1980–83 and 1987, the net financial flow to Africa dropped from $19.6 to $13 billion. In real terms, the erosion is even more noticeable; since 1981, it has been on the order of thirty percent. And if one looks at the net transfers and no longer just at the net flow, the loss of resources is even greater. From $8 billion in 1980, they dropped to $4 billion in 1987. By assessing the annual resource needs of Africa at $9 billion, the deficit increases to $5 billion, that is, to the amount of the debt service discharged annually by the African states. In 1988, the net transfers of the World Bank to Africa hardly surpassed $600 million, that is, barely five percent of the current deficit of African states. Worsening the situation, the role of traditional mediators between Africa and the international environment seems increasingly compromised.

The French Decline

This new reality directly affects France. To be sure, on the face of it, nothing has changed. France's military guarantee is still strong and effective, as Chadian events have shown. French economic aid is still the highest in Africa; and Franco-African networks still seem alive and well, as witnessed in Franco-African and francophone summits. But keeping to this level of things neglects the considerable shift of stakes from the classic diplomatic-strategic sphere to the economic sphere. On this level, the French model is in crisis. The system of the Franc Zone, on which the model is largely based, is increasingly challenged. This monetary union is based, we must remember, on three major principles: a fixed exchange rate since 1948 between the French franc and the CFA franc; the total freedom of transfer within the zone; and the unlimited convertibility of CFA francs by the French Department of the Treasury, prorated according to the resources in French francs held by the states. Today, two problems assail the Franc Zone. The first is the growing gap between the exchange rate of francophone countries and that of other African countries. Between 1985 and 1987, the effective exchange rate of the Franc Zone appreciated 21.8 percent, while that of the majority of African countries depreciated 21.3 percent—that is, a split of more than 40 percent in four years. The result is that the cost of labor is three times higher in Abidjan than in Accra. The second problem is the slippage between the base currency (the French franc) and the currency in which the ever-increasing, extra–Franc Zone exchanges are drawn up (the dollar). With an overvalued currency, francophone countries lose on two counts: their exports are more expensive and therefore less competitive; but on the other hand, their imports are not any less so, for they come in large part from France.

Should one therefore devaluate? The question is an economic one, but it is also an eminently political one. The classic effects of devaluation are well known; it should permit reducing global demand through the increase in the price of imports, and rebalancing public finance by valorizing budgetary receipts tied to foreign relations. But the risks are proportional to the stakes. In the African economies dominated by primary exports, devaluation has little chance of leading to an increase in receipts, since prices are determined by the world market. Besides, the difficulty most African states have controlling inflation has always been offered, on the French side, as a sound reason not to devaluate the CFA franc. But today the context has changed. The refusal to devaluate the CFA franc is a result of political conservatism and not of any rational economic calculation. What is at stake is the protection of a French model of consumption in Africa, where importing products is not tied to having currency. Moreover, a recent confidential French study has stressed that the performances of Franc Zone states have been in the process of declining compared to extra–Franc Zone countries that have devalued their currency. Based on four criteria (imports, trade balance, current cash balance, and growth of the gross domestic product), Franc Zone countries are encountering a more negative evolution than other countries. There is thus economic penalization of francophone countries.

France, which envisioned relations with Africa based on protectionist conceptions (Franc Zone, "*pré carré*"), is proving to be increasingly in-capable of making its strategy evolve. Its economic failings are spectacular in that respect. On the macroeconomic level, France has nothing with which to counter the IMF and the World Bank rigorously. It is torn between its interests as a major Western power in favor of the logic of structural adjustment and as a vigorous defender of the "protected interests" of African elites and French economic groups. In fact, Africa is of increasingly marginal economic interest to France. And, to be sure, economic rationality never did dominate French strategy in Africa. But will the hiatus between the economic insignificance of the continent and the power reserve it supposedly provides France be durable?

The future of the superpowers in Africa is not written anywhere. But whatever the strength of foreign control, that control will hardly in and of itself be able to counter the international logic of Africa's loss of status.

Notes

INTRODUCTION

1. Throughout this book we will refer, improperly, to "Africa" as meaning only the sub-Saharan area, thereby excluding from our field the western Sahara, Morocco, Algeria, Tunisia, Libya, and Egypt. Although in certain respects this division is purely artificial, it seems relatively convenient for understanding the game the superpowers play. We would have been forced to extend our problematics to the conflict in the Middle East if we had included Arab Africa.

2. M. Amondji, *Felix Houphouët et la Côte d'Ivoire: L'envers d'une légende* (Paris: Karthala, 1984).

3. These different biases and real difficulties should not, however, obscure the profound effort at renewal of africanist political analysis. Undertaken by both French and African researchers, this work tends to make visible the limits of state political control on subordinate actors and to understand the behaviors the latter engage in to resist authoritarian modernization projects. Cf. J.-F. Bayart, "L'Etat en Afrique" (Paris: Fayard, 1989), and C. Coulon, *Les Musulmans et le pouvoir en Afrique noire* (Paris: Karthala, 1983).

CHAPTER 1

1. W. Williams, *Black Americans and the Evangelization of Africa (1877–1900)* (Madison: University of Wisconsin Press, 1982).

2. M. Charles, *The Soviet Union and Africa: The History of an Involvement* (Boston: University Press of America, 1984), 7.

3. A. Gromyko, "Soviet-Ethiopian Relations Today" (paper presented to the Eighth International Conference on Ethiopian Studies), 6.

4. *Bibliografia Afriki* (Moscow, 1964, 76–79); quoted in Charles, *The Soviet Union and Africa*, 7.

5. J. Kenyatta is said to have traveled to the Soviet Union on two occasions, the first in 1929 and the second in 1932–33. J. Murray-Brown, *Kenyatta,* 2d ed. (London: Allen & Unwin, 1979), 168.

6. Declaration made by C. Hull, *Department of State Bulletin* 10 (248), March 28, 1944, 276.

7. J. Penfield, "The Role of the US in Africa: Our Interests and Operations," *Department of State Bulletin* 40 (1041), June 8, 1959, 845.

203

8. J. Spencer, *Ethiopia, the Horn of Africa, and US Policy* (Cambridge: Institute for Foreign Policy Analysis, 1977), 23.

9. H. Carrère d'Encausse, *La politique soviétique au Proche-Orient, 1955–1975* (Paris: Presses de la Fondation nationale des sciences politiques, 1975), 27–42.

10. F. Bolton, *Report of the Special Study Mission to Africa,* US House of Representatives, 1956, 13.

11. R. Packenham, *Liberal America and the Third World: Political Development Ideas in Foreign Aid and Social Science* (Princeton: Princeton University Press, 1973).

12. B. Badie, *Le développement politique,* 3d ed. (Paris: Economica, 1984).

13. *Sovietskaya Etnografiya* 4 (1957). Quoted in *Mizan,* July–August 1960, 12.

14. Ismagilova, "Composition ethnique du Tanganyka," in *Des africanistes russes parlent de l'Afrique* (Paris: Présence africaine, 1960), 157.

15. E. Shils, *Political Development in the New States* (The Hague: Mouton, 1962), 90.

16. J. Coleman, "The Character and Viability of African Political Systems," in W. Goldschmidt, *The United States and Africa,* 43.

17. *International Affairs* 2 (1959): 106.

18. *Pravda,* March 3, 1960, quoted in *Mizan,* July–August 1960, 19.

19. *New Times (Novoë Vremya)* 25 (June 1960): 24.

20. *Trud,* April 2, 1960, quoted in *Mizan,* July–August 1960, 23.

21. USET (US Embassy Telegram), Addis Ababa, March 18, 1960 ("declassified" confidential document), 16.

22. Ibid., 2.

23. *Pravda,* March 27, 1960, quoted in *Mizan,* July–August 1960, 18.

24. USET, Addis Ababa, May 18, 1960 ("declassified" confidential document), 3.

25. G. Staruchenko, *Le principe d'autodétermination des peuples et des nations dans la politique étrangère de l'Etat soviétique* (Moscow: Progress, 1962), 186.

26. T. Farer, *War Clouds on the Horn of Africa* (Washington: Carnegie Endowment for International Peace, 1979), 115.

27. *Pravda,* July 20, 1960, quoted in *Soviet Documents on the Congo* (supplement to *Mizan,* July–August 1960), 9.

28. *Izvestia,* November 20, 1960, quoted in *Mizan,* December 1960, 24.

29. *The Great Soviet Encyclopedia, 1961* (in Russian), quoted in *Mizan,* December 1961, 29.

30. Y. Etinger and O. Milikyan, *Neutralism and Peace: Neutralist Policy in African and Asian Countries* (in Russian) (Moscow, 1964), quoted in *Mizan,* September 1964, 13.

31. *Pravda,* August 26, 1960, quoted in *Mizan,* October 1960, 3.

32. J.-F. Bayart, "La politique extérieure du Cameroon, 1960–1971," *Revue française d'études politiques africaines* 75 (March 1972): 56.

33. *Study Mission to Africa,* US Senate, January 14, 1962, 17.

34. *US Security Agreements and Commitments Abroad,* US Senate, June 1, 1970, 25.

35. USET, Addis Ababa, December 14, 1960 ("declassified" secret document).

36. USET, Addis Ababa, December 15, 1960 ("declassified" secret document).

37. USET, Delhi, February 24, 1962 ("declassified" secret document), 4.

38. USET, Addis Ababa, July 18, 1961 ("declassified" secret document), 11.

39. *Ethiopia and the Horn of Africa: US Relations with Ethiopia and the Horn,* Hearings, US Senate, August 1976, 36.

40. S. Weissman, *American Foreign Policy in the Congo, 1960–1964* (Ithaca: Cornell University Press), 44.

41. L. Battle, "Analytical Chronology of the Congo Crisis," White House, National Security Files, and USET, Brussels, September 28, 1960 ("declassified" secret documents).

42. DOS (Department of State), "Talking Paper for the President," November 17, 1961 ("declassified" confidential document).

43. Idem.

44. USET, Leopoldville, December 1962 ("declassified" secret document).

45. R. Hilsman, *To Move a Nation: The Politics of Foreign Policy in the Administration of J. F. Kennedy* (New York: Doubleday, 1967), 267.

46. USET, Leopoldville, February 8, 1964 ("declassified" secret document).

47. USET, Leopoldville, February 12, 1964 ("declassified" secret document).

48. DOS, "National Security Series: South Africa," intermediate draft, October 28, 1963 ("declassified" secret document), 197.

49. JCSM (Joint Chiefs of Staff Memorandum), "US Policy toward Portugal and South Africa," July 10, 1963 ("declassified" secret document).

50. DOS, "National Security Series: South Africa," 196.

51. "Report to the Chairman of the Task Force on Portuguese Territories in Africa," July 4, 1961 ("declassified" secret document), 2.

52. L. Crollen, *Portugal, the US, and NATO* (Louvain: Leuwen University Press, 1973), 127–28.

53. DOS, "National Security Series: South Africa," 163.

54. DOS, Rusk, Memorandum, June 15, 1963 ("declassified" secret document).

55. I. Potemkhin, *Ghana Today* (in Russian) (Moscow, 1959), 42, quoted in *Mizan*, July–August 1960, 15.

56. W. Scott Thompson, *Ghana's Foreign Policy, 1957–1966* (Princeton: Princeton University Press, 1969), 186.

57. C. Stevens, *The Soviet Union and Black Africa* (London: Macmillan, 1976).

58. Thompson, *Ghana's Foreign Policy*, 450.

59. This advantage was, however, reduced by the commitment made by Ghana to acquire, in exchange, expensive and poor quality Soviet products, not to mention the profit made by certain socialist countries through re-exporting Ghanian cocoa. I. Outters-Jaeger, *L'incidence du troc sur l'économie des pays en voie de développement* (Paris: OCDE, 1979), 81.

60. Thompson, *Ghana's Foreign Policy*, 274.

61. H. Chambre, *Union soviétique et développement économique* (Paris: Aubier-Montaigne, 1967), 383.

62. *Pravda*, May 31, 1962, quoted in *Mizan*, June 1982, 18.

63. Communist Party of the Soviet Union (CPSU) program adopted by the Twenty-second CPSU Congress, October 31, 1961. Supplement to *New Times* 8 (November 1961), 44.

64. *Pravda*, January 25, 1963, quoted in *Mizan*, February 1963, 10.

65. D. Goldsworthy, *Tom Mboya: The Man Kenya Wanted to Forget* (London: Heineman, 1982), 168–69.

66. USET, Accra, February 4, 1961 ("declassified" secret document).

67. DOS, "Memorandum to the President," September 24, 1961 ("declassified" top secret document).

68. USET, Conakry, "The Current Situation in Guinea and Its Implications for US Policy," May 12, 1961 ("declassified" secret document).

69. W. Attwood, *The Reds and the Blacks* (New York: Harper & Row, 1967), 63.

70. Ibid., 127–28.

71. E. Carrère d'Encausse and S. Schram, *L'URSS et la Chine devant les révolutions dans les sociétés préindustrielles* (Paris: Presses de la Fondation nationale des sciences politiques, 1970), 70.

72. As an example of revolutionary action, Chou En Lai cited the Moroccan decision to

shut down American bases. Reported by the Chinese agency NCNA, quoted in *Mizan*, May 1964, 49.

73. C. Cheng, *The Politics of the Chinese Red Army: A Translation of the Bulletin of Activities of the People's Liberation Army* (Stanford: Hoover Institution, 1966), 484.

74. N. Khrouchtchev, "Rapport à la session du Soviet suprême de l'URSS du 12 décember 1962" (Paris: collection Etudes soviétiques, no date), 45.

75. Quoted in A. Hutchinson, *China's African Revolution* (Boulder: Westview Press, 1975), 43.

76. *Pravda*, December 22, 1963, quoted in *Mizan*, June 1964, 1.

77. DOS, *Portuguese Africa: Background Papers,* July 10, 1963 ("declassified" confidential document). Note, however, that the absence of official American support was compensated for by the discreet involvement of nongovernmental agencies such as the African American Institute. The latter inaugurated the "East African Training Program" in Tanzania in 1963 for the children of Mozambican refugees. The Ford Foundation's contribution in Dar es Salaam was the creation of the Institute of Mozambique, directed by Frelimo.

78. Cf. G. Ball, *The Discipline of Power: Essentials of a Modern World Structure* (London: The Bodley Head, 1968).

79. DOS, G. Mennen Williams to the Secretary for Portuguese African Territories: Action Memorandum, April 29, 1964 ("declassified" secret document), 1.

80. DOS, G. Mennen Williams, Letter to US Ambassadors, March 19, 1964 ("declassified" secret document).

CHAPTER 2

1. J. Levesque, *La politique internationale de l'URSS* (Paris: Armand Colin, 1979), 229.

2. R. Tucker, "The American Outlook," in R. Osgood et al., *America and the World: From the Truman Doctrine to Vietnam,* vol. 1 (Baltimore: Johns Hopkins University Press, 1970), 38.

3. *Department of State Bulletin*, June 6, 1966, 54 (1406): 877.

4. After A. Ogunsanwo, *China's Policy in Africa, 1958–1971* (Cambridge: Cambridge University Press, 1974), 269–70.

5. R. Legvold, *Soviet Policy in West Africa* (Cambridge, MA: Harvard University Press, 1970), 240.

6. Ibid., 241.

7. *MEIMO* (5), May 1965, in C. McLane, *Soviet-African Relations,* 52.

8. *Azia i Afrika Segodnia* 11 (1965), cited in McLane.

9. Legvold, *Soviet Policy in West Africa,* 244.

10. American diplomatic archives reveal clearly the continued rapport maintained by the CIA with certain higher-ups of Nkrumah's regime. It had specific information available on the strategies of such men as Kewsi Armah (Minister of Foreign Trade) and Quaison-Sackey (Minister of Foreign Affairs). According to the CIA: "Background to President Nkrumah's Second Letter to President Johnson," Intelligence Information Cable, August 16, 1965 (partially "declassified" secret information).

11. *Pravda*, June 14, 1966, quoted in *Current Digest of the Soviet Press* (*CDSP*) 18 (24): 25.

12. *Izvestia*, March 12, 1967, quoted in *CDSP* 19 (10): 35.

13. *Izvestia*, April 20, 1966, quoted in *CDSP* 18 (16): 38.

14. *Izvestia*, May 25, 1966, quoted in *CDSP* 18 (21): 40.

15. D. Hall, "Naval Diplomacy in West African Waters," in S. Kaplan, ed., *Diplomacy*

of Power: Soviet Armed Forces as a Political Instrument (Washington: Brookings Institution, 1981), 528.

16. C. Gertzel, *The Politics of Independent Kenya* (London: Heineman, 1970), 67.

17. Kenyan African National Union.

18. J. Orwenyo, "The Soviet Union and Communism as Factors among Kenyan Intelligentsia in Kenya's Internal Problems, 1966–67" (Ph.D. diss., Georgetown University, 1973), 235.

19. *Pravda,* April 9, 1966, quoted in *Mizan,* May–June 1966, 99.

20. *Izvestia,* April 15, 1966, quoted in ibid., 98.

21. Houphouët-Boigny would say of the Soviet Union in 1965 that it had given up its ambitions to dominate. Radio Abidjan, September 28, 1965, quoted in McLane, *Soviet-African Relations,* 74.

22. Tass News Agency, January 10, 1972, quoted in ibid.

23. *Izvestia,* November 26, 1965, quoted in *CDSP* 27 (42): 26.

24. J. Mulira, "Soviet Bloc: Trade, Economic, Technical and Military Involvement in Independent Africa: A Case Study of Uganda, 1962–79," *Genève-Afrique* 19 (1): 53 (1981).

25. For details about the renegotiation of Soviet aid, see Tom Mboya's report after his return from Moscow. In C. Gertzel, *Government and Politics in Kenya* (Nairobi: East African Publishing House), 586–87.

26. *Izvestia,* January 6, 1966, quoted in *CDSP* 17 (1): 24.

27. *Pravda,* January 22, 1966, quoted in *CDSP* 18 (3): 26.

28. *Pravda,* August 3, 1966, quoted in C. McLane, *Soviet-African Relations,* 104.

29. *Za Rubežom* 19, April 25, 1967, quoted in *Mizan,* January–February 1969, 32.

30. A. Klinghoffer, "The USSR and Nigeria: The Secession Question," *Mizan,* March–April 1968, 65; and A. Stent, "The Soviet Union and the Nigerian Civil War: A Triumph of Realism," *Issue* 3 (2): 44 (Summer 1973).

31. O. Ojo, "Nigerian-Soviet Relations: Retrospect and Prospect," *African Studies Review* 9 (3): 55 (December 1976).

32. *Izvestia,* October 11, 1968, quoted in *CDSP* 20 (41): 20.

33. R. Ofoegbu, "Foreign Policy and Military Rule," in O. Oyediran, *Nigerian Government and Politics under Military Rule, 1960–1979* (London: Macmillan International College Editions, 1979), 139.

34. B. Porter, *The USSR in Third World Conflicts: Soviet Arms and Diplomacy in Local Wars, 1945–1980* (Cambridge: Cambridge University Press, 1984), 111.

35. G. Hudson, "Soviet Naval Doctrines and Soviet Politics, 1953–1975," *World Politics,* October 1976, 104.

36. *Izvestia,* May 26, 1970, quoted in McLane, *Soviet-African Relations,* 125.

37. G. Fawaz, "Le Soudan, le Parti communiste soudanais et le camp socialiste: Relations internationales et relations internationalistes" (doctoral diss., University of Paris), 189–90.

38. Proceedings of the CPSU–Syrian CP talks, quoted in G. Fawaz, "Le Soudan, le Parti soudanais," 196.

39. Cf., for example, the difference in the texts between the Russian version of *New Times (Novoë Vremya)* published July 23 and its English version after the failure of the putsch. *USSR and Third World* 1 (7): 414 (July 5–August 15, 1971).

40. Cf. the Moscow Radio commentaries of February 6 and October 8, 1971, quoted, respectively, in *USSR and Third World* 2 (3): 88 (January 11–February 14, 1971) and *USSR and Third World* 1 (9): 56 (September 20–October 24, 1971).

41. According to *Proposed Expansion of US Military Facilities in the Indian Ocean,* Hearings, US House of Representatives, February–March 1974, 159.

42. M. Mamdani, *Imperialism and Fascism in Uganda* (London: Heineman, Educational Books, 1983), 69–70.

43. "Bringing the officers' corps to the forefront is a remarkable phenomenon in the history of the struggle for national liberation," E. Joukov et al., in *Le Tiers Monde: Problèmes et perspectives* (Moscow: Moscow Editions, 1969), 64–65.

44. DOS, October 29, 1964 ("declassified" confidential document).

45. A. Lake, *The Tar Baby Option: US Foreign Policy towards Southern Rhodesia* (New York: Columbia University Press, 1974), 121.

46. *Sunday Times,* September 21, 1975.

47. G. Idang, *Nigeria: International Politics and Foreign Policy, 1960–1966* (Ibadan: Ibadan University Press, 1973), 63.

48. B. Ate, *Effects of Nigerian-US Bilateral Ties on Nigeria's Decolonization Policy, 1960–1966, 1970–1976* (Ph.D. Diss., Columbia University, 1980), 188.

49. USET, Lagos, March 26, 1964 ("declassified" confidential document).

50. R. Morris, *Uncertain Greatness: Henry Kissinger and American Foreign Policy* (New York: Harper & Row, 1977), 19.

51. S. Cronje, *The World and Nigeria: The Diplomatic History of the Biafran War, 1967–1970* (London: Sidgwick & Jackson, 1972), 228.

52. CIA, Intelligence Memorandum, "The Food Crisis in Eastern Nigeria," March 1969 ("declassified" secret document).

53. C. Ogene, *Interest Groups and the Shaping of Foreign Policy: Four Case Studies of US-African Policy* (New York: St. Martin's Press, 1983), 89.

54. *National Security Study Memorandum* 39.

55. Cf. B. Cohen and H. Schissel, *L'Afrique australe de Kissinger à Carter* (Paris: L'Harmattan, 1977).

56. A. Hartley, *American Foreign Policy in the Nixon Era* (London: IISS 110, 1975), 10–11 (Adelphi Papers).

57. Lake, *The Tar Baby Option,* 124.

58. Ibid., 125–26.

59. Morris, *Uncertain Greatness,* 111.

60. P. Hassner, "A la recherche de la cohérence perdue: Du côté de la semi-péripherie," *Revue française de science politique,* April 1980, 241.

61. S. Hoffman, *Primacy of World Order: American Foreign Policy since the Cold War* (New York: McGraw-Hill, 1977), 47.

62. R. Smith, "The Nature of American Interests in Africa," *Issue,* Summer 1972, 37.

63. *Africa: Report from the Continent: Report of a Special Study Mission to Africa,* November–December 1972 and November–December 1973, US House of Representatives, 1974, 141.

64. D. Newsom, "American Interests in Africa and African Development Needs," *Issue,* Spring 1972, 45.

65. *Boletin mensual de estatistica* (Lourenço Marques), no. 4, April 1973, and no. 6, June 1973.

66. *Area Handbook for Rhodesia* (Washington: American University, 1975), 239.

67. *African Contemporary Record, 1970–1971,* B436.

68. *African Contemporary Record, 1969–1970,* C42.

69. Ibid., C43.

70. Between 1968 and 1973, 43% of the total nationalizations in the Third World occurred in Africa. D. Jodice, "Sources of Change in Third World Regimes for Direct Investment, 1968–1976," *International Organization,* Spring 1980, 43.

71. *On Doing Business in Cabinda,* updated statement by Gulf Oil Co., no date.

72. *The Complex of US-Portuguese Relations before and after the Coup,* Hearings, US House of Representatives, March and October 1974, 186–87.

73. Ibid., 191.

74. *South Africa,* Hearings, US Senate, September 1976, 557ff.

75. Morris, *Uncertain Greatness,* 110.

76. *Implementation of US Arms Embargo against Portugal and South Africa and Related Issues,* Hearings, US House of Representatives, March–April 1973, 52.

77. Ibid., 58.

78. Lake, *The Tar Baby Option,* 36.

79. Ibid., 141–42.

80. *US Policy towards Southern Africa,* Hearings, US House of Representatives, June–July 1975, 179.

81. Ibid., 185.

82. *African Contemporary Record, 1972–1973,* A75.

83. See G. McGee, "The US Congress and the Rhodesia Chrome Issue," *Issue,* Summer 1972.

84. Henry Kissinger, *American Foreign Policy* (New York: Norton & Co., 1974), 233.

85. Conversations.

86. *Review of State Department Trip through Southern and Central Africa,* Hearings, US House of Representatives, 1974, 35.

87. *Washington Post,* February 22, 1975.

CHAPTER 3

1. The discussion that follows here on the weaknesses of Angolan nationalism owes a great deal to the research of C. Messiant, *1961: L'Angola colonial, histoire et société: Les prémisses du mouvement nationaliste* (doctoral diss., Paris, EHESS, 1983).

2. J. Marcum, *Exile Politics and Guerrilla Warfare: The Angolan Revolution, 1962–1976,* vol. 2 (Cambridge, MA: MIT Press), 48.

3. USET-Leopoldville, July 7, 1963 ("declassified" secret document).

4. See *Pravda,* March 11, 1961.

5. Marcum, *Exile Politics and Guerrilla Warfare,* 131.

6. *International Affairs* (Moscow), March 1963, 116.

7. J. Marcum, "Communist States and Africa: The Case of Angola," unpublished article, 8.

8. N. Valdes, "Revolutionary Solidarity in Angola," in C. Blasier and C. Mesa-Lago, eds., *Cuba in the World* (Pittsburgh: University of Pittsburgh Press), 85.

9. USET-Leopoldville, March 10, 1964 ("declassified" secret document).

10. Marcum, *Exile Politics and Guerrilla Warfare,* 172.

11. See *Pravda,* April 22, 1965.

12. Marcum, "Communist States and Africa," 8.

13. B. Davidson, *L'Angola au coeur des tempêtes* (Paris: Maspero, 1972), 253.

14. S. Weissman, "The CIA and US Policy in Zaire and Angola," in *Dirty Work (2): The CIA in Africa,* 196.

15. *Daily News* (Dar es Salaam), July 29, 1973.

16. Marcum, *Exile Politics and Guerrilla Warfare,* 201.

17. *The Times,* May 20, 1974.

18. *US-Angolan Relations,* Hearings, US House of Representatives, May 25, 1978, 11.

19. *New Times* 46 (November 1974): 16.

20. J. Valenta, "Soviet Decision Making on the Intervention in Angola," in D. Albright, ed., *Communism in Africa* (Bloomington: Indiana University Press, 1980), 22.

21. *New Times* 43 (October 1974): 21.

22. G. Bender, "Angola: The Anatomy of a Failure," in R. Lemarchand, *American Policy in Southern Africa: The Stakes and the Stance* (Washington: University Press of America, 1978), 257–58.

23. Conversations.

24. *New Times* 10 (March 1975): 8.

25. T. Watson, *The Angola Affair, 1974–1976, Research Report 257* (Maxwell Air Force Base, AL: US Air Force Air War College, Air University, April 1977), 22.

26. Ibid., 22.

27. *US-Angolan Relations,* HR Hearings, loc. cit., 12.

28. Notably at the time of Cuban Major Bravo Flavio's visit to Brazzaville.

29. *New Times* 23 (June 1975): 11.

30. The name of the South African Secret Service.

31. J. Stockwell, *In Search of Enemies: A CIA Story* (New York: Norton, 1978), 187.

32. Ibid., 164.

33. *US-Angolan Relations,* HR Hearings, loc. cit., 13.

34. *Tass,* quoted in *Le Monde,* November 13, 1975.

35. Stockwell, *In Search of Enemies,* 206.

36. *New Times* 51 (December 1975): 16.

37. *US Involvement in Angola,* 9.

38. *US Policy in Angola,* 29.

39. Stockwell, *In Search of Enemies,* 54.

40. Ibid., 187.

41. *Newsweek,* May 17, 1976, 53.

42. *Trimfo* (Madrid) (730), quoted in "Cuba et l'Afrique," *Problèmes politiques et sociaux,* La Documentation française (347), 16.

43. R. Kapuscinski, *D'une guerre à l'autre* (Paris: Flammarion, 1989).

44. *Granma Weekly Review,* September 7, 1976, 8–9.

45. Quoted in C. Blaser and C. Mesa-Lago, eds., *Cuba in the World,* 105.

46. P. Hassner, "Intégration et coopération ou inégalité et dépendence," *Revue française de science politique,* December 1974, 1266.

47. H. Kissinger, quoted in *Department of State Bulletin* 74 (1913), February 23, 1976, 204.

48. *Angola: US Involvement in Civil War in Angola,* Hearings, US Senate, January–February 1976, 194.

49. W. Leogrande, "Cuban-Soviet Relations and Cuban Policy in Africa," *Cuban Studies* 10, 1 (January 1980): 3.

50. Quoted in J. Levesque, *L'URSS et la révolution cubaine* (Paris: Presses de la Fondation nationale des sciences politiques, Presses de l'Université de Montréal, 1976), 130.

51. J. Dominguez, "Cuban Foreign Policy" *Foreign Affairs,* Autumn 1978, 90.

52. The Clark amendment expressly prohibited all American aid to UNITA without the explicit consent of Congress.

53. This amendment was nevertheless repealed by the House of Representatives in June 1985.

54. The argument that the Cubans and the East Germans supported the FNLC is defended by General Gras, former head of the military mission in Zaire. See his testimony in S. Cohen and M.-C. Smouts, eds., *La politique extérieure de Valéry Giscard d'Estaing* (Paris: Presses de la Fondation nationale des sciences politiques, 1985), 230. On the other hand, C. Vance indicates in his memoirs (*Hard Choices*) that no tangible proof of direct Cuban involvement

with the FNLC was ever found. This piece of information was confirmed for us by P. Borg, United States Consul in Lumumbashi at the time of the second Shaba crisis.

55. A. Rouquié, "Cuba dans les relations internationales: Premiers rôles et vulnérabilité," *Problèmes d'Amérique latine* 2 (1982): 89.

56. J. P. Gilbert, "Les échanges économiques entre Cuba et l'Union soviétique," *Problèmes d'Amérique latine* 2 (1982): 109.

57. M. A. Crosnier, "La dépendence économique de Cuba," *Courrier des pays de l'Est,* April 1980, 19.

58. A. Rouquié, "Cuba dans les relations internationales," 88.

59. J. Dominguez, "Political and Military Implications and Consequences of Cuban Policy in Africa," *Cuban Studies,* July 1980, 52.

60. Indeed, Cubans cannot escape the reproaches generally addressed to all foreign expeditionary corps. The "lesson-giving" side of Cubans is sometimes similarly resented.

CHAPTER 4

1. See S. Krasner, *Defending National Interest: Raw Material Investment and US Foreign Policy* (Princeton: Princeton University Press, 1978), 31.

2. W. Foltz, "US Policy toward Southern Africa: Economic and Strategic Constraints," in R. Lemarchand, *American Policy in Southern Africa: The Stakes and the Stance* (Lanham, MD: University Press of America, 1981), 268.

3. In particular, J. Schneider, *Ideological Coalitions in Congress* (Westport, CT: Greenwood Press, 1979), and B. Russet and E. Hanson, *Interest and Ideology: The Foreign Policy Beliefs of American Businessmen* (San Francisco, 1975).

4. D. McHenry, W. Maynes, A. Lake, and R. Moose were among the principal architects of the Carter administration's African policy. Former diplomatic officers, they shared having resigned in protest against United States policy in Southeast Asia. A. Young, for his part, had actively participated in the struggle for civil rights beside Martin Luther King.

5. "In Atlanta, Georgia, when five banks decided that racial trouble wasn't good for business, racial unrest ceased. . . . From that day, everyone benefited from the prosperity of a market economy." A. Young, quoted in *The Sun* (Johannesburg), May 9, 1977.

6. See his testimony before Congress in *US Policy towards Rhodesia,* Hearing, US House of Representatives, September 7, 1977, 19.

7. See R. Moose's declaration in *US Policy towards South Africa,* Hearing, US House of Representatives, April–June 1980, 7.

8. C. Crocker, "Regional Stability in Southern Africa," *Department of State Bulletin,* October 1981, 24.

9. Such a measure would nonetheless be largely symbolic: while three hundred American companies are officially represented in South Africa, fifty-seven hundred other companies are active there without being officially represented.

10. We are referring specifically to a study by the Carnegie Foundation ("Public Opinion Poll on American Attitudes toward South Africa") and a study directed by W. Foltz, *Elite Opinion on United States Policy toward Africa,* for the Council on Foreign Relations.

11. The Carnegie study demonstrates that this image predominated among 11% of blacks polled. It also corroborates perfectly what Malcolm X had said already in his autobiography: "I don't know why, but for me Africa was a place full of naked savages, of cannibals, of monkeys and tigers, of jungles where heat oozed."

12. W. Foltz, *United States Policy towards South Africa: Is an Effective One Possible?* ACIS Working Paper no. 413 (Los Angeles: UCLA Center for International and Strategic Studies, 1983), 21.

13. See S. Weissman and J. Carson, "Economic Sanctions against Rhodesia," in J. Spanier and J. Nogee, *Congress, the Presidency and American Foreign Policy* (New York: Pergamon Press, 1981), 145–47.

14. *South Africa: Time Running Out,* Report of the Study Commission on US Policy toward South Africa (Berkeley: University of California Press, 1981), 315.

15. Ibid., 320.

16. *US Mineral Dependence on South Africa,* US Senate, October 1982, 16.

17. *Imports of Minerals from South Africa by the United States and the OECD Countries,* Congressional Research Service, September 1980, 11.

18. Foltz, *US Policy towards South Africa,* 4.

19. See *The Possibilities of a Resource War in Southern Africa,* Hearing, US House of Representatives, July 8, 1981, 52–56.

20. R. Rotberg, "Confronting the Common Danger: South Africa and the US in the Reagan Era," in A. Hero and J. Barratt, eds., *The American People and South Africa* (Lexington, MA: Lexington Books, 1981), 206.

21. *US Interests in Africa,* Hearing, US House of Representatives, 1979, 140–45.

22. However, taking into account indirect investments, that is to say, American participatory activity in South African firms, the global volume of American investments would reach $15 billion.

23. Fifty percent of American investments were in the hands of four large firms whose presence in the Republic of South Africa represents but an infinitesimal portion of their assets.

24. D. Myers, "US Domestic Controversy over American Business in South Africa," in Hero and Barratt, *The American People and South Africa,* 70.

25. Foltz, *United States Policy towards South Africa,* 3.

26. *Eximbank and Trade in South Africa,* Hearing, US House of Representatives, February 9, 1978, 75.

27. From $1.5 billion in 1981, the volume of loans by American banks to the private sector in South Africa rose to $4.6 billion in 1984. On the other hand, American bank loans to the South African government seem to have virtually ceased to exist in 1985 after having reached $343 million in 1983.

28. *US Corporate Activities in South Africa,* Hearings and Markup, US House of Representatives, September–June 1982, 31.

29. C. Crocker, *From Rhodesia to Zimbabwe: The Fine Art of Transition* (Washington: Georgetown University), 21.

30. Interview with Henry Kissinger in the *Washington Post,* July 3, 1979.

31. *South Africa: Time Running Out,* 354.

32. Especially since the closing of the Mozambican border in March 1976, which left Rhodesia totally dependent on South African ports.

33. D. Martin and P. Johnson, *The Struggle for Zimbabwe* (London: Faber & Faber, 1981), 263.

34. D. Clark, *Africa,* Report to the Committee on Foreign Relations, US Senate, July 1977, 17.

35. The Kissinger plan nevertheless foresaw that the more the colonialists prolonged their stay in Zimbabwe, the more the basis of their indemnification would be advantageous from the start.

36. Crocker, *From Rhodesia to Zimbabwe,* 19.

37. *US Policy towards Rhodesia: A Report on the New Anglo-American Initiative,* Hearing, US House of Representatives, September 7, 1977, 8.

38. C. Vance, *Hard Choices: Critical Years in America's Foreign Policy* (New York: Simon & Schuster, 1983), 271.

39. *Recent Developments in Rhodesia,* Hearing, US Senate, July 23, 1979, 108.

40. S. Low, "The Zimbabwe Settlement," unpublished article, 24.

41. Ibid., 20.

42. Vance, *Hard Choices*, 263.

43. Ibid., 266.

44. Ibid., 268–69.

45. *Washington Post*, March 17, 1978.

46. Vance, *Hard Choices*, 268.

47. See President Nyerere's remarks to Senator Clark in *Africa*, 21.

48. See McHenry's testimony in *US Policy towards Namibia*, Spring 1981, Hearing, US House of Representatives, June 17, 1981, 21.

49. *US Policy toward Africa*, Hearing, US House of Representatives, 1978, 214.

50. Interviews, Washington, August 1980.

51. G. Cros, *Chroniques namibiennes: La dernière colonie* (Paris: Présence africaine, 1983), 151.

52. Interviews.

53. Vance, *Hard Choices*, 277.

54. Ibid., 306.

55. Cros, *Chroniques namibiennes*, 165–66.

56. "Muldergate" by analogy to Watergate. From the name of Connie Mulder, communications minister of the Vorster government, who was accused of having improperly used government funds to promote international propaganda.

57. Vance, *Hard Choices*, 308.

58. This decision was made in the hope of softening the position of those South Africans who were particularly hostile to McHenry.

59. According to D. McHenry, in *The Current Situation in Namibia*, Hearing, US House of Representatives, May 7, 1979, 24.

60. J. Seiler, "South Africa in Namibia: Persistence, Misperception and Ultimate Failure," *Journal of Modern African Studies* 4 (December 1982): 702.

61. C. Crocker, "Regional Strategy for Southern Africa," *Department of State Bulletin*, October 1981, 27.

62. In an article written before he attained an official position of responsibility, C. Crocker had defined the terms of the policy perfectly: "The real choice we will face in southern Africa in the eighties concerns our readiness to compete with our global adversary. . . . The choice has global implications, but the immediate decisions are, more often than not, regional ones," "South Africa: A Strategy for Change," *Foreign Affairs*, Winter 1980/81, 345.

63. C. Crocker's testimony to Congress, in *US Policy toward Namibia*, Hearings, US House of Representatives, June 17, 1981, 3.

64. See Zaki Laïdi, "Washington a surestimé ses moyens de pression sur l'Afrique du Sud et l'Angola," *Le Monde*, December 30, 1982; and J. de Saint-Jorre, "Crisis of Confidence," *Foreign Affairs (America and the World)*, 1982.

65. *Ethiopia and the Horn of Africa*, Hearings, US Senate, August 1976, 114.

66. *Izvestia*, February 8, 1975, cited in CDSP 27 (13).

67. D. Borisov, "The Development in Ethiopia," *New Times* 8 (February 1975): 11.

68. Radio Peace and Progress (in Arabic), March 1, 1975, quoted in *USSR and Third World*, February 24–March 31, 1975, 117.

69. T. Farer, *War Clouds on the Horn of Africa* (Washington: Carnegie Endowment for International Peace, 1979), 122.

70. Conversations.

71. M. Tuscherer, "L'unité yéménite," *L'Afrique et l'Asie modernes* (124), 1st trimester 1980: 14.

72. Vance, *Hard Choices*, 74.

73. *Washington Post*, September 27, 1977.

74. The only exception to this rule is Nigeria because of its disproportionate demographic weight. *Liberia and Ghana: Policy Challenges in West Africa*, US Senate, June 1982, 4.

75. *AID Congressional Presentation, FY 1985*, appendix 1, "Africa," 389.

76. C. Rossiter, *The Conflict of Development and Diplomacy: American Assistance to Southern Africa, 1973–1981* (Ph.D. diss., Cornell University, 1983), 42.

77. See, in particular, *Foreign Assistance Legislation for Fiscal Year 1983 (Part 7)*, Hearings and Markup, US House of Representatives, April 1982, XIII.

78. *Weekly Review (Nairobi)*, February 8, 1980.

79. The United States maintains one of its largest contingents of Peace Corps volunteers in Kenya (four hundred). It also welcomes more than four thousand Kenyan students.

80. *Standard (Nairobi)*, December 5, 1980.

81. P. Jacquemot, "Le FMI et l'Afrique subsaharienne: Une critique des politiques d'ajustement," *Problèmes économiques*, October 26, 1983, 15–16.

82. Details of this program can be found in *AID Congressional Presentation, FY 1985*, loc. cit.

83. Ibid., 14.

84. OCDE, *Coopération pour le développement: Examen, 1983*, 155.

85. J.-F. Bayard, *La politique africaine de François Mitterand* (Paris: Khartala, 1984), 92.

86. The political, financial, and economic risk run by foreign investors in South Africa is tending to increase. The risk rating established by the *International Report* on the basis of a graded scale from 0 (maximum risk) to 100 (minimum risk) rated South Africa at 58.5 in June 1983, as opposed to 63.5 six months earlier. For the sake of comparison, the risk rating is rising in most black African states. In June 1985, Kenya's risk was rated at 58, Cameroon's at 56, and Nigeria's at 45.5.

87. *An Assessment of AID Activities to Promote Agricultural and Rural Development in Sub-Saharan Africa*, AID, April 1988, 4.

88. Ibid., 104.

89. *US Aid to Senegal: Its Impact on Agricultural and Rural Development*, MADIA, World Bank, 1987, 59.

90. *US Aid to Cameroon: Its Impact on Agricultural and Rural Development*, MADIA, World Bank, 1987, 58ff.

91. *US Aid to Nigeria: Its Impact on Agricultural and Rural Development*, MADIA, World Bank.

92. *An Assessment of AID Activities*, 155.

93. J. Mudgr, "Implications of the Agenda for US Aid Policies and Priorities in Agriculture," *Rural Africana*, Spring–Summer 1984.

94. General Accounting Office (GAO), *US Use of Conditions to Achieve Economic Reforms*, August 1986, 17.

95. *An Assessment of AID Activities*, 64.

96. *Washington Post*, February 2, 1989.

97. Z. Laïdi, *Enquête sur la Banque Mondiale* (Paris: Fayard, 1989), 81ff.

98. GAO, *Improving the Impact and Control of Economic Support Fund*, June 1988, 37.

99. Ibid., 38.

100. GAO-Liberia, *The Need to Improve Accountability and Control over US Assistance*, July 1987.

101. *An Assessment of AID Activities*, 114.

102. Idem.

103. *Cereals Marketing Liberalization in Mali: An Economic Policy Reform Assessment*, AID, March 1987, 15.

104. E. Simmons, "Policy and Structural Reform of Grain Markets in Mali," ODI, Regent's College, London, September 10–11, 1987, 18.

105. *United States Military Posture for Fiscal Year 1979,* Washington, Department of Defense, 55.

106. *New York Times,* July 23, 1978.

107. *Washington Post,* May 24, 1978.

108. As stressed in the memorandum on the Crocker-Botha conversations of June 1981, *Covert Action,* July–August 1981, 38.

109. Conversations.

110. *World Military Expenditures and Arms Transfers, 1971–1980,* Arms Control and Disarmament Agency, 1983, 117.

111. The "two wars" hypothesis refers to America's ability to carry on a war in Europe and a war in the Persian Gulf.

112. US Department of Commerce, *Nigeria: A Survey of US Business Opportunities* (Washington: Government Printing Office, May 1976), 1.

113. Conversations.

114. R. Ofoegbu, "Foreign Policy and Military Rule," in D. Oyediran, *Nigerian Government and Politics under Military Rule, 1960–1979* (London: Macmillan International College Editions, 1979), 138.

115. O. Aluko, "Nigeria, the United States and Southern Africa," *African Affairs,* January 1979, 94.

116. Conversation.

117. Conversations.

118. R. Libby, *Towards an Africanized US Policy for Southern Africa: A Strategy for Increasing Political Leverage,* Policy Papers in International Affairs (Berkeley: Institute of International Studies, 1980), 119.

119. In 1980 nearly two thousand Nigerian officers were in various American military schools.

120. Pierre Hassner has written before about "incomplete domination and imperfect reciprocity."

121. *Annual Energy Outlook, 1982: With Prospects to 1990* (Washington, Government Printing Office, 1984), 66.

122. D. Bach, "Nigeria et Etats-Unis: Convergences d'intérêts et relations de pouvoir," *Politique africaine* 2 (1980): 16.

CHAPTER 5

1. The Soviets are careful to give the limited list of socialist-oriented states. Among those repeatedly mentioned are Angola, Benin, Congo, Ethiopia, Guinea, Madagascar, Tanzania, and Mozambique. On a more intermittent basis, the following countries also appear on the list: Cape Verde, Guinea-Bissau, Mali, São Tomé and Princípe, and the Seychelles Islands. Finally, one can foresee including Burkina-Faso and Zimbabwe in a future list.

2. A. Kiva, "Orientation socialiste: Théorique et pratique," *Sciences sociales* 2 (1978): 134.

3. E. Primakov, "La politique et le développement socio-économique des pays d'Orient," *Asie et Afrique aujourd'hui* 6 (1982): 20.

4. G. Boudarevski, "Les non-alignés dans le monde contemporain," *New Times* 9 (February 1983): 5.

5. G. Kiva, "Le mouvement de libération nationale à l'étape présente," *La vie internationale,* April 1981, 31.

6. N. Simonia, "Les problèmes du développement des pays libérés," *La vie internationale,* May 1982, 90.

7. Kiva, "Le mouvement de libération nationale," 40.

8. R. Ulianovsky, "The Twentieth Century and the National Liberation Movement" (in Russian: *Narodi Azii i Afriki* 2 [1980]), quoted in Joint Publication Research Service (JPRS), *USSR Report*, Political and Sociological Affairs (PSA); quoted later in JPRS, *USSR Report-PSA*, August 8, 1980, 23.

9. Conversations.

10. A. Gromyko, "L'orientation socialiste en Afrique," in *Idéologie de la démocratie révolutionnaire africaine* (Moscow: Académie des Sciences de l'URSS, 1984), p. 13. One nonetheless should note that the nationalization of the economy is not, for the Soviets, a sufficient condition for a socialist orientation. For Smirnov, "the difference between developing countries of socialist orientation and those of capitalist orientation resides not in the volume of state enterprise in areas characterized as productive but rather in the state's participation in the development of the non-productive social sphere of the economy." *Sciences sociales* 2 (1980): 154.

11. Y. Gavrilov, "Problems of Training Parties of the Avant-Garde in Countries of Socialist Orientation" (in Russian: *Narodi Azii i Afriki* 6 [1980]); quoted in JPRS, *USSR Report-PSA*, March 24, 1981, 6.

12. V. V. Luchkov, *National-Democratic Revolutions: Some Questions of Theory and Practice* (in Russian: Moscow-Nauka); quoted in JPRS, *USSR Report-PSA* 1, no. 10 (1982): 29.

13. Ibid., 30.

14. P. Chastitko, "Le révolution doit savoir se défendre," *Asie et Afrique aujourd'hui* 3 (May–June 1982): 7.

15. E. Primakov, "Countries of Socialist Orientation: A Difficult but Achievable Transition" (in Russian: in *MEIMO* 7 [July 1981]); quoted in JPRS, *USSR Report-PSA,* October 22, 1981, 12.

16. Thus C. Legum, in *Politique étrangère* 4 (1984), defines Ethiopia as a country having "rallied the Soviet camp to the sides of Cuba and Vietnam." Moscow establishes a crucial difference between "socialist orientation" and "world socialist system."

17. P. Wiles, *A New Communist Third World* (London: Croom-Helm, 1982), 15.

18. J. Copans, "L'URSS, alibi ou instrument des états d'Afrique noire?" in Z. Laïdi, ed., *L'URSS vue du tiers monde* (Paris: Karthala, 1984), 53.

19. J. Leca, "Préface," in Laïdi, ed., *L'URSS vue du tiers monde,* 14.

20. H. Ossebi, "Affirmation ethique et discours idéologique au Congo" (doctoral thesis, Paris-V, 1982), 197.

21. R. Lefort, *Ethiopie: La révolution hérétique* (Paris: Maspero, 1981), 164.

22. C. Baeckman, "L'Ethiopie ou le socialisme impérial," *Le Monde diplomatique,* October 1982, 18.

23. "Mengistu Addresses WPE Constituent Congress," in *FBIS (Foreign Broadcast Information Service) Daily Report, Middle East Africa,* September 18, 1984, R1–R34.

24. See Ossebi, *Affirmation ethnique.*

25. J. Leca, "L'hypothèse totalitaire dans le tiers monde: Les pays arabo-islamiques," in G. Hermet et al., *Totalitarismes* (Paris: Economica, 1984), 227.

26. J. L. Domenach, "Le totalitarisme n'arrête pas l'histoire: Communisme et société en Chine," *Esprit,* September 1984, 23.

27. See T. Callaghy, "The Difficulties of Implementing Socialist Strategies of Development in Africa: The First Wave," in C. Rosberg and T. Callaghy, eds., *Socialism in Sub-Saharan Africa* (Institute of International Studies, 1979), 112–29.

28. Bayart, "L'hypothèse totalitaire dans le tiers monde: Le cas de l'Afrique noire," in G. Hermet et al., *Totalitarismes,* 212–13.

29. F. Furet, *Penser la Révolution française* (Paris: Gallimard, 1983), 72.

30. See Ossebi, *Affirmation ethique.*

31. See G. Kepel, "Les Oulémas, l'intelligentsia et les islamistes en Egypte: Système social, ordre transcendental et ordre traduit," *Revue française de science politique* 3 (June 1985): 424–25.

32. Furet, *Penser la Révolution française,* 81.

33. See Ossebi, *Affirmation ethique.*

34. The decision to bring P. Nzé before the Control Commission of the Party was eventually postponed to a later date.

35. T. Todorov, *Michaël Bakhtine: Le principe dialogique,* after *Ecrits du Cercle Bakhtine* (Paris: Seuil, 1981), 68.

36. *Third People's Congress of the PCT,* 180.

37. V. Sidenko, "Non-Aligned Movement: 20 Years," *New Times* 6 (February 1981): 6.

38. In the name of technical assistance, the Soviet Union had sent nearly four thousand advisers to black Africa in 1982 of whom two thousand were engineers, two hundred geologists, four hundred medical doctors, and one thousand teachers. P. Kochelev, "Coopération économique et technique entre l'URSS et les pays d'Afrique tropicale," *Commerce extérieur* 10 (1982): 11. In addition to the personnel sent in the name of technical assistance, there were technicians who were dispatched in the context of strictly commercial agreements. That was the case, for example, for six thousand Soviet technicians employed in Ajeokuta, Nigeria.

39. A. Gromyko, *Africa: Progress, Problems, Prospects* (Moscow: Progress, 1983), 154.

40. *Sunday New Nigerian,* September 13, 1981, cited in JPRS, *Africa Report* 8 (October 1981): 86.

41. Gromyko, *Africa,* 172–73.

42. *AFP-BQA,* September 18, 1984.

43. The deliveries of Soviet equipment planned in the aid contracts were integrated into commercial statistics. This is also true of the deliveries of raw materials to the USSR that function as a reimbursement of loans.

44. The Malagasy government is said to have nevertheless asked the USSR to dismantle its surveillance stations; *Le Monde,* March 23, 1985.

45. Conversations.

46. See J. L. Domenach, "L'URSS et l'Asie," *Le Débat,* September 1985.

47. *African Countries' Foreign Policy* (Moscow: Progress, 1983), 43.

48. *Pravda,* August 27, 1981, in CDSP 33, no. 34: 23.

49. *Rand Daily Mail,* December 5, 1983.

50. See N. Tikhonov's speech at the time of L. Lara's visit to Moscow; *Pravda,* January 21, 1982.

51. Whereas the South African aggression of August 1981 had given rise to an authorized commentary by the Tass News Agency (*Pravda,* August 27, 1981), that of 1982 was reported only through press commentary (*Pravda,* August 20, 1982).

52. Reflecting the Angolan point of view rather well, the bimonthly *Afrique-Asie* evaluated Soviet-Angolan relations on the eve of Dos Santos's trip to Moscow in the following terms: "Will the Soviet Union, which is tied to Angola by a friendship and cooperation treaty, accept granting indispensable armaments . . . in order to stand up to the aggressors . . . , armaments that are nonetheless dispensed to Libya and to Syria?" *Afrique-Asie* 295 (May 9–22, 1983).

53. See "President Dos Santos Pays Working Visit to the USSR," *FBIS Daily Report, Middle East and Africa,* May 18, 1983, U1.

54. *Noticias,* July 10, 1982, quoted in JPRS, *Africa Report,* August 26, 1982, 44.

55. *Noticias,* September 15, 1980, quoted in JPRS, *Africa Report,* October 30, 1980, 35.

56. *Noticias,* December 5, 1981, quoted in JPRS, *Africa Report,* December 29, 1981, 38.

57. *Service of the World Broadcast,* SWB-SU/WII 8_2/A$_5$/2, April 23, 1982.

58. *Noticias,* July 10, 1982, quoted in JPRS, *Africa Report,* August 26, 1982, 44.

59. *Afrique-Asie* 309 (November 21–December 4, 1983): 25.

60. G. Prunier, "La Guerre aérienne sur la frontière Angola-Namibie," *Politique africaine* 16 (January 1985): 143–44.

61. *The Economist,* March 30, 1985.

62. *Pravda,* January 13, 1984, quoted in *FBIS Daily Report, Soviet Union,* J1.

63. According to *The Economist* (March 30, 1985), the USSR is said to have dissuaded SWAPO from exploring paths to an agreement with Pretoria at the time of the Lusaka meetings in May 1984.·

64. Soviet TV, quoted in SWB-SU-$_{7597}$/A$_5$/$_2$, March 21, 1984.

65. See *Pravda,* October 14, 1979; October 22, 1980; October 11, 1981; and October 17, 1982.

66. O. Bogomolov, "CMEA and the Developing World," *International Affairs* 7 (1979): 31.

67. The Soviets admit that the gift element of their assistance to Africa is between 38% and 58%. *Commerce extérieur* 10 (1982): 11.

68. D. Pineye, *Le facteur marchand dans les relations économiques Est-Sud* (Paris: CEPII, September 1984), multigraphed, 8.

69. C. Lawson, "Revealing Preferences: The East in North-South Negotiations," European Consortium for Political Research (ECPR), March 1985, 20.

70. Madagascar's President, D. Ratsiraka, has recently damaged this perception by citing, with evidence, the advantages of Soviet-Malagasy cooperation: "Since 1978, Soviet aid has become important and precious. Globally it has risen to $446.33 million, of which $350 million is in economic aid. . . . Moscow has furnished us free of charge with 200 tractors and we have bought 1,000 of them under excellent long-term payment conditions. The Soviets lent us 150,000 tons of oil last year and 250,000 tons this year; their technicians are currently on location to develop rice production over 2,000 hectares. . . . As for the credit they are allowing us, the long-term interest rates vary from 2.5% and 3%, with a two-year postponement clause." *Afrique-Asie* 351 (July 1–4, 1985): X.

71. *Marchés tropicaux et méditerranéens,* February 15, 1980, 378.

72. *Pour la paix et le progrès social* (Moscow: Nauka, 1983), 42.

73. M. Skak, "Disparity and the Merging of Systems: The Case of CMEA Relations to Africa," ECPR, March 1985, 19.

Select Bibliography

Besides a few general works on the East-West relationship in Africa, among which is V. Nielsen's *Great Powers and Africa* (New York: Praeger, 1969), none exist that offer the problematics of the whole Soviet-American relations in Africa. On the other hand, there are an impressive number of sovietological, americanist, and africanist works, as well as articles that deal with one or several aspects of the subject.

Primary Sources

The study of American policy is based on three major primary sources: "declassified" diplomatic documents, Congressional documents (reports and hearings), and conversations. Diplomatic archives, which are increasingly available to the public, are of great interest because of the relative speed (twelve years) with which they are made available.

Although done selectively, the "declassification" of American documents is a precious source for analysis of decision-making mechanisms and for understanding actors' perceptions. This mass of documents, accessible at the Library of Congress in Washington, D.C., and through inter-

Readers interested in having an exhaustive bibliography on the subject can refer to the notes and bibliography of our thesis, *Les deux grandes puissances et l'Afrique, 1960–1977* (Bibliotheque de l'Institut d'études politiques de Paris). They can also refer to several bibliographical works: *African International Relations: An Annotated Bibliography,* the Westview Press Special Studies on Africa, which covers the whole period from 1960 to 1977; *Bibliographie des travaux en langue française sur l'Afrique du Sud du Sahara,* published regularly by the Centre d'études africaines de l'EHESS; *La bibliographie internationale des sciences sociales* (CIDSS). *La revue française de science politique,* whose June issue is devoted each year to the publication of unpublished work in political science, and the *International African Bibliography* will also be found to be extremely useful.

library loan systems, is quite heterogeneous. It runs from the simplest diplomatic telegram to the lengthy reports of *ad hoc* committees, including diplomatic reports to the State Department, instructions for the chiefs of diplomatic posts, correspondence between the White House and the State Department, preparatory memoranda for official meetings, mission reports, CIA reports, internal State Department memos, and so on.

Reports and hearings constitute the second primary source indispensable to an understanding of United States policy. The impressive number of them (approximately one hundred) makes it impossible to cite all here. We can, however, recommend to researchers that they read the annual *Hearings* that are devoted to aid programs (*Foreign Assistance Legislation for Fiscal Year . . .* = Part 7).

Over the course of the last ten years, the number and the quality of hearings on Africa have noticeably increased. *US Interests in Africa* (1979) most precisely captures America's image of Africa at the end of the seventies. Nonetheless, it is on southern Africa that the greatest effort to gather information can be detected. On American policy in southern Africa before, during, and after the decolonization of Angola, we recommend reading *The Complex of US-Portuguese Relations before and after the Coup* (1974); *Implementation of US Arms Embargo against Portugal and South Africa and Related Issues* (1973); *Angola: US Involvement in Civil War Angola* (1976); and *US-Angolan Relations* (1978).

On the relations of the United States with the Republic of South Africa, *US Policy towards South Africa* (1980) and *US Corporate Activities in South Africa* (1982) are obligatory reading. The Carter administration's policy in the region is well delineated in *US Policy towards Africa* (1978); that of the Reagan administration is clearly defined in *Namibia* (1982).

On strategic problems, the hearings on *The Possibility of a Resource War in Southern Africa* (1981) deal with alarmist Western arguments on the subject in a carefully thought-out manner. On the question of raw materials, one can usefully refer to the *Congressional Handbook on US Material Import Dependency/Vulnerability* (1981) and to the indispensable *Mineral Commodity Summaries,* Bureau of Mines (1984). A reading of *Defense Appropriations* and the *Annual Report to the Congress* by the Secretary of Defense sheds interesting light on American military strategy. *Building Trade with Africa* (1983) offers a synthesis of debates on new prospects for the American economy in Africa. In this specific area, readers can usefully supplement their information by consulting official publications of the Department of Commerce, especially *Business America.*

From the evidence, the study of Soviet policy does not offer the same resources. Entire areas of this policy, such as the decision-making process, are totally unavailable to sovietological analyses of Africa. With but a few

exceptions (official statistical series and speeches), "gray literature" *
from the Soviet Union is extremely limited. The few undistributed Soviet
studies on Africa (economic reports, for example) are more easily available
in Africa than in the Soviet Union.

That being the case, Soviet literature on Africa is sufficiently plentiful
and codified to offer a grid for analysis and interpretation. From that point
of view, the mastery of the Russian language offers the analyst an unquestionable advantage. Nevertheless, nothing suggests that access to all
translated Soviet sources would introduce a bias that might preemptively
invalidate a study of Soviet policy.

Among these translated sources, which are with only a few exceptions
the only ones used for this work, one can cite *La vie internationale, New
Times (Novoë Vremya), Sciences sociales, Commerce international,* and
Asie et Afrique aujoürd'hui. For the entire Khrushchev era, the journal
Mizan systematically translated most Soviet writings on Africa. The *Cur-
rent Digest of Soviet Press* also offers a large range of translations of the
Soviet press. The BBC's *World Service* and the *Daily Report* (Soviet
Union) enable one to keep track of the day-to-day developments in official
Soviet positions. But the most important source, and the best known, for
Soviet translations comes from the various series of the JPRS (Joint Publication Research Service) devoted to the Soviet Union. The series International Economic Relations offers a very broad panorama of Soviet
writings on the topic. It usefully supplements a monthly reading of *Commerce extérieur.* The series World Economy and International Relations is
even more useful. It is exclusively devoted to translations of the most important Soviet journal on international relations, *MEIMO.* Finally, the
journal *Political and Sociological Affairs* offers access to translations of
Narodi Azii i Afriki.

An inventory of the main primary sources on this topic would be incomplete without the African sources. On this central matter, nearly all sovietological and americanist works are often silent. Use of the African press
and recourse to conversations with actors on the African continent are
hardly more frequent. The difficulty of taking into account the constraints
of the African field nevertheless seems less pronounced in the work of
specialists on American policy (who are most often American africanists)
than in that of their Soviet counterparts, who are on the whole ill-informed
about Africa. In a limited number of countries (Kenya, Nigeria), the quality of the press does offer the analyst some unquestionable resources. In
other cases, the dogmatism of the official press must not be allowed to

---

*By "gray literature" one should understand files, documents, or reports that are not
subject to official distribution (as opposed to newspaper or journal articles).

discourage essential efforts to decode information (such is the case, for example, with the Mozambican weekly *Tempo*). In addition, newspapers like *Jornal de Angola, Diario de Moçambique,* and *Ethiopian Herald,* to cite but three, offer extremely valuable empirical information. Their selective translation in the JPRS series Sub-Saharan Africa Report is in this regard salutary.

Secondary Sources

On the historical dimension of the relations between the superpowers, one can refer to the works of E. Wilson, *Russia and Black Africa before World War II* (New York: Holmes and Meïr Publishers, 1974), and of M. Charles, *The Soviet Union and Africa: The History of an Involvement* (Lanham, MD: University Press of America, 1980); to those of F. Arese, *La politique africaine des Etats-Unis* (Neuchâtel: La Baconnière, 1945), and E. McKinley, *The Lure of Africa-American Interests in Tropical Africa—1919–1939* (Bobbs-Merrill, 1974).

On the problematics of development and the ideological foundations of Soviet and American behavior at the beginning of the sixties, one can profitably read *Des africanistes russes parlent de l'Afrique* (Paris: Présence africaine, 1960); Z. Laïdi, *Les grandes puissances et l'Afrique* (Paris: Cahiers du CHEAM, 1984); B. Badie, *Le développement politique* (Paris: Economica, 1984); and R. Packenham, *Liberal America and the Third World: Political Development Ideas in Foreign Aid and the Social Sciences* (Princeton: Princeton University Press, 1973).

Although limited to western Africa, R. Legvold's *Soviet Policy in West Africa* (Cambridge, MA: Harvard University Press, 1970), is probably the best written on Khrushchev's policy in Africa. The works of S. Weissman, *American Policy in the Congo, 1960–1964* (Ithaca: Cornell University Press, 1974), and of M. Kalb, *The Congo Cables: The Cold War in Africa from Eisenhower to Kennedy* (New York: Macmillan, 1981), offer valuable detailed analyses of Kennedy's policy in the Congo.

Research on American-African relations under Kennedy is usefully enriched by Ambassador Attwood's testimony, *The Reds and the Blacks* (New York: Harper & Row, 1967). W. Scott Thompson's *Ghana's Foreign Policy, 1957–1960: Diplomacy, Ideology, and the New State* (Princeton: Princeton University Press, 1969) makes possible a better understanding of relations between the two superpowers and Ghana under Nkrumah.

Relations between the United States and Portugal in the sixties are exhaustively analyzed in the works of L. Crollen, *Portugal, the US, and NATO* (Louvain: Leuven University Press, 1973), and W. Minter, *Portuguese Africa and the West* (New York: Monthly Review Press, 1972).

Although devoted to the sole problem of Rhodesia, A. Lake's work *The Tar Baby Option: US Policy toward Southern Rhodesia* (New York: Columbia University Press, 1976) is without a doubt the most rigorous treatment of American policy in Africa between 1965 and 1974.

It is especially through analyses of economic and social development ("the noncapitalist way of development") that one can best evaluate the evolution of the Soviet position on Africa.

During the entire period from the end of the sixties to the Angolan crisis, the slimness of the Soviet diplomatic stakes in Africa stimulated "realist" thinking free of Khrushchevian optimism: N. Garilov, *The National Liberation Movement in West Africa* (Moscow: Progress); A. Iskenderov, *Africa: Politics, Economy, Ideology* (Moscow: Novosti, 1972); N. Simonia, *Socialist Oriented Development and National Democracy* (Moscow: Novosti, 1974); V. Solodovnikov, *The Present Stage of Non-Capitalist Development in Asia and Africa* (Budapest: Institute of World Economy, 1973); V. Solodovnikov and N. Bogoslovsky, *Non-Capitalist Development: An Historical Outline* (Moscow: Progress, 1975); E. Tarabrin, *The New Scramble for Africa* (Moscow: Progress, 1974); and R. Ulianovsky, *Le socialisme et les pays libérés* (Moscow: Progress, 1975).

For a more recent analysis of Soviet positions on the same subject, one can refer to the publications of the Academy of Sciences devoted to African affairs (*Idéologie de la démocratie révolutionnaire africaine,* Moscow: Sciences sociales d'aujourd'hui, 1984; *L'URSS et l'Afrique,* Moscow: Sciences sociales d'aujourd'hui, 1982; *Aspects économiques du développement des pays de l'Afrique,* Moscow: Sciences sociales d'aujourd'hui, 1981). One can read with interest the documents of the Soviet-African science and politics conference (October 1981) included in *Pour la paix et le progrès social* (Moscow: Nauka, 1983), as well as the annual publications of *Africa in Soviet Studies* (Moscow: Nauka). On Soviet-African diplomatic relations, one can find two works by A. Gromyko. The first, published under his leadership, is devoted to *African Countries Foreign Policy* (Moscow: Progress, 1981). The second is entitled *Africa: Progress-Problems-Prospects* (Moscow: Progress, 1983).

The different African conflicts and crises, and the conditions of interventions by the superpowers have been abundantly studied.

Of all of the African crises, the Congo crisis has received the best treatment. The extensive publication of American diplomatic archives by M. Kalb, *The Congo Cables: The Cold War in Africa from Eisenhower to Kennedy,* has made a contribution to it; but the important elements of this crisis had already been dealt with in S. Weissman's *American Policy in the Congo, 1960–1964* and in C. Hoskyns, *The Congo since Independence* (London: Oxford University Press, 1965).

The Nigerian civil war also gave rise to numerous writings. The central work devoted to the international dimension of this conflict is J. Stremlau's *The International Politics of the Nigerian Civil War* (Princeton: Princeton University Press, 1978). On the same theme, one can read S. Cronje's very useful *The World and Nigeria: The Diplomatic History of the Biafran War, 1967–1970* (London: Sidgwick & Jackson, 1972). Good analyses devoted to American policy in Nigeria can be found in G. Idang, *Internal Politics and Foreign Policy, 1960–1966* (Ibadan: Ibadan University Press), and O. Oyediran, ed., *Nigerian Government and Politics under Military Rule: 1960–1979* (London: Macmillan, 1979).

On the 1975 Angolan civil war and its internationalization, one can profitably turn to J. Stockwell's testimony, *In Search of Enemies* (New York: Norton, 1978), on CIA action and American policy; to A. Klinghofer's study on Soviet policy, *The Angolan War: A Study in Soviet Policy in the Third World* (Boulder: Westview Press, 1980); to B. Porter's complementary analysis in *The USSR in Third World Conflicts: Soviet Arms and Diplomacy in Local War, 1945–1980* (Cambridge: Cambridge University Press, 1984); and to the interpretation of Cuban policy that C. Mesa-Lago and J. Belkin, eds., give in *Cuba in Africa* (Pittsburgh: Center for Latin American Studies, 1982).

An in-depth study of this crisis, however, requires taking into account endogenous factors. On this matter, J. Marcum's *The Angolan Revolution: Exile Politics and Guerrilla Warfare, 1962–1976* (Cambridge, MA: MIT Press, 1978) seems indispensable. It can be supplemented by the original work of C. Messiant, *1961: L'Angola colonial, histoire et société* (doctoral dissertation, Paris, EHESS, 1983).

For researching the conflicts on the Horn of Africa, one can profitably refer to two essential works on the Ethiopian revolution: F. Hallyday and M. Molyneux, *The Ethiopian Revolution* (London: Verso, 1981), and R. Lefort, *Ethiopie: La révolution hérétique* (Paris: Maspero, 1981. The international aspects of the Somali-Ethiopian confrontation were treated more specifically in T. Farer, *War Clouds on the Horn of Africa* (Washington: Carnegie Endowment for International Peace, 1976); M. Ottoway, *Soviet and American Influence in the Horn of Africa* (New York: Praeger, 1982); and B. Porter, *The USSR in Third World Conflicts;* as well as J. Spencer, *Ethiopia, the Horn of Africa and US Policy* (Cambridge, MA: Institute for Foreign Policy Analysis, 1977). On the historical aspects of the Soviet-American rivalry in this area, and especially in Kenya, one can turn to W. Attwood, *The Reds and the Blacks*, to D. Goldsworthy, *Tom Mboya: The Man Kenya Wanted to Forget* (London: Heinemann, 1982), as well as to primary documents in C. Gertzel et al., *Government and Politics in Kenya: A Nation Building Text* (Nairobi: East African Publishing House, 1972). Finally, G. Staruchenko's *Le principe de l'autodéter-*

mination des peuples et des nations dans la politique étrangère de l'Etat soviétique (Moscow: Progress, 1962) offers the Soviet point of view on the delicate question of borders in the area.

As one might expect, southern Africa has also stimulated an abundant production of works stressing the regional dynamics here or the integration of external powers there. On American policy in the region, R. Lemarchand, ed., *American Policy in Southern Africa: The Stakes and the Stance* (Washington: University Press of America, 1981), offers a good critical interpretation of American behavior. The strategic stakes of this policy have been clearly and relevantly summarized by R. Price in *US Foreign Policy in Sub-Saharan Africa: National Interest and Global Strategy* (Berkeley: University of California Press, 1978). A conservative counterpoint on American–South African relations is given by R. Bissel in *South Africa and the US: The Erosion of an Influence Relationship* (New York: Praeger, 1982). A reading of that book can be supplemented by A. Hero and J. Bratt, eds., *The American People and South Africa* (Lexington, MA: Lexington Books, 1981). Nonetheless, the best analysis of American–South African relations to our mind is that of W. Foltz, *US Policy towards South Africa: Is an Effective One Possible?* (Los Angeles: UCLA-ACIS, 1983).

The articulation between regional dynamics and foreign intervention is excellently presented in T. Callaghy, ed., *South Africa in Southern Africa: The Intensifying Vortex of Violence* (New York: Praeger, 1983), and in G. Carter and P. O'Meara, *International Politics in Southern Africa* (Bloomington: Indiana University Press, 1982).

Seen from the South African perspective, problems in southern Africa and foreign intervention have been well posed by R. Schrire, ed., *South Africa: Public Policy Perspectives* (Capetown: Juta & Co. Ltd., 1982), M. Hough, *National Security in the RSA: The Strategic Importance of South Africa and Southern Africa, the Pretoria View* (University of Pretoria, June 1981), and D. Geldenhuys, *The Diplomacy of Isolation: South African Policy-Making* (New York: St. Martin's, 1984).

The problems of decision-making in foreign policy are totally absent from Western sovietological works. On the other hand, the broad scope of testimony by the actors and the great transparency of the American political system enable a good comprehension of the mechanisms that shape United States African policy. On the Kennedy period, the most significant statements are those of A. Schlesinger, *Les mille jours de Kennedy* (Paris: Denoël, 1966), and W. Attwood, *The Reds and the Blacks.* On the behavior of the Nixon administration, and the rivalries between the White House and the State Department, R. Morris's report *Uncertain Greatness: Henry Kissinger and American Foreign Policy* (New York: Harper & Row, 1977) is very useful. The work of C. Ogene, *Interest Groups and the Shaping of*

Foreign Policy: Four Case Studies of US African Policy (New York: St. Martin's Press, 1983), is also valuable in grasping American bureaucratic conflict. Finally, the conflict in interpretation of the African crises by Vance and Brzezinski under the Carter administration is very clearly discussed in C. Vance's "memoirs," *Hard Choices: Critical Years in America's Foreign Policy* (New York: Simon & Schuster, 1983).

The relations of the superpowers to other foreign powers in Africa have been more or less well studied. Soviet-Cuban relations have been very well defined by J. Levesque's *L'URSS et la révolution cubaine* (Paris: Presses de la FNSP, 1976). They are also dealt with in C. Blasier and C. Mesa-Lago, eds., *Cuba in the World* (Pittsburgh: University of Pittsburgh Press), and in C. Mesa-Lago and J. Belkin, *Cuba in Africa*.

The Sino-Soviet conflict in Africa is directly addressed by H. Carrère d'Encausse and S. Schram in *L'URSS et la Chine devant les révolutions dans les sociétés pré-industrielles* (Paris: Presses de la FNSP, 1970), B. Larkin, *China and Africa, 1949–1970: The Foreign Policy of the PRC* (Berkeley: University of California Press, 1971), and A. Ogunsanwo, *China's Policy in Africa, 1958–1971* (Cambridge: Cambridge University Press, 1974).

Index